# A COOK'S BOOK

## THE ESSENTIAL NIGEL SLATER

Also by Nigel Slater:

*Greenfeast*
*The Christmas Chronicles*
*The Kitchen Diaries III*
*Eat*
*The Kitchen Diaries II*
*Tender, Volumes I and II*
*Eating for England*
*The Kitchen Diaries*
*Toast – the story of a boy's hunger*
*Appetite*
*Real Food*
*Real Cooking*
*The 30-Minute Cook*
*Real Fast Puddings*
*Real Fast Food*

NIGEL SLATER is an award-winning author, journalist and television presenter. He has been the food columnist for the *Observer* for over twenty-five years. His collection of bestselling books includes the classics *Appetite* and *The Kitchen Diaries* and the two-volume *Tender*. He has made cookery programmes and documentaries for BBC1, BBC2 and BBC4. His memoir *Toast – the story of a boy's hunger* won six major awards and became a film and stage production. His writing has won the James Beard Award, the National Book Award, the Glenfiddich Trophy, the André Simon Memorial Prize, the British Biography of the Year and the Fortnum & Mason Best Food Book. He lives in London. He was awarded an OBE in the New Year Honours in 2020 for services to cookery and literature.

nigelslater.com
Instagram @nigelslater

# A COOK'S BOOK

## THE ESSENTIAL

## NIGEL SLATER

Photography by Jonathan Lovekin
and Jenny Zarins

4TH ESTATE · *LONDON*

4th Estate
An imprint of HarperCollins*Publishers*
1 London Bridge Street
London SE1 9GF
www.4thEstate.co.uk

HarperCollins*Publishers*
1st Floor, Watermarque Building, Ringsend Road
Dublin 4, Ireland

First published in Great Britain in 2021 by 4th Estate

1

Text copyright © Nigel Slater 2021
All recipe photographs © Jonathan Lovekin 2021
Except p. 79 and p. 444 © Nigel Slater 2021
Location and portrait photographs © Jenny Zarins 2021

Howard Hodgkin, *A Pale Reflection*, 2015–2016, hand-painted sugar-lift aquatint
©The Estate of Howard Hodgkin, courtesy Cristea Roberts Gallery

A catalogue record for this book is available from the British Library
ISBN 978-0-00-821376-3

Always follow the manufacturer's instructions when using kitchen appliances.

Design by David Pearson
Typeset by GS Typesetting
Printed in Bosnia and Herzegovina

**MIX**
Paper from
responsible sources
**FSC** www.fsc.org **FSC™ C007454**

This book is produced from independently certified FSC™ paper to ensure
responsible forest management.

For more information visit: www.harpercollins.co.uk/green

*To Louise Haines,*
*who first encouraged me to put pen to paper*

# Acknowledgements

*A Cook's Book* was written at my kitchen table during the pandemic of 2020–21, but the stories and recipes between these covers go back a long way before that.

A book of recipes and meals shared is, inevitably, a collaborative affair, and I have many wonderful people to thank.

To Louise Haines, my editor for over thirty years.

To Allan Jenkins and to Harriet Green, Martin Love, Gareth Grundy and everyone at the *Observer*, I simply cannot thank you enough for your continuing support. Thank you to Araminta Whitley, Marina de Pass and everyone at the Soho Agency, and a huge appreciation to the *Observer* readers and to my followers on Instagram and Twitter.

Many hands have been involved in this book, but none more so than James Thompson's. Whether he is cooking with me or working with The Great Oven – his international network for refugee aid and emergency food relief – his work and inspiration run deeply through the pages of this book. I can never thank him enough. A round of applause to Giles Cooper, who worked painstakingly on many of the recipes in this book, testing and retesting, and to Nicola Lamb for her wisdom and baking expertise.

To everyone at 4th Estate, especially Charlie Redmayne, Michelle Kane, Julian Humphries, Chris Gurney and Mia Colleran; to Gary Simpson, Annie Lee, Laura Nickoll, Alex Gingell and Louise Tucker, my thanks.

It has been a joy, as always, to work with Jonathan Lovekin, who has photographed not only the food in this book and my weekly *Observer Magazine* columns but all of my cooking for as long as I can remember. I am so grateful to Jenny Zarins for photographing me and my kitchen, and for giving the stories and recipes in this book a sense of place. I think of each of my books as having its own character, which is why each has its own format. I thank David Pearson once again for his thoughtful design and am grateful to GS Typesetting and everyone at GPS Group.

As always, there are no stylists or 'props' involved in my books. If you recognise plates and bowls and pots and pans it is because they are part of my life. The ceramics from which we eat are important to me and I would like to mention all those whose pieces I use regularly in my kitchen, especially Florian Gadsby, Steve Harrison, Anne Mette Hjortshøj, Rupert Spira, Teppei Ono, Darren Ellis, Jono Smart and Emily Stephen, and the late Richard Batterham.

I have long been an admirer of the late Howard Hodgkin and am lucky to have some of his paintings in my own collection. I am indebted to Antony Peattie and the Howard Hodgkin Legacy Trust for their permission to use Howard's painting *A Pale Reflection*, 2015–16, on the cover of this book.

Many have encouraged, inspired or helped with this book more than they would ever know. A shout out to Dalton Wong and George Ashwell, Richard Stepney, Tim d'Offay, Jonathan Nunn, Edmund de Waal and Takahiro Yagi; to Katie Findlay, Jack McGuigan, Tok and Hiromi Kise; Takako Seito; Maureen Doherty, Lyn Harris, Kyoko Kuga and Mitsue Iwakoshi. Thank you and much love to you all.

Nigel Slater, London, October 2021

# Contents

# Introduction

I am a cook who writes. You could measure my life in recipes. Each one a letter to a friend, a story of something I have made for dinner, the tale of how it came to be on my table. A salad tossed together with broad beans, salted ricotta and the first white-tipped radishes of spring; a roast chicken, its crisp skin served with a fat jug of its roasting juices on an autumn day; or a gloriously messy platter of grilled aubergines, hummus and torn flatbread shared with the best of friends.

That letter might accurately chronicle the details of a cake with which I am quietly pleased, tell the reader of a quince that has simmered peacefully in lemon juice and orange blossom honey on my hob on a winter's afternoon or mention a pillowy dumpling I have just lifted from a steaming bamboo basket. Sharing food with those at your table – passing round a bowl of late autumn raspberries or a slice of sugar-encrusted blackberry and apple pie – is heart-warming enough, but a recipe posted in a newspaper, ephemerally on social media or in more lasting form in the pages of a book, has the chance to be shared even more widely. It is just a recipe, a suggestion for something you might like to make for others, but it is what I do.

The first recipe I encountered – for a Christmas cake – belonged to my mother. Handwritten on a piece of ruled Basildon Bond notepaper, it lived in the bowl of the electric mixer that only saw light of day once a year, when I helped her make The Cake. The first cooking I did on my own was a tray of jam tarts – blackcurrant, marmalade and raspberry. The ghost of them lingers still, me standing on a stool in an attempt to reach the kitchen table, rolling out scraps of pastry into a craggy rectangle with a red-handled wooden rolling pin, pressing Mum's crinkle-edged cutters into the pale dough and filling the little tarts with jam as bright and clear as jewels. The jam boiled over and glued the tarts to the tin, but peeling off the chewy crumbs and eating them was a delight.

There is something – and this is the point really – that goes hand-in-hand with making something to eat, that transcends putting the finished dish on the table. Cooking – for me at least – is about making yourself something to eat and sharing food with others but is also – whisper it – about the quiet moments of joy to be had along the way. Watching the progress of dinner as you stir onions in a pan, at first crisp, white and pungent – you may have shed a tear – then slowly becoming translucent gold, darkening to bronze, all the time becoming softer, sweeter. Take them too far though, and those sweet onions will turn bitter. And that is where a good recipe comes in and partly the point of what I do, to guide a new cook towards a pleasing dinner, and for those who have been cooking for years, to share a recipe that they may not know.

I am not a chef and never have been. The word means 'chief' and is therefore somewhat inappropriate. It is no secret that I ran away from the heat of the professional kitchen. The stress and frenetic speed of the work, the dedication required to be really good at what you do and the relentlessness of that life, simply wasn't for me. I wanted to cook for a living but without the seasoning of stress and adrenaline. I fell into writing about food by accident – whilst working in a rather lovely café – so it is odd to think I have had a cookery column for nigh on thirty years, written ten cookery books and penned a memoir (which itself spawned a film and stage play). My respect for professional chefs not only remains undimmed, but I find myself in awe of what they do. It just wasn't my thing.

# How I cook

I am a home cook. I have cooked for half a century and still love every slow turn of the wooden spoon. Simple food, nothing fancy. Just something to eat really. Yes, I go out to dinner or bring home a tray of sushi; I will phone for gyoza or biang biang noodles but even then I will probably have cooked lunch at home. I once described my cooking as 'straightforward, everyday stuff, the sort of thing you might like to come home to after a busy day'. I still stand by that.

Making a few ingredients into something good to eat continues to give immeasurable pleasure. Making dinner for others even more so. I love the deep reassurance that comes from cooking and eating something familiar, a dish I know well, but I also possess an endless curiosity with the new – an insatiable hunger for what is to come. I am never going to be someone who repeats the same old dishes year in year out as if on some sort of culinary treadmill. There is far too much fun to be had for that.

As cook and writer I have got things right, wrong and somewhere in between. I know my faults – in particular my ability to be contradictory, by turns pedantic (handmade basil pesto is better than that made in a food processor, broad beans are much nicer to eat if you take the time to pop them out of their papery skins), and can at other times be happily laid-back (it truly doesn't matter if the fruit sinks to the bottom of your cake; it is just as delicious). We are what we are.

I enjoy eating complex, exquisitely presented food. I just don't like cooking it. More truthfully, I can't. I leave such delicate artistry to the professionals.

## So, back to simple

Dinner is rarely more than a single dish in this house. A bowl of noodles with chilli and greens; plump, garlicky beans slowly cooked in the oven, a boned chicken leg on the grill brushed with thyme and lemon. Sometimes we feast: a vast dish of pasta with mussels and prawns; a steaming pie of sweet potatoes and lentils; baked fatty pork with butter beans and broth. Even then, this is straightforward eating. The nearest you will get to a 'starter' is a bowl of olives. Dessert or cake is more often a mid-morning thing. Tiramisu, after all, means 'pick-me-up' – a neat, sweet punch of energy for when we start to flag. Come to dinner and you are just as likely to get your food in a bowl as on a plate. And those bowls won't match either.

But casual does not mean careless. There is much pleasure to be had from doing a little thing meticulously – taking your time to perform a kitchen task that could be done more quickly. There is a lot of satisfaction in slowly, carefully unfurling and washing salad leaves. Drying them too. If I am enjoying a specific kitchen task – making a salad dressing, shaping a loaf or grating a lemon – I will often slow down, taking a minute or two more to enjoy the process. It is why my pestle and mortar gets as much use as my food processor. Both have a place in the kitchen, but one is about getting something done, the other about enjoying doing it.

It is true that I like to keep things minimal. I often look at a recipe and consider what I can take out rather than what else I can put in. Following a recipe with nineteen ingredients is rather like walking into a room where every surface is awash with 'ornaments'.

I have little truck with perfection. I would rather have a good time round a table with friends and some rough-edged cooking than marvel in silence at the cook's technical precision. I have been to too many dinners like that and they are painful – it is almost a relief to go home. To put it another way, let's just make something good for dinner and enjoy ourselves.

My cooking is free, without being constrained by the rather tiresome idea of doing something as it has always been done, or worse – how someone else feels it 'should' be done. Unfettered by the chains of classical cooking or misplaced authenticity, I am free to enjoy myself in the kitchen.

I couldn't care a jot what is, or is not, considered fashionable. I only care whether or not it is delicious. When some keyboard warrior – or heaven forbid 'influencer' – decides that 'sourdough is so yesterday, gochujang is a passing fad,' I just find myself laughing at the ridiculousness of it all. Something is either good to eat, or it isn't.

## A cook's book – a kitchen chronicle

I am a writer who cooks. It is as simple as that. Not a day goes by when I am not grateful for being able to make a living out of it.

I keep notes, handwritten scribbles in scruffy food-speckled notebooks. Annotations on what I make for dinner, which I then turn into a hopefully clear and workable recipe. I test it to make sure it will work for others, then cook it again so it can be photographed. I then do the washing-up.

Often a published recipe is mine and mine alone; sometimes it is something I work on with my long-time friend and collaborator James. Kindred kitchen spirits, we constantly bounce ideas off one another and have had, and continue to have, many good times at stove and table. I hope we always will.

Food is the way I make a living; it is literally how I put food on the table, but I slightly wince when I hear people say they think about food all day – or that they 'live, eat and dream food'. I know I am not that guy. Food is just part of the ebb and flow of my life; it is both a pleasure and a privilege, but not all-consuming. As I see it, making something nice to eat should not be an obsession, it should simply be part and parcel of everyday living.

Between these covers is a collection of the recipes I make most frequently. Recipes that have stood the test of time in my own kitchen and that I make

again and again. This collection is very much a roll call of those that have become an essential part of my life. There are many new ones too (I couldn't resist). Eagle-eyed readers will notice that some of the recipes appear here with slight alterations from the original. This has been one of the unexpected perks of writing this book, the ability to be ruthless with an unnecessary step or an ingredient that wasn't pulling its weight. The chance to illuminate a crucial detail, to find a way to do something more efficiently, or to take a more sustainable route.

I have incorporated the jottings I have made in the margins of my own books into the recipes that I feel might be helpful to others. (My cupboards have decades of kitchen chronicles, thin pages of fading pencil notes, studded with Post-it notes and marbled with butter or oil.) Every recipe has been retested, and not just by me. Sometimes, the recipe has simply been updated because I felt it needed refreshing. Cooking should not stand still. Eating, cooking and therefore recipes move on.

*A Cook's Book* is a diary of sorts, a chronicle of a life spent mostly at the stove but also a conversation with the reader. It is a collection, a celebration, of the intimate details of hands-on cooking, the small pleasures that are often overlooked in our quest to get food on the table. (I leave the bigger picture – the politics, science and provenance of food – to those who do it better.) All I have done for years is write about my supper.

# A note about the recipes

A recipe must work. Otherwise, what is its point? At its most basic, it is simply a set of instructions for making something to eat. Fine, if that is all you want. Such recipes are concise, neat, spare. But I also enjoy those that are more than just cold instructions, those that are more generous, more than simply 'do this, do that'. The best recipes are those that not only work but are a delight to read, contain a useful tip or two and guide the reader to a good result with ease. I like to hear the voice of the cook who has tempted me to follow their recipe, to feel they are beside me in the kitchen as I cook, a guide and a friend. It is my greatest hope that you feel I do just that.

A recipe must be clear and precise. It is perhaps worth remembering they were once known as 'receipts'. A recipe can contain the grace of accuracy yet without being authoritarian. When I transcribe a recipe from notebook to printed page I like to keep the tale of how the idea came about – its back-story if you like – in a preamble which can be read or ignored as the reader wishes. I don't want anyone to have to extract the instructions on how to boil an egg from a five-hundred-word ramble.

I have never gone in search of 'authentic' recipes. To be honest, authenticity is a bit of a red herring. 'Authentic' is simply to repeat one person's way of doing something. It is unlikely they were the first to ever make that recipe. The fact is that everyone can argue theirs is the 'authentic' version. Every cook tweaks a classic dish to suit their own taste, so who is to say which is the 'right' one. Every bowl of ash reshteh in Iran, every shepherd's pie in Britain, each French coq au vin is a variation on a theme, and no one can claim true 'authenticity'.

## All you need is a good recipe (well, actually, no)

It is an arrogant cookery writer who insists that their way is the 'only' way to do something. Ask forty cooks the 'correct' way to make a classic recipe and you will get forty different answers. Some of them will go on to insist that their way, and only their way, is right. (Indeed, some seem to have made a career out of it.) The fact is that no recipe can work every time for everyone.

As I said in *Appetite*, there are many variables. Your pan may have a heavier base than mine (which makes giving exact cooking times tricky), your oven may run at a slightly different temperature (you have no idea how common that is) and one person's tablespoon may be slightly more heaped than another's. No two pork chops are ever the same, because they come from different animals. Each variety of potato will cook differently, and a winter onion and a summer onion will produce sometimes strikingly dissimilar results. (The summer one has more water in it so it will take considerably longer to caramelise, if at all.)

I have said, many times, that it is unwise to cook by the clock alone. Cook instead by using your sense of smell, touch and eye. To put it bluntly, use your good sense. That said, there is nothing to beat experience. Following the timings for a cheesecake, a first-time cook may think it isn't ready because the filling is still awobble. A helpful writer will tell you not to worry as that is how it should be, because it will thicken on cooling. (It is the same story with custard tarts and quiches. Some things need time to settle.) And sometimes, ingredients are just

plain naughty. A cake that is usually cooked in 40 minutes will, on other days, take 45. Same oven, same cake tin, same recipe. No one knows why. Sometimes ingredients play up. We shouldn't get into a fizz about it.

A cookery writer's job can occasionally be a frustrating one. We can suggest, perhaps inspire and lend a hand, but we can also only go so far. No one likes to have their hand held too tightly, or to have a set of instructions barked at them. The line between being helpful and patronising is sometimes a thin one, especially when you are writing for people with vastly differing levels of experience. Every cookery writer I know works hard to ensure that a recipe makes sense, that the outcome will be successful. Some of us like to go the extra mile, to give the reader details that are more than just a set of weights and timings opposite a picture, and that is what I have always tried to do and hope that I have continued to do here, in this book.

## The quiet table – the unshakeable importance of breakfast

My day starts at the kitchen table. It always has done. Espresso. Make that two. Then breakfast. I cannot remember the last time I failed to eat breakfast.

As a child, breakfast meant cereal. A bowl of porridge with a scandalous pool of golden syrup or perhaps a patterned china dish ('Midwinter', the willow-pattern of the 1960s) of honey-coated puffed rice. Once I left home, the first meal of the day was all about the bacon sandwich – of varying levels of quality, depending on my means at the time – the arrival of which I still regard as a moment of unsurpassable merriment.

Breakfast takes a full hour in my house. During the week there will be (unfailingly) a tiny bowl of kefir or yoghurt. A single piece of fruit. (As I write, mangoes and cantaloupes have just come into season; there is no better start to the day.) There is always, always, toast.

On a Sunday, there will be a small bowl of sticky rice with iridescent Japanese pickles of radish, cabbage or ginger. A lacquer bowl of miso soup. I take my time, I turn the pages of a book. I will not be hurried. Sixty precious minutes in which I organise the day ahead, write my diary, read a book, drink coffee and eat breakfast. If this sounds indulgent, so be it. This is my version of meditation. The entire day is about other people. This single hour is mine.

I love breakfast almost more than any other meal. Staying in a hotel, I will always come down first thing and most probably tuck into a full English. (Hell is a basket of miniature croissants, pain au chocolat and Danish pastries.) My favourites are those in Scotland where good thick sausages come with fried bread and haggis and a fat coin of black pudding. There will be toast wedged tightly in a silver rack and a pot of orange marmalade of whose bitterness I am inordinately fond. Such breakfasts are a treat beyond measure. The icing on the cake is that someone else cooks it.

If I am far from home, I will drop my early morning habits in favour of theirs. What is the point of travel, only to take your own culture with you? Rust-coloured kimchi with my breakfast soup and rice in Korea – you bet. Warm sheets of softly puckered flatbread with sour cherry jam and cream cheese in Lebanon – most certainly. A silent bowl of butter-soft pumpkin in a puddle of dashi in Japan – yes, I'll take that too. Other countries' breakfasts have informed my own and are probably why mine now resembles something of a hybrid.

I am at my desk by seven-thirty.

It should be noted that we don't always eat in the kitchen, cosy though it is. There is a room upstairs that doubles as office, study and photographic studio, in which there is also a large table. It is here that we have meetings and eat. It is also where Jonathan has taken pictures of everything we cook, for as long as I can remember. On fine days, at every possible opportunity, I will eat outside, either in the overgrown courtyard outside the kitchen or in the garden proper.

## The joyous sound of dinner

The kitchen may have a sense of order and calm, but I keep a noisy table. I thrive on the sound of dinner. The clatter of plates, the tinkle of knives and forks, the chink of glasses. A table which, when food is placed upon it, comes to life. Can someone pass me the mayonnaise? Would anyone like some of this? Hands reach across. Bread is torn. Bottles are opened. The table, once so precisely laid, becomes untidy, messy even. (You can leave your table manners at home.)

There is no real plan to the way food appears. Most times, I put a large serving plate or bowl in the middle and let everyone help themselves. Occasionally

I will serve, passing plates and bowls down the table, but it feels too much like being school prefect. If there are just two of us, then supper will often be plated at the stove. Sometimes, eaten there too. Each meal is treated differently, a fluid, open-ended event. To a cook, this, the sound of everyone tucking in, having a good time – the happy thrum of dinner – is the pay-off. A plate licked clean is thank you enough, although those two little words rarely go amiss.

Occasionally, I dine alone. It is one of life's unsung luxuries, especially in a restaurant or, better still, a hotel dining room. Now and again, I will order a home delivery – a massive treat. There may be plump and jolly dumplings with a mysterious liquorice-coloured sauce, slices of sashimi with wasabi paste or skeins of noodles wolfed from a waxed cardboard carton with chopsticks.

## In the kitchen

You'll usually find me in the kitchen. They are those most genial of spaces, somewhere you can cook, eat and drink, where you can gossip and console, laugh and feast. A place to share food and drink with others. I can cook pretty much anywhere, and indeed have done, but some spaces are easier, more pleasurable to work in than others. Maybe now, the kitchen is an even more important place to us than ever? A space whose purpose as the heart and soul of the home is even more evident. I know that time spent in my kitchen means more to me than it has ever done. The space is even more cherished.

My first kitchen, a small, low-ceilinged space with dark wooden beams and a stone floor, led on to a raggedy kitchen garden. My childhood home, a kitchen of Pyrex, melamine and Formica in which the days were marked less by the calendar than by the food cooked in it. Wednesday for ham and parsley sauce spied through the fugged-up kitchen window, faggots and thick gravy from a foil container on a Friday and if there was a pork pie or a rust- and cream-coloured crab on the table it must be a Saturday lunchtime. For a kid trudging back from school in all weathers, the repetition of a cycle of half a dozen meals came in warm, reassuring waves. Balm for a teenager's simmering discontent.

Once I left home, 'my' kitchens, or at least the ones I found myself cooking in, varied from a redundant fisherman's loft in Cornwall to a mullion-windowed castle in Somerset. There was a sixteenth-century pub in Worcestershire and a frenzied and intimidating restaurant kitchen in Yorkshire. There was the tiny kitchen – the size of a fireside rug – of my first London flat. There are cupboards larger than that kitchen, but we had some good times there, and some good food.

I have now cooked in the same space for two decades.

You walk down a flight of worn stone steps. The long, slim kitchen runs the full length of the house. It enjoys both early morning sun and soft evening light, a room as good for breakfast as it is for dinner. A room which, even on the hottest days of the year, has the cool, calm air of a dairy. The colours – milky white, grey stone and shades of celadon – accentuate a feeling of peace. I loathe clutter, so the space is kept open and airy. Plates and pots and pans and cooking ephemera live behind cupboard doors; bare essentials (olive oil, sea salt, wine vinegar and such-like) reside in tall cupboards by the cooker; other less regularly used ingredients in a little larder down the hall. A clean and gentle room in which to make food.

When I bought this old house, twenty years ago now, the basement had become a separate dwelling – a granny flat. The space intrigued. Adjacent to the one large room were several smaller ones whose layout didn't really make sense until I realised (a lightbulb moment if ever there was one) that the space had originally been the kitchens of the house, with a cluster of store rooms attached. I knew, from that moment, that one day it would be so again.

Over the course of a long, long year I turned the space back to being somewhere in which to cook and eat. Walls were stripped in the main room, revealing a pair of hidden fireplaces, one large enough to stand up in, each flanked by the original cupboards. Stone floors and shelves appeared, wooden laths and lime plaster were restored, as was a tiny room that contained ceiling hooks and a fireplace and whose original purpose remains a mystery to this day. It is now, unromantically, the boiler room. The bedroom has its original life back as a scullery and the bathroom is once again a small larder lined with narrow wooden shelves, a marble slab and racks in which to store a few bottles of wine. I sometimes think, on a winter's afternoon, of those who lived and cooked here before me (the house has previously been a hospice, a slum and an art gallery) and wonder what 'they' made for dinner.

As anyone who has restored a house knows, you sometimes wish you hadn't started. The dust, the mushroomy dampness of old wood – and yet more dust – can seem endless. I won't pretend it was an easy year; there was no heating, the winter damp went through to my bones and I twisted my ankle more than

once balancing on heavy scaffolding boards over the dug-out floor. I watched every penny of my savings dissolve. Once the dust had settled, I rather liked that the kitchen had been returned to its former use. Twenty years on it feels right. As I said, I can cook pretty much anywhere, but you need to cook in a collection of places before you can really decide what works best for you. (And to anyone in the midst of kitchen renovation and wishing they hadn't started, I say keep going. Just keep going. It'll be fine.)

This is a kitchen of stone, oak and zinc, with deep fireside cupboards for odd plates and bowls, one for tea caddies and coffee pots and another for 'slow-cooking' stoneware casseroles and a handful of cookbooks. There is a drawer for the bottle opener and corkscrew, napkins and flea-market wooden trays. Another for cookie cutters and rolling pins. Everything in this kitchen has its place but for no other reason than I genuinely feel time is getting short and I am not going to waste 20 minutes of my life looking for the bloody bottle opener.

The aesthetics of a working environment are important, though more so to some than to others. I value a workspace that is uplifting. Which, to me, means light, clean and 'relatively' tidy. Yes, there is art on the walls, music and pale, beautiful ceramics. Such details matter to me. Sadly, there are no plants (my green thumb is confined to outdoors – I can kill a houseplant at twenty paces).

The kitchen is an important space in my life – I spend much of my day there – it is where I take breakfast and bake bread, make tea and dinner and feed friends. It is crucial to me that every piece of kit, no matter how mundane or basic, is well made, pleasing to use and good to hold. Why would I want to cook or even wash up with something made of plastic when it can have the gentle tones of wood or porcelain or clay? It is, I suppose, rather old-fashioned but I don't miss having a microwave or a rice cooker, a deep-fat fryer or a bread-maker or any other 'essentials' of the modern kitchen. For this cook, they take away rather than add to the pleasure of cooking. The fewer things I own with a plug the better.

I do, however, need light. (I speak as someone whose first kitchen had no window – it was like cooking in a cupboard.) As I chop and peel and knead and stir, I want to know what is going on outside. I need to see the sky change colour and to know if it is raining. There is a window with an old horsehair blind that looks out over a tiny brick-floored courtyard. A rescued basement space, once rubble and bins, now home to a second-hand zinc-topped table, white jasmine and a rampant climbing rose. There are wayward pelargoniums in old terracotta and a potting table where I keep rosemary and thyme and several mint plants for tea. It's a small space, now greened – almost wild – and I love it.

As with so many others, my kitchen doubles as a dining room. There is much to be said for this. It feels right to me that food is eaten in the same room in which it is cooked. The journey from stove to table is short, the food arrives hot on your plate. The economy of space appeals. But there is more to it than that. I like the feeling that cook and eaters are more connected. That perhaps, just perhaps, those at the table will understand a bit more of the story of what is on their plate.

Perhaps surprisingly, it is the table, not the cooker, that is the heart and soul of my kitchen. It is the point of it all. The point of everything. It is where what I do for a living begins to mean something. Where I can share what I have been doing all my working life with others. It is also where I sit down and write my letters to you.

# A few essentials

I may, one day, stop making notes and writing down recipes. Who knows? But it is my belief and hope that I will always cook. The idea of not making myself and others something to eat each day seems unthinkable now. I may end up living on grilled chicken and green salad and that would be no bad thing. But that grilled chicken will be basted as it cooks with a marinade of lemon and dried thyme or of miso and honey. The salad will come with a thoughtfully made dressing. I will char lemons to squeeze over my dinner and maybe make a pot of golden, glossy mayonnaise.

There are a few basics, a handful of what I think of as 'essentials', that I would genuinely hate to live without. Small things, but to my mind important. I offer some of those here – not so much recipes as ideas – a salad dressing; a bowl of mayonnaise; an instant green sauce and a nutty, herby cream. They are small details that make a big difference. But then, there is so much else to celebrate, so much pleasure to be had. Making something delicious for someone to eat really is as good as life gets.

# Salad dressing

There is not a day when I don't toss salad leaves in a bowl, but not every salad is dressed. A few are shown little more than the olive oil bottle, and maybe a sprinkle of vinegar. Bitter leaves – chicory, watercress – may get a thick vinaigrette dressing made with twice as much mustard as usual. When a dressing is made, there will be enough to last a day or two, stored in a glass jar in the fridge.

I put the smallest clove of garlic I can find into a mortar, a pinch of salt, then smash the garlic to a paste. Four tablespoons of red wine vinegar are poured over the garlic and then it is set aside for 10 minutes. A short time, but enough to take the heat and crude pungency out of the garlic. A teaspoon of soft, smooth Dijon mustard and then I beat in 175ml of olive oil with a small whisk, a few twists of the peppermill, pour it into a screw-top jar or Kilner and keep it in the fridge. This is enough for 4 bowls of salad leaves, generously dressed.

My dressing is a variant of that of Chez Panisse, Alice Waters's legendary restaurant in Berkeley, California, simply the best dressing I have ever come across. The ratios of oil to vinegar are theirs, but I use different vinegar and a little less garlic.

# Mayonnaise

I make my own mayonnaise... sometimes. A big shining bowl of it, glossy and upright for when it is almost the whole point of the meal – to serve with asparagus or radishes or a bowl of hot and salty chips. When mayonnaise is to be used as a dressing – a supporting role – then it invariably comes from a bottle. Mayonnaise made at home is a very different beast from that you can buy. Thicker, a shimmering crocus yellow, it will come with a deep flavour of olive oil. I sometimes loosen the mixture with a little warm water, add lightly steamed wild garlic leaves, finely chopped, or basil leaves I have pounded to a verdant paste with a pestle. I use two different oils. To use exclusively olive will give a too strong and rasping mayonnaise. A more pleasing result is to be had using half and half with another more neutral oil.

I start with two egg yolks in a deep bowl. The sort of yolks with a proud, upstanding dome, more orange than yellow. I beat in a teaspoon of smooth Dijon mustard, a pinch of sea salt, 2 teaspoons of white wine vinegar (sometimes I use tarragon vinegar), then add 250ml of oil – half groundnut, half olive – at first drop by drop then, as the mayonnaise thickens, a thin but steady stream. I finish with a squeeze, no more, of lemon. The mixture should stand in thick, shiny peaks; it should wobble when shaken, almost like a jelly.

# Marinades

A basic marinade, a sloppy paste in which to soak vegetables, fish or meat before cooking under a grill. A quick, no-messing way to transform your dinner into something really rather wonderful. I use two basic mixtures, using them to soak the ingredients for half an hour before cooking, but, just as importantly, with which to baste them as they cook. They couldn't be simpler or more effective. They are little kitchen lifesavers.

## The miso marinade

This is the marinade I use for chicken, for slices of aubergine, for pork chops. I toss everything in it until thoroughly coated, then cook in a foil-lined grill pan under a hot grill.

In a mixing bowl, stir together 135ml of mirin, 4 tablespoons of white miso paste, 4 tablespoons of honey and a splash of vegetable or groundnut oil. As the ingredients cook, they get a further basting with the remaining marinade.

## The za'atar marinade

Again, a marinade for chicken, for aubergine and pork chops, but also for lamb cutlets, courgettes and mushrooms.

In a medium-sized mixing bowl, mix together 50ml of olive oil, the juice of a large lemon, 2 large cloves of garlic and a tablespoon of za'atar. Marinate, grill and baste.

# Burnt lemons

The difference a scorched lemon – its juice hot, sweet, smoky and sour – can make to a grilled aubergine is extraordinary. Slice a lemon in half, place it cut side down on a hot griddle and leave it there until the cut side is almost burnt. The juice will enhance almost anything you care to squeeze it over.

# A green sauce for almost everything

A chuck-it-in-a-blender sauce for serving with whatever you like, from grilled fish and prawns to baked tomatoes. In a jug blender, mix together 10g of basil leaves, 15g of parsley and 10g of mint, 3 tablespoons of red wine vinegar, 6 anchovy fillets, a teaspoon of Dijon mustard and 2 tablespoons of lemon juice. Pour in 100ml of olive oil and process to a thick, emerald paste. Stir in a tablespoon of capers. It works without the anchovies too if you are looking for a vegan version, though you will need to add a little salt. This will keep for a day or two in a jar in the fridge.

# A herb cream

An invaluable cream to accompany grilled and baked vegetables, fish and meat. It melts softly when spooned on top, forming an effortless, impromptu sauce. This is what I add to baked aubergines, each one cut in half, brushed with olive oil generously, then seasoned and baked till the flesh is soft and silky. When stirred with chopped dill, I use it with grilled salmon or mackerel; with chopped tarragon leaves it becomes something to melt over baked mushrooms.

Put 200ml of thick yoghurt in a bowl, then stir in 4 tablespoons of tahini and a squeeze of lemon juice. (I like it especially with the burnt lemons above.) I prefer to do this lightly, leaving ribbons of the sesame paste marbling the snow-white yoghurt. To this add shredded basil leaves (about 10 medium-sized), a handful of finely chopped dill fronds or a mixture of 12 finely chopped leaves of mint and 20 of coriander.

To use it as a dressing (shredded cabbage, crisp white or red; shaved fennel and sliced orange), whisk in a couple of tablespoons of iced water.

# A cucumber labneh

A cool, pale green summer accompaniment to serve chilled alongside lamb cutlets from the grill, a dish of devilled crab or a plate of roast root vegetables. If I can't find labneh, then I make my own: you stir a teaspoon of sea salt and a little lemon juice into a tub of yoghurt, pour it into a sieve lined with muslin and let it quietly drip overnight into a bowl. The next morning there is a pool of the milky whey that has seeped drop by drop through the cloth, and a snow-white parcel of curds firm enough to spread.

Halve a piece of cucumber weighing 250g lengthways and scoop out the seeds with a teaspoon. Using the coarse side of a grater, grate into a sieve then suspend it over a bowl and leave to drain.

In a dry, shallow pan toast 3 tablespoons of pumpkin seeds over a moderate heat for a few minutes till fragrant. Add 2 tablespoons each of white and black sesame seeds and continue toasting for a couple of minutes, then tip the lot into 400g of labneh.

Squeeze the grated cucumber between your hands to remove as much of the moisture as you can, then add the cucumber to the labneh. Stir everything gently together with a fork, then trickle 4 tablespoons of olive oil over the surface.

# Kitchen kit – the essential knives, pots, pans and cake tins

I loathe gadgets of any sort, especially those made of plastic. That drawer crammed with bits and bobs, those that only come out once a year, doesn't exist in my kitchen. I decided decades ago that there is no place here for a piece of kit that takes longer to find than it does to use. What works for me is a humble collection of well-made pieces of kitchen equipment and little else. Nothing matches. Everything sports the dents, chips and scars of battle. I guess we find space for what we need (my oyster opener is essential; others may use theirs only for opening tester pots of paint). If you get your jollies icing cakes then you will obviously need piping bags, nozzles and other fun bits of kit. Bakers will need a dough scraper (also good for getting ice off a car windscreen). Preservers might need a cotton jelly bag. My advice though is to edit your kit ruthlessly, if only for the relief of seeing your kitchen drawers half-empty. Oh, and always to the charity shop, not the bin.

## In search of the perfect knife

There have been very few knives in my life. One, a thin, flexible filleting knife, has been with me since cookery school. I look after them, keep them clean and sharp(ish) and treat them with respect. I know cooks with a different knife for every task. (They tend to take themselves rather seriously.) There are just two or three I use all time, for pretty much everything.

The best knife is one with which you feel the most comfortable. The one that makes chopping or slicing almost effortless. That knife may be large or small, cheap as chips or eye-wateringly expensive. It could be the one whose purchase you agonised over in Kappabashi in Tokyo or it could simply be the one you inherited from your gran. What matters is that it works for you.

A good strong bread knife with a serrated edge is a must if you like to make toast as much as I do. A small all-purpose knife is invaluable. (Mine is as old

as the hills and something of a workhorse.) My larger 'cook's knives' – one with a stainless-steel blade, the other carbon steel – are used every day. I am enormously fond of them. I like that each has its own story – the handle of one, made by Dan Prendergast, is from an old oak beam that came out of a cottage dated 1757. Everything about his knife works for me. By which I mean it is neither too big or too heavy and I love knowing that it had a previous life. It just feels right in my hand.

# Pots and pans

My pans are few and much used. A couple of wide, shallow pans, 22cm to 30cm in diameter, some with handles, others without – a couple of which are non-stick, others that have developed their own patina through constant use. There is a set of Italian stainless-steel saucepans, each with two handles and a hidden layer of copper, that I have had for about thirty years. I guess they will be with me till I hang up my apron. My cupboards also contain a collection of deep earthenware casseroles for the slow baking of beans and meat on the bone and a couple of large Italian tin-lined copper casseroles for feasting. The assorted cast-iron pans, made in Shropshire, and a set of obscenely heavy enamelled pans, are endlessly useful.

Almost permanently on the hob is a French cast-iron griddle and a smaller Japanese grill pan. Both are much cherished and have developed a natural patina from years of smoke and caramelised food, which stops the meat and vegetables sticking. They are used almost daily for long-stemmed broccoli or cauliflower, for asparagus or thin, young leeks. A steak perhaps, a fillet of mackerel. Before their first use, both griddles were 'seasoned', an essential process that encourages the formation of a natural non-stick layer. I recommend anyone buying a cast-iron griddle goes through this. You brush the piece generously with oil, warm over a low flame or in a hot oven, then allow to cool. There is often quite a bit of smoke, so do put the extractor on. I completed this three times before showing the griddle any ingredients. The process works, and it would be difficult to imagine cooking without them.

Copper outside, stainless steel within, with stocky brass handles, my roasting tin weighs a ton and is even heavier with a fat chicken in it. Like every other pot and pan, it is well used and cared for. If something gets burned on, then

I pour boiling water into it from the kettle and leave it to soak briefly. It is worth investing (and it IS an investment) in a couple of cast-iron baking sheets. Mine are constantly in and out of the oven and under the grill. They never buckle or bend, rust or split. I would be lost without them. Never is the saying 'buy cheap, buy twice' truer than on the subject of pots, pan and oven trays. I can't even remember the last time I bought one. All have served me well.

## A few notes about tart and cake tins

There are two non-stick tart tins with loose bottoms (20cm and 22cm in diameter) that have become invaluable; a wide-rimmed cast-iron pie plate (20cm across the base and 27cm from rim to rim) – the perfect apple pie plate – and a couple of deep-sided round cake tins with removable bases (the 20cm is the most used). Oh, and a square aluminium one for traybakes and brownies. Cared for, they will last you a lifetime. The trick with any pie or cake tin – and especially those of cast iron or tin – is to make sure you dry them thoroughly before putting them away. Obvious I know, but they have a habit of holding water in their corners. Being an old fusspot, I dry mine in the residual heat of the oven to make doubly sure.

Not being a hobby baker, cake decorator or home preserver, I find this thoroughly honed capsule collection more than enough. But then there are anomalies: I might not need a honey dipper or a pizza slice, a piping bag or a garlic press, but my fancy-schmancy Kugelhopf tin, the sort that makes the plainest of cakes look like a Bavarian fairy castle, is a keeper.

# A bowl of soup

It is the humblest of suppers, yet soup has always felt like a luxury to me. We never had soup at home. Soup was something to be chosen from a menu and brought by a waiter. Part and parcel of the treat of going to a restaurant. Oxtail, cream of mushroom, Scotch broth, with its tiny diced carrots and swedes, or cream of chicken. All of which were eaten at a table with a starched white tablecloth from a wide-rimmed soup plate with a round spoon.

Even now, soup comes with hints of indulgence. The velvet texture of puréed pumpkin. A wealth of beans in a crystal broth. The New Year lentil soup whose round pulses were supposed to represent coins and wealth. The most basic recipe in my collection, leek and potato with Parmesan, has the texture of silk, despite the limited ingredients. Whether embellished with cream or strips of chicken or plump dumplings or glistening with pools of goose fat on its surface, even a small bowl of soup seems to speak in generous tones.

Occasionally, on a visit to my godmother the two of us would share a tin of Campbell's asparagus, smiling at each other at the sheer extravagance of it. One I make now is with leeks or onions, softened till they can be crushed with finger and thumb, joined by leftover vegetables and stock, cooked till soft, then blended. The flavours change depending on whether there are more carrots than kale, more peas than parsnips.

Bean soups, green soups, thin, clear broths, nubbly bowls of lentils and cheerful purées of scarlet and ochre, rust and mustard – there is a soup for every mood. In summer, I will happily take a bowl of chilled soup, by which I mean iced, into the garden. A green bowl of quiet contentment. In winter, soup is all about warming our soul, a bowl to bring colour to our frozen cheeks.

I stir soup with a wooden spoon but serve it with a ladle. A ladle carries with it a certain generosity. The volume of soup it holds, the capacious bowl, the implication that there is always more in the pot. A life-enriching thought on a winter's night. The exceptions to all of this are the sachets of instant Japanese miso soup, which I have for breakfast or late in the evening, when in an 'I'm-hungry-but-can't-be-bothered-to-cook' mood.

# Pumpkin soups

There are, at the last count, eight pumpkin soups in my archive: the noodle-rich pumpkin laksa in *Appetite*; the golden squash puréed with lentils, its surface a tangle of fried onions (*The Kitchen Diaries*) and another with bacon and cream; with tomatoes, rosemary and cannellini beans (*The Kitchen Diaries II*); and finally a smooth and silky version with tahini and butternut (*Greenfeast: autumn, winter*). Favourite of all is the stew-like offering in *Tender, Volume I*, where the squash's golden flesh is cooked with chickpeas, ginger, cardamom and coconut. Good luck working out the inspiration for that one.

At its simplest, when the pumpkin's sugary flesh is simmered with onions and perhaps dried chilli, you get a soup that warms and consoles. It fulfils your aim with minimal additions. In some ways, the soup is perfect as it is, and yet the sweet blandness is a perfect point for additions that are spicy, savoury or crisp. Out come the cumin and the coriander, the chickpeas and tahini, the bacon and the Parmesan. (You really must try slipping a piece of Parmesan rind into your pumpkin soup.) Smooth though the golden purée is, you can turn the texture from mere wool to cashmere with the addition of cream or coconut milk.

A straightforward pumpkin or butternut squash soup can be made by simmering 1kg of flesh (skin and seeds removed) with a litre of vegetable stock for 15 minutes till soft enough to crush, then blending till super-smooth. Salt, black pepper, toasted sesame seeds, tahini or grated cheese can be added as you think fit.

# Roast butternut soup with mushrooms and ginger

Rather than the usual velvet-textured pumpkin soup, I have kept the pieces of squash in large pieces, served in a broth red with paprika and hot with shredded ginger. You end up with a textural soup with deep bosky notes, a pleasing change from the usual deep orange, silky soup.

*Serves 6*

butternut  1kg
shallots  6, medium
olive oil  5 tablespoons

sweet paprika  1 teaspoon
hot smoked paprika  1 teaspoon
vegetable stock  1 litre

*For the mushrooms:*
chestnut mushrooms  200g
olive oil  3 tablespoons

ginger  a 10g piece
soured cream  150g

Set the oven at 200°C. Peel the butternut, halve it lengthways and discard the seeds and fibres. (There is no real necessity to peel a butternut, but mine had very hard skin.) Cut the flesh into large chunks, then place in a single layer on a baking sheet or roasting tin. Peel the shallots, halve them, then tuck them among the squash.

Mix the olive oil and the paprikas then spoon over the squash, slide the dish into the oven and bake for about an hour or until the squash is patchily browned but thoroughly soft and tender.

Warm the vegetable stock in a large saucepan. Add the squash and shallots to the stock, place over a moderate heat (use a few spoonfuls of the stock to deglaze the roasting tin if there are any interesting bits of roasted squash and shallot left), then season with salt and a little pepper and bring to the boil. Partially cover the pan with a lid and simmer for 20 minutes until the squash is falling to pieces. Crush a few pieces of the squash into the liquid with a fork to thicken it slightly.

Slice the mushrooms thinly, then fry them in the olive oil in a shallow pan until golden. Peel the ginger and shred it into very fine matchsticks, then add it to the mushrooms and continue cooking for a minute or two. When all is golden and sizzling, remove from the heat. Ladle the soup into deep soup bowls, then spoon over the soured cream and the mushrooms and ginger.

# A pumpkin laksa

At first glance, this noodle-rich supper may seem complicated. It isn't. It is just a lot of ingredients, many of which you may well have in the fridge anyway. The point here is getting the balance to your liking. Something I have spent much time on. The considerations are the sourness and freshness (lime juice, mint, coriander), the body and sweetness (pumpkin, coconut milk) and the heat (ginger, garlic and chillies).

*Serves 4, generously*

| | |
|---|---|
| pumpkin, skinned weight 350g | tamari 1–2 tablespoons |
| chicken or vegetable stock 600ml | the juice of a lime |
| coconut milk 400ml | dried noodles 100g cooked as it |
| nam pla (fish sauce) 2–3 tablespoons | says on the packet, then drained |

*For the spice paste:*

| | |
|---|---|
| red bird's-eye chillies 2 or 3 | coriander roots 5 or 6 |
| garlic 2 cloves | coriander leaves 20g |
| ginger a 35g piece | groundnut oil 2 tablespoons |
| lemongrass 2 plump stalks | sesame oil 2 teaspoons |
| ground turmeric 2 teaspoons | |

*To finish:* a handful of coriander and mint leaves

Remove the seeds from the pumpkin and cut the flesh into large chunks. Cook in a steamer or colander over a pan of boiling water for 10 minutes or so until tender. Remove from the heat.

For the spice paste, remove the stalks from the chillies, peel the garlic, peel and roughly chop the ginger and lemongrass. Put them all into a food processor with the turmeric, coriander roots and leaves and the oils and blitz till you have a rough paste.

A pumpkin laksa

Heat a large, deep pan and add the spice paste. Fry for a minute, then stir in the stock and coconut milk and bring to the boil. Allow to simmer for 7–10 minutes, then stir in the nam pla, tamari, lime juice, cooked pumpkin and the cooked and drained noodles. Simmer briefly, then serve in deep bowls with the coriander and mint leaves over the top.

# Bean soups

My interest in bean soups was initially spiked by Patience Gray, in particular the story of her life with her sculptor husband living around the Mediterranean. Her beautiful, grounding book *Honey from a Weed* (Prospect Books, 1986) talked of soup born from marbled beans simmered with stock and a ham bone; of pesto swirled through fresh bean soups; and of *la pignata*, the tall earthenware cooking pot used for simmering all manner of legumes over the open fire. By the time I arrived at 'The Threatened Bombardment', her rather splendid chapter about the beans' side effects, she had ignited my interest.

There are two forms of bean soup. The first is made from scratch, by soaking dried haricot or cannellini beans overnight and slowly cooking them with aromatics and a good stock, and there is the sort I make more often, using tinned or bottled beans. They both have a place in my life, and therefore this book.

Twenty years ago, I made my first long-cooked bean soup. The kitchen filled with steam, an almost silent blip, blip coming from the big pot with its gently simmering cargo of onions, carrots, leeks, herbs and beans. Few moments in the kitchen have felt the way this did. It is a simple soup, born out of a need to feed ourselves in the depths of winter with a few very basic ingredients. The broth bubbled up, the smell of bay and thyme and sweet root vegetables teased us long before the soup was ready. We made toast, cut thick like a book and raggedly torn, to slide deep into the bowls of hot soup.

The recipe has changed a little over the years. The ham bone replaced by thick rinds of Parmesan; more sweet roots; a little longer on the hob. The soup will be made in this kitchen for ever.

Long, slow-cooked bean soup

# Long, slow-cooked bean soup

*Serves 4, generously*

dried cannellini beans  200g
oil, butter or fat  a little
bay leaves  3
thyme  6 sprigs
pancetta  250g
carrots  1 large or 2 smaller
swede  250g

celery  1 stick
leek  1, large
garlic  2 or 3 fat cloves
Parmesan rind  75g
   (plus grated Parmesan to serve)
parsley  a small bunch

Soak the beans overnight in cold water. The next day, drain them, then tip them into a large, deep pan and cover with water. Add a drop or two of olive oil and the bay leaves and thyme sprigs. Boil hard for 10 minutes, then turn down the heat and simmer briskly until the beans are tender but far from squashy. The exact time will depend on the beans, but you can expect them to take anything from 30 minutes to an hour.

Cut the pancetta, carrot and swede into small dice, cut the celery quite finely and shred the leek into thin coins, discarding the tough green leaves. Peel and chop the garlic.

Warm a couple of tablespoons of olive oil in a deep pan, add the diced pancetta and cook over a moderate heat for a minute or two till the fat is translucent. Add the carrot, swede, celery, leek and garlic, and continue cooking for 7–10 minutes till the vegetables have softened and brightened, stirring regularly.

Drain the beans, bay and thyme and add them to the vegetables. Add the Parmesan rind, then pour in enough water to cover – a good 1.5 litres – and bring to the boil. Turn the heat down so the soup is bubbling gently, partially cover with a lid and leave for at least an hour and a half. Leave it for longer if you can.

Fish out the soft, gooey Parmesan rind, the bay leaves and the thyme sprigs. Check the seasoning, roughly chop and add the parsley and serve in deep bowls with a little more Parmesan.

A quick pancetta and bean soup with spaghetti

There is a bean soup I make when I am short of time. It lacks the soaking of dried haricot and the clouds of aromatic steam they produce as they cook. There are no onions to chop and soften, or long, slow simmering. This is a soup that needs little attention. But it is still a worthwhile contender for supper on a cold night. Bean soup without the fuss. I finish it with a trickle of olive oil, a flourish I love, the oil pooling on the surface in glowing emerald bubbles.

## A quick pancetta and bean soup with spaghetti

*Serves 4*

pancetta in one piece  250g
a little olive oil
garlic  2 cloves
chopped tomatoes  1 x 400g tin
chicken stock  600ml

haricot or cannellini beans
  1 x 400g tin
spaghetti  125g
parsley  a small bunch
extra virgin olive oil

Chop the pancetta into small pieces, then fry for a minute or two in the olive oil over a moderate heat. Once the pancetta starts to turn golden, peel and crush the garlic and add to the pan, followed by the chopped tomatoes, stock and the drained beans. Bring to the boil and season with salt and pepper. Lower the heat so the mixture simmers gently, slowly thickening, for about 15–20 minutes.

Break the spaghetti into short 2cm lengths and boil in deep, salted water for 8–9 minutes till tender, then drain. Roughly chop the parsley and stir into the soup together with the spaghetti. Add a trickle of olive oil to each bowl at the table.

The colder the weather, the thicker the bean soup I need. My last recipe (*Greenfeast: autumn, winter*) had the classic aromatics of onion, garlic, carrot and celery cooked with stock, black-eyed beans and kale. The structure was almost thick enough for you to stand your spoon up in.

The pulses change with the weather. Slim cannellini for a light, golden broth. Brown or green lentils for a thick bacon or mushroom rich soup-stew.

Fat, mealy Judión beans for the coldest nights. The latter come from jars rather than tins, their flesh smooth as a sea-washed pebble. A butter bean of sorts.

I like running my fingers through jars of lentils, especially masoor dal, the tiniest of orange pulses. That they collapse with too much cooking is a good thing. The resulting purée is particularly soothing.

The underrated orange lentil (masoor dal) makes a soup that will become smooth and luscious in texture with just a rigorous stirring from a wooden spoon or brief pressure from a potato masher. I often make a soup similar to the southern Indian soup rasam with split red lentils, tomatoes, ginger and tamarind.

You can use chana dal (split chickpeas) and small yellow lentils (moong dal) if you prefer, but I feel I should mention that they take twice as long to reduce to a velvety purée.

# A spicy red lentil soup

From time to time I find myself with a bag of curry leaves. This soup is a good place for them. Crisped in a little oil in a shallow pan, then drained on kitchen paper and scattered over as you serve, like aromatic crisps.

*Serves 4*

| | |
|---|---|
| red split lentils  175g | ground turmeric  1 teaspoon |
| cumin seeds  1 teaspoon | chillies, small, hot  2 |
| black peppercorns | groundnut oil  3 tablespoons |
|  half a teaspoon | yellow mustard seeds  1 teaspoon |
| cardamom pods  8 | tomato purée  1 tablespoon |
| ginger  a 35g piece | tomatoes  250g |
| garlic  3 cloves | tamarind paste  3 teaspoons |

*To finish:*

| | |
|---|---|
| yoghurt  120ml | groundnut oil  a little |
| mint leaves  12 | curry leaves  8 |
| coriander leaves  a small handful | |

A spicy red lentil soup

Wash the lentils in cold running water. Put the cumin seeds and peppercorns in a spice grinder. Crack the cardamom pods, extract the black seeds from within and add them to the cumin. Grind to a coarse powder. (You can also do this with a pestle and mortar.) Tip the ground spices into a food processor, then add the ginger and garlic, both peeled and cut into pieces, the turmeric and the chillies. Pour in a tablespoon of the oil and process to a coarse paste.

Pour the remaining oil into a deep saucepan over a moderate heat, add the mustard seeds and let them cook for a minute, shielding with a lid should they start to pop. Stir in the spice paste and fry for a minute or two till fragrant. Add the tomato purée. Chop the tomatoes and add to the pan, continue cooking for a few minutes, then as the tomatoes soften and collapse add the lentils, the tamarind paste, 750ml of water and a half-teaspoon of salt. Lower the heat and leave to simmer for 25 minutes. Stir regularly.

Put the yoghurt into a small serving bowl. Finely chop the mint and coriander and stir into the yoghurt. Warm the oil in a small frying pan over a moderate heat, drop in the curry leaves and fry them till crunchy, taking care they do not burn, then add them to the yoghurt. Mash the soup with a potato masher till thick and creamy (alternatively, process half of the soup through a blender until it is purée-like in texture, then return to the pan).

Ladle the soup into bowls and stir in the yoghurt and herbs at the table.


The small green and brown lentils, from Le Puy and Castelluccio, are the varieties I use for thick soups seasoned with herbs rather than spices. There will be garlic and onions amongst them, but instead of fiery chillies and earthy cumin you will find mint or tarragon, lemon, parsley or rosemary, and very often mushrooms of some sort. If my red lentil soups can be called hot and earthy, then those I make with green and brown lentils are bosky, like the woodland floor. They will often have spinach or chard stirred into them, and in winter, cavolo nero or crinkly-leaved Savoy cabbage.

A creamy green lentil soup

# A creamy green lentil soup

*Serves 4*

onions  2 small or 1 large
olive oil  3 tablespoons
garlic  3 cloves, sliced
mushrooms, brown  125g
parsley  a small bunch
Puy or Castelluccio lentils  250g

stock, or, at a push, water  1.5 litres
spinach  2 large handfuls, 150g
mint  a small bunch, leaves torn
lemon  1
double cream  100ml

Peel the onions and chop them finely, then let them cook in a large, deep saucepan over a low to moderate heat with a couple of tablespoons of the olive oil and the sliced garlic. The onions should be soft and pale gold in colour. Chop the mushrooms, stir them into the onions and continue cooking for 5 minutes or so. Chop the parsley and stir it in.

Wash the lentils thoroughly, then stir into the onions. Pour over the stock and bring to the boil, skimming off any froth that comes to the surface. You can add a bay leaf or two if you like. Turn the heat down so the lentils simmer merrily, then partially cover the pan with a lid and leave until they are tender but far from collapse – about 30 minutes.

Wash the spinach thoroughly and tear it up a bit. Whilst it is still wet and dripping, put it into a shallow pan over a high heat and shut the lid tightly – it needs to cook in its own steam. After a minute it will be limp and bright green. Lift it out, squeeze it dry, then stir into the lentil soup.

Season the soup with salt, black pepper, mint leaves, the lemon juice and the cream. Make sure it's hot, then serve.

# Green soup

Is there anything quite so spirit-lifting as a bowl of vivid green soup? Pea and parsley; broccoli and bacon; or greens and cheese. Bowls of vital, green energy. Recipes that are quick to execute if for no other reason than you want to cook green vegetables for as little time as possible.

There are some recipes that barely qualify as cooking. Emptying a packet of peas into a pan with a pot of stock and a potato is one of them. This is a soup I make regularly throughout the year, equally suited to celebrate the arrival of spring blossom as it is to cheer us on a grey winter's night.

I could have left the recipe where it was, a bowl of instant efficacy, but decided instead to give it a kick up the backside. If wasabi, the vibrant green Japanese horseradish root, does so much for the addictive little snack of crisp, dried wasabi peas, then could it do the same for my soup? On a whim, I squeezed the paste into my soup. Gingerly at first, a teaspoon of the hot paste at a time. I am not sure why I hadn't thought of it before, considering how fond I am of the ubiquitous Japanese snack. A verdant bowl of sweetness and heat.

## Pea and parsley soup

*Serves 6*

butter 60g
spring onions 75g
flat-leaf parsley 300g
a medium potato
peas 200g (shelled weight)

garlic 2 cloves, peeled
stock, chicken or vegetable
1 litre
wasabi paste

Melt the butter in a large, heavy-based pan. Chop the spring onions and stir them into the butter, letting them cook for 4–5 minutes over a moderate heat.

Chop 150g of the parsley, stalks and all, combine it with the spring onions and leave to cook for a minute or two till the colour has darkened. Peel, dice and add the potato. Add the peas and peeled garlic and pour in the stock. Bring to the boil, then lower the heat to a simmer and cook for 8–10 minutes.

Put a pan of water on to boil. Discard the stalks from the reserved parsley, add the leaves to the boiling water and leave for 2 minutes, then drain. Stir the leaves into the soup, then remove from the heat, process to a smooth, green purée in a blender or food processor and serve. At the table, pass the tube of wasabi paste, letting each stir in as much as they need. (Go gently with the wasabi. As a guide, my threshold is about half a teaspoon per bowl.)

# Gentle soups

Just as a bowl of soup can uplift and invigorate, it can also soothe and calm. I am thinking here of all white vegetable soups such as soubise, the ivory-hued onion soup, cream of cauliflower, and celery. (Why no one makes celery soup any more is beyond me; it is a graceful, quietly pleasing soup.) But I also include cheese soups, the fondue's thinner sister, the sort into which you want to dunk tufts of chewy bread.

# Cauliflower soup

A pale beauty. If you bake a cloud-like head of cauliflower under a blanket of cheese sauce, or deep-fry florets in a gossamer-textured tempura batter, then you can congratulate yourself. Cauliflower can also be sliced and roasted and eaten with a green sauce. The snow-white cap, stalks and small green leaves of a cauliflower make a soothing soup, though it may need a shot in the arm in the form of blue cheese or perhaps a little seafood, such as mussels, prawns or smoked oysters. I was quietly pleased with the one involving a few young leeks and a handful of toasted cheese croûtes.

Cauliflower soup

*Serves 4*

| | |
|---|---|
| leeks  3, medium | bay leaves  2 |
| butter  30g, plus a little extra | parsley leaves  a good handful |
| for the toast | sourdough bread  4 slices |
| olive oil  2 tablespoons | cheese (any good melting type) |
| cauliflower  1kg | 100g |
| vegetable stock  1 litre | |

Discard the coarse part of the green leaves from the leeks and roughly chop them. Warm the butter with the olive oil in a deep pan. Add the leeks and cover with a lid. Cook over a low to moderate heat, stirring and checking their progress regularly, until the leeks are soft but without browning them.

Trim and thickly slice the cauliflower and add to the leeks. Stir briefly, then pour in the vegetable stock and bring to the boil. Add the bay leaves and a little salt, then lower the heat and leave the leeks and cauliflower to simmer for 15–20 minutes, until soft. Remove and discard the bay leaves. Process half the mixture in a blender until really smooth. Add the handful of parsley to the remainder and process it to a thick, rough-textured consistency. Mix the two together and check the seasoning, adding salt and ground pepper as you think fit.

Spread the sourdough with a little butter or olive oil and place under a hot grill, toasting one side to a light crispness. Turn the bread over and cover the other side with thick slices of cheese, then return to the grill until melted. Cut the cheese croûtes into small pieces, divide the soup between bowls and float them on top.

Cheese, the ultimate enrichment for soup. The floating croûte on the cauliflower soup above. The crust of grated Gruyère entwined with onions and slices of bread on a bowl of classic onion soup. A golden lid to crack with your spoon. Grated Parmesan in your bean broth. Or we can take it one step further. An entire soup of cheese.

I have taken this recipe on by toasting thick – and they must be thick – slices of bread, and placing them in the bottom of the soup bowl and by letting the soup soak into them, I had something pretty special in front of me. Silken and

A soup of bread and cheese

soothing, a soup with which to thaw a frozen soul. Cheese on toast you eat with a spoon. Wait for a frosty night.

# A soup of bread and cheese

*Serves 4–6*

onions 2, medium
butter 30g
olive oil a little
carrots 2, medium (100g)
celery 1 stick
milk 400ml
plain flour 45g

vegetable stock 400ml
cider 350ml
Dijon mustard 1 tablespoon
Cheddar 400g
bread a couple of thick slices
chopped parsley a small handful

Peel and roughly chop the onions. Warm the butter and oil in a deep saucepan over a moderate heat, then add the onions and cook till soft. Scrub and finely dice the carrots, finely dice the celery, then add to the softening onion and continue cooking for 10 minutes or so till tender.

Warm the milk in a small saucepan and set aside. Stir the flour into the vegetables and continue cooking for 2–3 minutes, then add the milk and stir to make a thick sauce. Pour in the vegetable stock and cider, bringing it to the boil, then lower the heat and let the mixture simmer for a few minutes. Stir in the mustard and check the seasoning. (It may want pepper, but probably very little salt.)

Grate the cheese and stir into the soup, leaving it to simmer (it is crucial it doesn't boil) for 5 minutes, until the soup has thickened. Toast the bread on both sides till crisp. Tear it into pieces, then put in the bottom of your soup bowls and add the parsley. Ladle the soup over the bread and let it soak in.


There are, I am sure, plenty of cooks who enjoy making fish soup. An entire meal in a large, open bowl, thick with shells and croûtes of bread. I am not one of them. The rust-red soups with their catch of red mullet and clams, prawns and pieces of monkfish, rarely seem worth the enormous amount of faff involved. And my word, the expense! Even if you find a kindly fishmonger, your soup will cost a small fortune, and that's before you've put the saffron in. On a minor domestic note, I also resent the endless amount of washing-up involved. And yet, I rather like eating the occasional bowl of fish soup.

I get round this by making a simple chowder of mussels. It fits the bill both financially and in culinary terms. It smells like a day at the seaside. I use buttery leeks rather than onions, which I feel marry more sweetly with the shellfish, and serve the mussels minus their shells. The result is a charming little bowl of piscine joy. (And very little washing-up.)

## A chowder of mussels and leeks

*Serves 4*

| | |
|---|---|
| leeks 3 | potatoes 450g |
| smoked streaky bacon 150g | double cream 200ml |
| butter 40g | bay leaves a couple |
| mussels 1kg | thyme 4 sprigs |
| white vermouth 2 glasses | parsley a few sprigs, chopped |

Thinly slice the leeks and rinse them very thoroughly. (No vegetable holds grit like a leek.) Cut the bacon into short, thin strips and put them in a deep, heavy-bottomed pan with the butter. Let the bacon colour lightly over a moderate heat. Turn down the heat, add the leeks and cover with a lid. Leave them to cook for 20 minutes or so, with an occasional stir, until they are soft and sweet – they should not colour. Remove from the heat.

Check the mussels and pull away any beards. Discard any mussels that are broken, open or exceptionally heavy. Put them in a large pot, pour in the vermouth and cover tightly with a lid. Place over a high heat till the mussels have opened (a matter of minutes), then remove each mussel from its shell and set aside.

Peel the potatoes and cut them into large dice. Put them in a saucepan with 400ml of the mussel cooking liquor, drained through a sieve. Add the cream, bay, thyme and a little pepper (no salt). Bring to the boil, then reduce the heat so the potatoes simmer gently for about 10 minutes.

Add three-quarters of the cooked potatoes to the leeks and bacon. Put the remainder in a blender with the cream (pick out the herbs first) and blitz briefly till smooth. Too long and it will turn gummy. Return to the pan and add the mussels and parsley. Bring to the boil and serve.

In the freezer, tucked behind the tubs of ice cream and boxes of puff pastry, are bags of dumplings. Prawn gyoza, wontons, delicately pleated zheng jiao filled with pork and chives and almost translucent har gow, their pink and green filling visible through the skin like fish in a frozen pond. They are not homemade. They come from one of the grocers' shops in Chinatown, hidden in the banks of freezers in the back of the shop. I keep them as a squirrel store of emergency solace.

I have never met a dumpling I didn't like. A plump, chewy wrapper of minced prawns or pork and sometimes both; coriander and spring onion, parsley and cracked pepper. If you told me I had to eat nothing but dumplings for the rest of my life, I would still die content. I like them steamed with a chilli dipping sauce or fried with Chinese black vinegar. Best of all, I like them in broth. Deep, golden chickeny broth with tiny, perfectly round puddles of oil dancing on its surface. All of which must be eaten too hot. The rule is that your eyes must water twice. Once when you sip the soup, and again when you bite into the dumpling.

My soup of solace is not the bland, nannying cream soup that works for others, but a bowl of clear, jewel-bright chicken broth, deeply savoury from the addition of fish sauce and citrus-sharp from lime leaves and lemongrass. I use frozen lime leaves if I'm out of fresh, but the lemongrass must be young, plump and supple.

For a supper as simple as this, you cannot get away with lacklustre stock. Believe me I have tried. It just doesn't hit the spot. But here's a neat little trick. If your broth isn't quite up to scratch, add a drop or two more fish sauce. It adds deep waves of umami.

# A simple, clear dumpling soup

*Serves 2*

| | |
|---|---|
| chicken stock, a good one 500ml | dumplings, prawn or vegetable, frozen or fresh  10 |
| lemongrass  2 stalks | fish sauce  about 2 teaspoons |
| lime leaves  6 | coriander leaves  2 handfuls |

Pour the stock into a deep saucepan and bring to the boil. Crush the lemongrass stalks with a pestle or other heavy kitchen object till they splinter, then put them into the pan together with the lime leaves, crushing them in the palm of your hand as you go. Turn off the heat, cover with a lid and leave for 20 minutes.

Place the dumplings in a steamer basket and cook over a pan of boiling water, covered with a lid, for 5–7 minutes till translucent. (I use my bamboo steamer for this, placing a piece of greaseproof paper or baking parchment in the steamer basket then laying the dumplings snugly on top before placing the basket on top of a pan of boiling water and covering with a lid.)

Remove the leaves and stalks from the stock, bring back almost to the boil, then season with the fish sauce, tasting as you go. Pile the dumplings and the coriander leaves into two bowls, then ladle in the stock.

And lastly, a chilled soup for high summer. Gazpacho, a soup that I first tasted in my teens (I think we pronounced it gaz-patch-io), was all the rage at the time, though rarely made with any understanding. It remains a soup whose success depends as much on the weather as it does on the recipe.

Spanish friends argue even within their own families as to the perfect mixture of tomatoes, green peppers and cucumber, to the inclusion of bread and whether contemporary versions are fun or an aberration. Even the texture is up for heated discussion. And then I come along and change the green peppers to red because I don't like the green ones (more accurately, they don't like me).

I am far from a kitchen pedant, and actually enjoy the fact that there are local or familial variations of a classic and no one single recipe. Indeed, not all gazpacho is even red, as some forms don't contain the tomato that one could assume lies at the heart of this chilled summer soup.

The consistency of a gazpacho is down to personal preference and local tradition. Most teeter on the edge of a coarse purée, but it is rarely a smooth soup. No matter how much you chop and blitz the soup, it is always more interesting for retaining a faint element of crunch from the raw ingredients; otherwise you might as well go the whole hog and turn it into a smoothie. Those that never see the inside of a blender can be particularly welcome, the tomatoes, peppers and cucumbers chopped very finely, giving more of a fine salsa than a soup.

Whether you take the rough route or the smooth, you will need a little vinegar in there. First choice is generally red, but a sherry vinegar is favoured to mellow the rawness of the peppers. Add it a spoonful at a time, tasting as you go.

And when I say chilled, I mean it. Few dishes are more welcome on a scorching summer's day than a dish of iced scarlet soup. Yet few things make me gag more than one at room temperature. You will need ice cubes if this soup is to truly hit the spot.

# Gazpacho

You could, if you wish, add a little Serrano ham to the soup at the last minute. Two or three cubes or a shredded slice or two is enough in each.

*Serves 6*

| | |
|---|---|
| tomatoes  6, large, but not beefsteak | spring onions  3 |
| | garlic  2 cloves |
| red peppers  3 | sherry vinegar  2 tablespoons |
| yellow peppers  3 | smoked paprika, mild  1 teaspoon |
| red onion  1 | olive oil  1 tablespoon |
| half a cucumber | caster sugar  2 teaspoons |

Cut a small cross in the bottom of each tomato, then put them in a heatproof mixing bowl. Put the kettle on and when it boils pour the water over the tomatoes and leave them for a minute or so. Lift each one out with a draining spoon and slip off the skins. They should come away easily.

Cut each tomato in half, discard the seeds and core, then put them in a blender. Chop the peppers, discarding the seeds, and add them to the tomatoes together with the onion, peeled and chopped, and the roughly chopped cucumber. Remove most of the green shoots from the spring onions, then roughly chop the white and add to the tomatoes with the peeled garlic.

Blitz the mixture until it is at the consistency you like. It's obviously up to you. Only you know how thick you like your soup. Now start to season your soup to taste with salt, the sherry vinegar, smoked paprika, olive oil and sugar. Start with the amounts in the list, then tweak to your own liking.

# Breaking bread

It started with a baguette. That first loaf, bought at dawn from a boulangerie on my way home after a night out in Paris, still warm, its crust crackling. The floury, craggy point of the bread – more crust than crumb, more air than loaf – wrenched off as I walked, and eaten (sans beurre, sans confiture, sans jambon) in the street will never leave me. There is more interesting bread than a baguette, but that memory has never dimmed, like the first forkful of chargrilled steak or the first (illegal) sip of beer. Even now, forty years on, retrieving the early morning round of bread from the toaster, juggling it from one hand to another on its way to the plate, I wish every slice could be the crust. It is the bread's crown, its point of glory.

At home, making my weekly sourdough, I will risk the searing heat of my oven cranked to its highest setting, the occasional piercing burn to my wrist, just to get the crust as crisp as possible. It is what makes bread worth eating, and worth baking. I can buy better bread now than at any point in my life. It is one of those things that is, without question, better than it used to be. The cottage loaf of my childhood, with its wonky topknot, may have disappeared in favour of the gnarled, oven-scorched crust of the sourdough loaf, but so toothsome is some of the bread now that you might wonder why anyone would ever bake at home.

Baking bread is time-consuming and, making one loaf at time, probably costs more than buying it from a shop. And yet we still do. I do. Weekly. As cooking goes, there is nothing more basic than forming and baking a loaf of bread. You don't do it for yourself. You make a loaf to share. You convince yourself, as you pull your proud piece of artistry out of the oven, that you and those you love could survive on that alone. A hand-raised loaf is not just a thing of beauty; it is testament to our ability to turn the most basic ingredients – flour, yeast, salt and water – into sustenance for those we love.

I bake bread. Not every day, but usually once a week. I bake when I need to feel dough in my hands or to relish the joy that is holding a handmade loaf. Baking at home is inevitably something for the weekend, when I can be more generous with my time. It also very much a winter activity for me. Possibly because, as a household, we eat less bread in summer.

Working with yeast can seem like sorcery. (I do believe there is a certain magic involved.) But it is also straightforward and deeply satisfying once you get the hang of it. That said, the capriciousness of yeast can be off-putting to the first-time baker. (I fully remember the loaves I made as a teenager ending their days turfed onto the lawn for the birds. What is more, as if my feelings weren't hurt enough already, the blackbirds, starlings and sparrows would then proceed to ignore them.)

You can make a good loaf without yeast. A quickly made bread, whose crust is risen not with the miracle that is yeast but by bicarbonate of soda, and needs no proving or shaping, might be a useful recipe to master. The speed appeals, but more than that, it is the fact that I can bake midweek (I can have a loaf in the oven within 15 minutes, baked in thirty, sliced, toasted and buttered just a heartbeat or two later).

The structure of soda bread is close-textured and mealy. As much cake as bread. It is fragile to the touch yet sustaining. A humble loaf.

## Seeded soda bread

I do like a seeded loaf, especially when sliced and toasted. Pumpkin, linseed, sunflower or hemp seeds introduce some interest to a standard soda bread. Linseeds should be crushed if we are to make the most of their plentiful omega-3 fats, but I use them simply for their nutty taste and silky texture.

*Makes 1 × 500g loaf*

wholemeal flour  225g
plain flour  225g
bicarbonate of soda
   1 level teaspoon
sea salt  half a teaspoon

caster sugar  1 teaspoon
golden linseeds  3 tablespoons
sunflower seeds  3 tablespoons
pumpkin seeds  2 tablespoons
buttermilk  350ml

Set the oven at 220°C. Place a heavy casserole, about 22cm in diameter, together with its lid, in the oven to heat up.

Sift the flours, bicarbonate of soda and salt into a large bowl. Stir in the caster sugar. Add the linseeds, sunflower and pumpkin seeds and fold evenly through the flour. Pour in the buttermilk and mix thoroughly to a slightly sticky dough.

Dust a pastry board or the work surface generously with flour. Working fairly quickly, pat the dough into a round large enough to fit snugly into the casserole. Remove the hot pan from the oven, dust the inside generously with flour, which will prevent the loaf from sticking, then lower the dough into the casserole. Cover with the lid, then return to the oven and bake for 20 minutes.

Remove the lid and continue baking a further 5 minutes, then lift the dish from the oven and leave to rest for 10 minutes, before freeing the loaf and placing on a rack to cool.

When I was writing *Appetite*, something of a magnum opus on basic home cooking, I was determined to offer a recipe for a white loaf. Uncomplicated, straightforward, simple to execute. I discounted using fresh yeast as it is far from easy to access, plumping instead for the dried, easy-bake granules in foil sachets. Easy buy, easy bake. The method was written in such a way that I felt anyone could do it. For many, it seemed, this was their first attempt at a loaf, and to this day I am told stories of people's success with it. There are certainly more inventive recipes using sourdough starters and any number of different flours, but the recipe remains what I set out to provide. A simple, no messing introduction to making your own loaf.

# A simple loaf

Or, as I called it in *Appetite*, 'A really good, and very easy white loaf'.

*Makes 1 very large loaf*

| | |
|---|---|
| white bread flour 1kg | sea salt 20g |
| instant dried yeast 2 × 7g sachets | water about 700ml |

Take your largest, widest mixing bowl and tip in the flour, yeast and salt. Pour in almost all of the water and mix it to a sticky dough. Keep mixing for a minute or so – the dough will become less sticky – then add a little more flour until you have a dough that is soft, springy and still slightly sticky to the touch.

Generously flour a large, flat work surface and scoop the dough out onto it. Work the dough, pushing it with your hands, pressing it flat with your palms. Fold the far edge towards you and push it back into the dough with the heel of your hand. Continue folding and pushing the dough. Work firmly but gently with none of that brutal banging people tell you about, folding and pushing the ball between your hands for 10 minutes.

It should feel soft, springy and alive (which, of course, being full of yeast, it is). The technique is less important than you may have been led to believe. What is important is that you carry on gently but firmly pummelling the dough. As you do so, you will feel it becoming lighter and springier. If you find it exhausting then you are pushing the dough too hard.

Place the ball of dough back in the bowl, cover it with a clean tea towel and put it somewhere warm, but not hot, for an hour or so. It should be well out of a draught. An airing cupboard is ideal. The dough should almost double in size. The time it takes will depend on how hot or moist your room is, the exact type of flour you have used and the age of your yeast, but it will probably be about 45 minutes to an hour.

Once the dough has almost doubled in size, you need to tip it out onto a floured surface again, scraping out any dough that has stuck to the bowl, and give it another short session of pushing and squeezing; a couple of minutes will do fine. Bring the dough into a ball again and place it on a baking sheet. Dust it heavily with flour, then cover with a tea towel and return it to the warm place to rise again.

Set the oven at 250°C. After an hour or so the dough will have spread, and somewhat alarmingly. You want it to be twice its original size, or as near as damn it. Gently, and I do mean gently, tuck it back into a neat, high ball, and place it softly in the oven. Don't slam the door.

Leave the loaf to bake for 10 minutes, then turn the heat down to 220°C. After 25–30 minutes you can check the loaf's doneness. It should sound hollow when you tap its bottom. Like a drum. Let the loaf cool on a cooling rack. Try not to cut straight into it; give it time to settle before slicing.

For all that I bang on about the crackling, flour-dusted crust, sometimes a soft roll is what you want. A crust that is pale, giving and pleasingly springy. A sweet and open crumb. A tender, plumptious bun.

You will get this sort of bread if you add yoghurt or kefir, or indeed milk, to a bread dough. Include a puddle of olive oil and you are well on the way to something altogether softer and richer. (Tread a step further and introduce eggs and you have brioche, but we are not going there.) I think of these enriched breads as something to make in spring, for no other reason than the time feels right. Their pleasingly yellow crumb feels in tune with what is happening in the garden. (There is a wonderful crocus-yellow saffron bread I long to make but have never got round to.) Buns that have an affinity with cream cheese or smoked salmon, with dill, rosemary and the tang of sheep's and goat's milk cheeses.

The buns that follow could hardly be easier. They rise like a dream and smell sweetly of snow-white cheese and mountain herbs.

## Soft rolls with feta and rosemary

*Makes 6 rolls*

plain flour  500g
fast-acting dried yeast
    1½ teaspoons
sea salt  half a teaspoon
kefir  200ml

olive oil  3 tablespoons
warm water  100ml
feta cheese  200g
rosemary  3 bushy sprigs
thyme  5 bushy sprigs

*To finish:*
thyme and rosemary  a few sprigs         olive oil  a little

You will need a deep-sided rectangular baking dish or bread tin, approximately 25cm × 16cm. Put the flour, yeast and salt in a large, warm mixing bowl. Put the kefir in a jug, add the olive oil and the warm water and stir well. Combine the kefir mixture and flour with a wooden spoon or your hands and mix until you have a soft and slightly sticky dough.

Crumble the feta into a small bowl. Remove the leaves from the rosemary and thyme, finely chop them and add to the crumbled cheese.

If you are making the dough by hand, tip on to a floured board and knead the cheese and herbs into it. If you prefer the easy way, use a food mixer fitted with a dough hook to knead the cheese and herbs into the dough. Continue kneading for a couple of minutes, adding a little more flour if necessary to stop it sticking, then put the dough back in its bowl, cover with a clean, warm cloth and put it in a warm place. Leave the dough in peace until it has risen to almost twice its original size.

Line the baking tin with a piece of baking parchment.

Cut the dough into six equal pieces, then shape each one into a round bun. Place the buns in the baking tin, three down each side, then return to the warm place, cover with the cloth and leave for about 30 minutes, until nicely risen and touching one another.

Set the oven at 220°C. Toss the herbs in the olive oil and scatter them over the rolls, then bake for about 20 minutes, until lightly golden brown.


Enriching a basic bread dough with olive oil gives a soft, open-textured bread that is sublime for tearing apart and thrusting into soft, fragrant mounds of hummus, beetroot or bean purée or just more olive oil. The oil you knead into the dough lends a richness that leaves traces of deliciously salty, herb-scented oil on your fingertips.

Focaccia is pretty easy to make to be honest. Baked in a deep tray, it is less demanding than a loaf, and surprisingly good-natured. It keeps for a day or two, prevented from drying out by its oil content, and is very good toasted.

My initial aversion was due to the 'cakey' quality of many I tried, and the inclusion of the sun-dried tomatoes. (Along with tomato purée and passata, sun-dried tomatoes are far from my favourite ingredients.) Baking my own, I could introduce briny green olives and a scattering of thyme leaves instead.

The best focaccia I have eaten was one made with a sourdough starter and begun three days in advance. Fine for the hobby baker and those who know what they want to eat days in advance. I like a quicker fix, so I have settled on a recipe that requires just one overnight spell in the fridge. Something of a compromise, I agree, but the result is a more open crumb and, I think, a better flavour than those that are risen and baked on the same day. Crisp on top and bottom, a good spongy, chewy crumb and satisfyingly olive-oily, this is seriously good focaccia.

I should add that I sometimes stir 2 tablespoons of sourdough starter into the warm water with the yeast and sugar. The inclusion is far from crucial, but it produces an even lighter, chewier loaf.

## Green olive and thyme focaccia

One for an early summer lunch – goat's milk cheese in thick, chalky slices, magenta ribbons of pickled red cabbage, and this focaccia, torn into oily tufts.

*Makes 1 large loaf*

warm water 400ml
easy-bake dried yeast 2 teaspoons
sea salt 1 teaspoon
caster sugar 1 teaspoon
sourdough starter 2 tablespoons
    (optional)
strong white bread flour 500g

olive oil 6 tablespoons, plus a little
    extra for the baking tin
green or lemon-marinated olives,
    stoned 100g
thyme the leaves from 6 bushy
    sprigs
sea salt flakes

You will also need a high-sided baking tin approximately 34cm × 24cm.

Put the water and yeast into a large mixing bowl and add the salt and sugar. If you are including a little of your sourdough starter, do so now, stirring it into the water till dissolved. Mix in the flour either by hand or with a wooden spatula. Add 2 tablespoons of the olive oil and mix loosely into the dough. Cover the bowl with a cloth and refrigerate overnight. (The dough will need a good eight hours.)

Next day, when the dough will have risen to about twice its original size, chop the olives and the thyme leaves and mix them into the dough along with another 2 tablespoons of the oil. Lightly oil the baking tin and turn the dough out into the tin. Push the dough out to fit the tin with your fist, gently pushing it almost into the corners – it will swell during the second proving – then wrap the tin in a cloth and place in a warm spot for a good hour, perhaps two, until it has risen to twice its size.

Set the oven at 220°C. When the oven is ready, use a floured finger to push several hollows into the dough, then scatter the surface lightly with sea salt flakes and bake for 30 minutes till golden. Remove from the oven, pour the remaining oil over the surface, then release from its tin with a palette knife and serve.

Green olive and thyme focaccia

It is 2017 and I am working in the Middle East, making a series of documentaries with James and a television crew. It is early morning in Tehran and we are filming at a bakery, where the bakers are lifting newly baked sheets of flatbread from the ancient and frankly terrifying brick ovens with long wooden shovels. Men are queuing at the door on their way back from the mosque. Each long, thin loaf is folded over and tucked under the buyer's arm like a broadsheet newspaper.

As I stand outside the bakery, waiting for the crew to wind up, I tear a jagged strip from my sheet of warm, blistered flatbread. The baguette moment I had forty years ago floods back, that single lump of bread that changed everything. Here was a revelation like the first sip of green tea (London, 2008), the first true espresso (Milan, 1979), that initial dunk of chewy, open-textured sourdough bread in jewel-bright olive oil (San Francisco, 1995). The seductiveness of good flatbread, the sheets of ubiquitous warm dough – blackened, blistered and puckered – was suddenly as clear as the morning call to prayer that had followed us throughout the Middle East. More crucially, nothing could be as far from those bendy slippers of damp dough I had previously known as flatbread.

At home I make my own flatbread in an everyday domestic oven. The result is less dusty, fragrant and interesting than that baked in an ancient brick oven, but it is what I have. No bread is simpler to make. No bread is more efficient for scooping up garlicky purées of chickpeas and tahini; nothing else seems quite right spread with soft, white cream cheese and a garnet spoonful of sour cherry jam. Even baked in a state of the art stainless-steel oven, it is bread that still feels as old as time.

## Herb flatbread

I see flatbread baked all over the world in brick ovens, on pebbles and on hot metal plates over an open fire. As you watch each piece puff up in the pan you know you are doing something that has barely changed in thousands of years.

Despite my respect for its simplicity, I also like moving things on a little – if only for myself – and have taken to adding some complementary seasonings to the basic dough: a sprinkling of the dried herb mix za'atar; replacing some of the water with yoghurt or pleasingly sour kefir. The result is a light, aromatic bread that is particularly good with whipped feta or mackerel pâté.

*Makes 12 flatbreads*

*For the basic dough:*

strong white bread flour  500g

salt  10g

caster sugar  a pinch

instant yeast  2 teaspoons

water  about 175ml

kefir or yoghurt  175ml

za'atar  3 teaspoons

Put the flour, salt, sugar and yeast in a large, warm mixing bowl, then pour in the water, kefir and za'atar. Mix thoroughly with a wooden spoon, then turn out onto a floured surface. Knead lightly for 5 minutes. (If you are using a food processor with a dough hook, you can knead for just 3 minutes.)

When the dough feels smooth and silky, place it back in the mixing bowl, cover it with a warm tea towel and leave it in a warm, humid place to rise for about an hour until the dough has almost doubled in size.

Tip the dough onto a floured surface, fold repeatedly until all the air is knocked out of it, then tear it into twelve equal pieces. Roll each piece into a ball. Lightly flour a baking sheet, then flatten each ball, with your hand or a rolling pin, into a round roughly 18cm in diameter, placing them on the baking sheet as you go. (By all means go for ovals or slipper shapes if that is what you want.)

Get a large, dry frying pan hot over a high heat, then place a disc of dough onto the hot pan. The warmth will make it first puff up, then start to brown patchily. Turn the bread over and let it colour on the other side. Lift it out and wrap in a clean tea towel. Repeat with the rest of the dough. You could have two or three pans on the go. The quiet rhythm of baking, turning and tucking them up in a cloth is positively pleasing.

This bread, warm from the oven, is at its best when used to scoop up whipped feta. Mix together equal quantities of mashed feta and thick yoghurt. Season with coarsely ground black pepper and beat lightly with a wooden spoon, stirring in a trickle of olive oil.

Sticky, seeded malt loaf

One of the rewards of my advancing years is that I feel free to enjoy the foods I once considered as being reserved for the elderly. Buttered crumpets and fruit cake, custard tarts and toffee, éclairs and toasted tea cakes. It also means, joy of joys, I can tuck into malt loaf. Everything about this curiously British fruit bread is worthy of our attention – its generous freckling of raisins and currants; the sticky top; and its back-notes of liquorice and hops. Dark and treacly, sweet (but not overly so) and a good keeper when wrapped in waxed paper or foil, malt loaf deserves to be better known.

When I put the recipe in my *Observer* column, I was inundated with notes from readers for whom it stirred memories. As I am now officially a pensioner, I intend to make it regularly, and rather wish I had done so all along.

## Sticky, seeded malt loaf

A cold winter's afternoon, almost dusk, is the time I need a slice of malt loaf. Cut thick and buttered, it is deliciously nostalgic. It occurred to me that the basic loaf could be embellished with seeds and more dried fruits, to give a treacly, almost cake-like bread suitable for eating with cheese, in the way an Eccles cake can be eaten with Cheddar.

*Makes 1 loaf*

malt extract  150g
light muscovado sugar  100g
black treacle  2 tablespoons
plain flour  250g
baking powder  1 teaspoon
salt  a pinch
rolled oats  50g

prunes  50g, stoned weight
black tea  125ml
eggs  2
sultanas or raisins  100g
pumpkin seeds  2 tablespoons
linseeds  2 tablespoons

*To finish:*
malt extract  a little more
pumpkin seeds  1 tablespoon
linseeds  1 tablespoon

full-flavoured blue cheese
  to serve

You will need a deep, rectangular cake tin measuring 20cm × 9cm lined with baking parchment.

Set the oven at 160°C. Gently warm the malt extract, muscovado sugar and black treacle in a small saucepan, without stirring, until the sugar has dissolved. Combine the flour, baking powder, salt and oats in a large mixing bowl. Cut the prunes into small pieces and stir them in. Make the tea. Break the eggs into a small bowl and beat lightly with a fork.

Pour the warm malt and sugar mixture into the flour together with the tea and the beaten eggs. Then fold the sultanas, pumpkin seeds and linseeds into the batter.

Scoop the mixture, which will be soft and runny, like a gingerbread batter, into the lined cake tin. Bake for an hour, until risen and lightly springy to the touch. Remove from the oven and leave to cool in the tin. While the cake cools, brush the surface with a little more malt extract and sprinkle with the extra pumpkin seeds and linseeds. Leave to thoroughly cool before slicing and serving with blue cheese.


'What do you always have in your freezer?' is a perennial interview question and one I answer dutifully despite its singular lack of originality. Ice cream – I have honestly never known my freezer without a tub (make that two); Chinese, Japanese or Korean dumplings (emergency dinner in 15 minutes); a roll of all-butter puff pastry; and almost always a supply of berries and stone fruits that are impossible to find out of season. By which I mean gooseberries, damsons and their kin. Most of the space, however, is taken up by freezer-boxes full of blackcurrants. I buy them in summer and freeze them for crumbles and pies, cakes and meringues, but more crucially, for simmering with a little sugar and water to have with yoghurt or thick kefir for a breakfast. Unseasonal, for sure. But on a bitterly cold winter's morning, when there is a fire in the hearth and frost ferns on the windows, I can think of few things more welcome than a jug of inky blackcurrant compote stirred into a bowl of porridge or thick yoghurt.

I am rarely happier than when I have flour on my hands. Dough made and rising under its snow-white tea towel, the possibilities become endless. We can stick to the classics, repeating our successes ad infinitum, or we can play a little. Happy with my focaccia recipe, I could go on tweaking its savoury elements for ever (black olives and feta; pancetta and thyme; sun-dried tomato and pine nuts) or I could rethink it altogether. My books have recipes for an apple and walnut variation, another with black grapes and one with blackberries. All made for eating with cheese. But what about a truly sweet version? Still with olive oil – its presence is what makes focaccia focaccia – but also with fruit for eating with cream or crème fraîche.

Blackcurrants are, I admit, a surprising addition to focaccia, but a good one. You could also use gooseberries or cherries. It does sound odd, but dipping fruit-freckled fingers of sugary, olive-oily focaccia into whipped cream is really rather wonderful.

# Blackcurrant focaccia

*Makes 1 large, rectangular loaf*

warm water  400ml
easy-bake dried yeast  2 teaspoons
sea salt  1 teaspoon
honey  1 tablespoon
sourdough starter  2 tablespoons
    (optional, but your loaf will be
    lighter for it)

strong white bread flour  500g
olive oil  6 tablespoons, plus a
    little extra for the baking tin
blackcurrants  fresh or frozen
    250g (blueberries, blackberries
    or cherries would also work)
granulated sugar  2 tablespoons

You will also need a high-sided baking or roasting tin approximately 34cm × 24cm.

Put the water and yeast into a large mixing bowl and stir in the salt and honey. (If you are using a sourdough starter, then add it now.) Incorporate the flour either by hand or with a wooden spatula. Add 2 tablespoons of the olive oil and mix lightly into the dough. Cover the bowl with a cloth and refrigerate for a good eight hours. (I leave it overnight.)

Next day, when the dough has risen to about twice its original size, remove the currants from their stems and add to the dough, with a further 2 tablespoons of olive oil, and mix lightly to avoid bursting the berries. Lightly oil the baking tin and turn the dough out into the tin. Push the dough out to fit the tin with your fist, gently pushing it almost into the corners – it will swell during the second proving – then cover with a cloth and leave in a warm place for an hour or so, until it has risen to twice its size.

Blackcurrant focaccia

Set the oven at 220°C. When the oven is up to heat, push several hollows into the dough with your floured finger, then scatter the surface lightly with the granulated sugar and bake for 30 minutes till golden. Remove from the oven, pour the remaining oil over the surface, then release from its tin with a palette knife and serve.

A note on cherry focaccia. Use juicy, ripe cherries and remove the stones before adding to the dough.


I spend as much time as possible in Finland. In Oulu, on the edges of Lapland, I am first down for breakfast. There is a fire lit on the hearth, fur rugs on the chairs and bowls of porridge with a compote of blackcurrants. There is glowing lingonberry juice in shot glasses with a dusting of spruce powder; smoked fish on a wavy-edged wooden board; and a whole side of dill-edged gravlax. Even then, I manage to tuck into venison black pudding and bacon and a dish of kale and potato hash.

Most of all there is bread. Dark rye the colour of black treacle; rye buns with a seeded crown; sheets of crispbread the size of a tabloid. This is bread that appears on the table as a whole napkin-wrapped loaf for you to slice as much as you wish. Bread that sets you up for the day with its scent of molasses and wholegrains. Damp, heavy, tobacco-coloured crumbs only a step away from Christmas cake.

There is much crispbread consumed here, and much consumed at home too. As often as not, it appears for breakfast with a soft curl of gravlax and a trickle of mustard and honey sauce. I am known for piling each jagged-edged sheet with ricotta, cottage cheese or goat's curd, with apricots in summer and autumn, blueberries for the rest of the year.

It took quite a while to get crispbread right. And by 'right' I mean light, dustily wholesome and easily shattered. I use seeds – pumpkin, linseed, poppy and sunflower – both in the dough and scattered on top. They add a satisfying crunch. The poppy seeds are especially beautiful, steely blue-grey, like driving Finnish rain.

# Three-seed crispbread

*Makes 24 crispbreads*

white rye flour  300g
wholemeal rye flour  150g
sea salt  1 teaspoon
sunflower seeds  2 tablespoons
pumpkin seeds  2 tablespoons

linseeds  1 tablespoon
honey  1 tablespoon
warm water  250ml
melted butter  2 tablespoons

*To finish:* poppy seeds, linseeds, sunflower seeds, sea salt

Put the flours into a large bowl and add the salt, the sunflower and pumpkin seeds and the linseeds. Stir in the honey, water and melted butter. Mix to a firm dough.

Turn the dough out onto a lightly floured board and knead for a full minute. Wrap in baking parchment and refrigerate for 30 minutes.

Line a baking sheet – or better still, two – with baking parchment. Set the oven at 220°C.

Divide the dough into 24 equal pieces. Have your jars of seeds and sea salt by your pastry board. Lightly flour the board and scatter generously with seeds and sea salt (I use about a teaspoon of each for every two breads) then place a piece of dough on top of the seeds and roll out to a rectangle roughly 12cm × 9cm. You don't want them to be too uniform, looking like they were made in a factory. Continue with the others, a few at a time, replenishing the seeds and salt after every two or three breads. Pierce the surface of the dough all over with holes, using a fork or skewer as you wish. Bake for 10–12 minutes until truly crisp. Watch carefully, as they are apt to burn in a heartbeat. Remove and continue with the rest of the dough. Once cool, the breads will keep in a biscuit tin for several days.

Three-seed crispbread

# The sourdough chronicles

In October 1995 I ate at Chez Panisse, Alice Waters's quietly lovely restaurant in Berkeley, California. It was a huge deal. The dinner was a thank you to my friend John for putting me up at his apartment for a while and was, to be honest, more than I could afford to spend. As we sat down and were handed the menu – decorated with a watercolour of radishes by Patricia Curtan – a basket of bread was set down on the table. Exhausted from a day spent walking San Francisco, we pounced.

I had never eaten bread quite like it. The crust was dark, almost black; the crumb was filled with huge air pockets. It was chewy, and deliciously so. Embarrassingly, we finished the entire basket even before we had finished our drinks. (We were young and hungry.) In a heartbeat, our empty basket was silently replaced with a full one. I don't always remember restaurant meals, even those I had last week, but this one – roasted figs and mozzarella, a seafood stew with almonds, sweet peppers and aïoli, and a hot tangerine crème brûlée – I doubt I shall ever forget. (I use their salad dressing recipe to this day.)

That was my introduction to sourdough bread. There was probably no better place to eat it at that moment. The sourdough I knew from Paris was unremarkable (in truth, it tasted like a bit of old cake). This San Francisco sourdough was something completely different.

Good sourdough can still fill me with sheer unbridled greed. I am not bored with it the way others are. I thank my lucky stars that it is here and bow to all those bakers who have mastered it. But it has to be said that there is a lot of poorly made sourdough around. The crust is weak, the baking timid, the inside spongy and dry.

Hobby baking really took off after we got hooked on *The Great British Bake Off*, and again, when we found ourselves in the midst of a pandemic. Homemade bread is both comfort and cure.

During the Covid pandemic sourdough became 'a thing'. I'm not sure why, but suddenly the internet was abubble with pictures of starters – the jars of

Sourdough starter

fermenting flour and water paste that make a sourdough loaf rise. Giles Cooper, who played the young me in the stage production of *Toast*, left a glass jar of his own starter on my doorstep. I made my first loaf, and with the encouragement of other kindred spirits, I kept on making them. Close friends started sending each other pictures of our latest bakes – for me, a Saturday morning thing – just as others post photographs of their children or their cats. We compared notes, sent ecstatic emojis applauding one another's handiwork and generally enthused and commiserated as seemed appropriate. Some loaves were (and still are) better than others, some make me proud, some make me feel like a total failure, but either makes great toast.

And whilst there must be a million sleeping sourdough starters at the back of the country's fridges, it is a habit that many have continued since life returned to near normal. And yes, my starter has a name. (Erik, since you're asking.)

I include my sourdough story here only because I probably get more enjoyment from making a good loaf than almost any other form of cooking and suspect that others might too. It's a bit geeky, an up-and-down time for the emotions (you feel like weeping when your first starter dies), but let me assure you that it is immensely, insanely rewarding when it works.

# A sourdough diary

THE FIRST DAY Weighed 100g of strong white bread flour and 100g of lukewarm water, then stirred them together in a sticky white paste in a white china bowl. Slipped the bowl inside a heavy-duty open freezer bag (I wouldn't normally have these in the house, but they work better than covering the dough with a tea towel because they encourage the humidity essential for the flour to ferment), then left it, the mouth of the bag gaping, in the laundry room. The location chosen for its warm, slightly humid quality. Failing that I would probably have chosen a window ledge above a radiator.

THE SECOND DAY Nothing much happening. The dough has softened enough that it can be poured, albeit slowly, from the bowl, and the smell is simply that of slightly porridge-like wet flour. Not a trace of sour or ferment. Doubts are setting in. Am I just being impatient?

THE THIRD DAY The starter has risen, the surface has a thin crust, and the smell is that of an untoasted crumpet. Below the surface there are bubbles and a sticky, ivory-coloured goo. It seems alive. I remove 30g of it, put it into a clean bowl, then stir in 100g of lukewarm water and 100g of strong white bread flour. I discard the rest. The bowl and resulting paste are returned to its warm home. I have a good feeling about this one.

THE FOURTH DAY A bit of a quandary. The mixture is certainly alive and kicking. Bubbles are breaking the surface, even bursting as I watch. What concerns me is the smell, which has a faint note of Parmesan. Some online research suggests I should chuck it and start again. Others suggest it is as it should be at this point. The smell will sweeten once I start feeding it regularly. So lively is it that I can't bear to throw it away. So once again I feed it, taking 30g of the starter (discarding the rest) and stirring in 100g each of strong white bread flour and water. This time I use bottled water, as some online suggestions say it will help. I lightly cover it and put it back in its safe place, the bag, as always, open.

THE FIFTH DAY Much jubilation this morning at the sight of a frothing starter. The whole bowl seems to be fizzing and bubbling, and smells yeasty, but not particularly sour. Once again, I feed it by mixing 30g of starter with 100g each of flour and water and return it to its warm place. Again, I discard the rest of the starter.

THE SIXTH DAY The starter is looking rather different now – a whole lot more alive. There is a thin crust, but beneath the surface the dough is stretchy and bubbly. I remove 30g of it, stir it into 100g each of warm water and strong white bread flour, then transfer it to a storage jar. I leave it out overnight, then loosely cover it and keep it in the fridge till the day before I need it. And that is it. A jar of bubbly, yeasty sourdough starter. A little pot of opportunity and joy.

## A few points I feel worth mentioning

· Not every starter succeeds. Be prepared to try more than once.
· At first, you will need to discard quite a bit of your starter each day. It is worth remembering, as you pour it down the sink, it is only a bit of flour and water.
· Every starter is different and some are stronger and more active than others.
· If you can't be bothered to make a starter from scratch, buy one online or beg some from a geeky baking friend. There's always one.
· Your jar of yeasty bubbles will keep in the fridge for weeks. Especially if given the occasional feed and a while out of the fridge. (I feed Erik once a fortnight, leave him out overnight, then pop him back in the cold once he's active again.)
· If it doesn't rise and bubble when removed from the fridge, then it has probably passed away, and you should pour it down the sink.
· Oh, and by the way, raw bread dough is the death to washing-up brushes. Don't use your best handmade wooden brushes to clean starter or dough bowls. Soak everything in warm, soapy water, pour it away, then wash the bowl before putting through the dishwasher as usual.

## For one large loaf

*First stage:*
sourdough starter  100g          strong white bread flour  550g
warm water  350g

*Second stage:*
sea salt  10g                    warm water  30g

The night before you plan to bake, remove the starter from the fridge and leave it loosely covered in a warm, but not hot, place.

The next day, weigh 100g of the starter into a mixing bowl, then pour in 350g of warm water. Stir until the starter has more or less dissolved, then stir in the flour. Don't knead. Just cover with a clean cloth and leave in a warm place for 30 minutes.

Dissolve the salt in the warm water, then pour over the dough and squish everything together with your hands. Wipe a little oil round the inside of a second, large bowl, then transfer the dough to it. Cover and set aside in a warm place for an hour.

Now there are many, many ways of incorporating air into your dough, but this is the way I do it. Place the dough on a very lightly floured board and gently pull it into a rectangle about 30cm × 18cm. (The measurements are only a rough guide; there is nothing crucial about this.) Now, with the short end facing you, fold the dough into three (I fold the top third down first, and then the bottom third over that). Now give the dough one quarter turn (as if you were turning it from 12 o'clock to 3 o'clock), tease it into a rectangle again, then, with the short side facing you, fold into three once more. Give it another quarter turn (as if you were turning it from 3 o'clock to 6 o'clock). Do this twice more, stretching, folding and turning one quarter turn each time. Be gentle, don't knead or tug the dough. You are simply trapping air between the folds.

Put the dough back in its oiled bowl, cover and leave for a further 30 minutes, then repeat all over again. Stretch, fold, turn and so on. Do this every half-hour for a further five times. Now, put the covered bowl of dough into the fridge and say goodnight.

Bring the dough from the fridge and turn out onto a lightly floured board. Shape into a neat ball and put it back in the oiled bowl, then leave it for an hour.

Set the oven at 230°C. Place a cast-iron casserole covered with its lid in the oven. Once the oven is up to temperature, very carefully (with good thick oven gloves, not a folded tea towel!) remove the pot from the oven, lift off the lid and tip the dough from its bowl into the pot. Cover with the lid, place the pot back in the oven and bake for 25 minutes. Remove the lid and continue baking for a further 20 minutes.

Remove the pot from the oven, tip the loaf out onto a cooling rack and leave to cool for at least 45 minutes before cutting. And I know it is tempting to cut a slice off while the loaf is still hot, but the loaf hasn't finishing baking until it has rested. Much magic happens during the resting period, and we must leave it to happen.

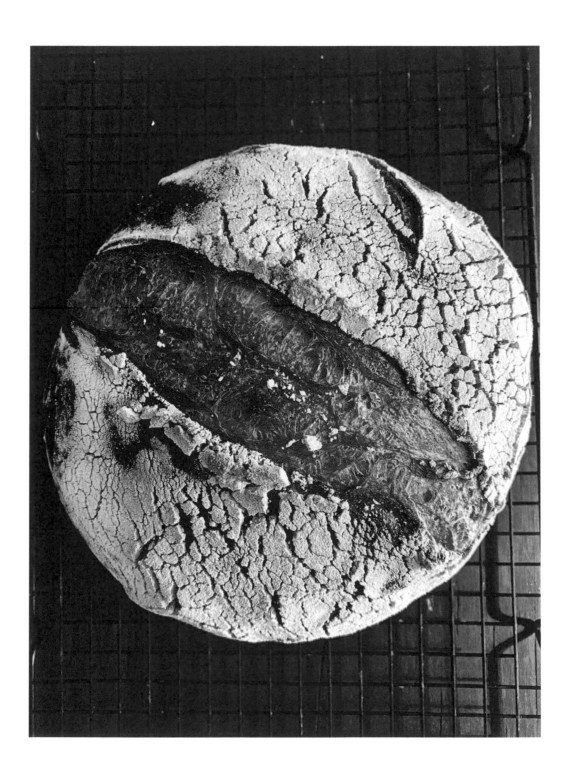

# Everyday greens

I take a couple of spring onions, a ripe chilli and a lump of ginger the size of my thumb. The onions are finely sliced, the chilli too, then I grate the ginger or cut it into matchsticks.

I warm a pool of oil – groundnut, vegetable, whatever – in a cast-iron pan over a high heat and fry the aromatics for a few minutes till they are soft and the kitchen is filled with the smell of somewhere far away. As they sizzle, I peel and finely slice a clove of fat, sweet garlic, stir it into the pan, then, as the garlic turns pale gold, I throw in handfuls – two, sometimes three or four – of shredded greens (by which I mean whatever is in the fridge, from cabbage to purple sprouting broccoli, sprout tops to bok choy, spinach or chard).

After the initial splutter of wet greens hitting sizzling oil, the scented steam makes me quicken my pace. I cover the pan with a lid and let the leaves and their seasonings cook for a minute or two. (Think stir-fry without the drama.) I turn the leaves with kitchen tongs, shake over a few drops of soy or ponzu sauce and sometimes a little fish sauce. I then dump everything into a bowl and eat it with chopsticks.

Sometimes I include tufts of coriander or leaves of Thai basil. The result is gentle (the low heat suits the delicate leaves better than a full-throttle wok job) and gives me a dinner or lunch that is restoring, invigorating, cheap as anything. It comes from nowhere in particular.

I couldn't tell you how many times I have cooked this for lunch when I'm working at home. It's a stir-fry without the endless chopping, softer-textured than the norm, lush and green, hot and fragrant. It works for me.

I eat a lot of vegetables, a lot of fruit. They are the anchor of my diet. And yes, I eat a little fish and meat too. What matters to me is simply whether something is delicious or not. What I have noticed, though, is the percentage of meatless meals I consume gets higher with each passing year. This is not, as I explained in *Greenfeast*, a deliberate choice, but simply the way my eating has changed, slowly, surely, unintentionally, over the years. My love for a bacon sandwich, a plate of oysters, a jagged strip of pork crackling or a tray of sashimi never diminishes. The difference is the regularity with which I eat it.

Over 75 per cent of the recipes in my weekly *Observer* column have been suitable for vegetarians and many of those work for vegans too. Those recipes have long been some of the most popular and I happily include my favourites, together with some new ones, here.

Carbs comfort and calm us with quick, cheap sustenance. For many years, they probably held the lion's share of my plate. That has changed in the last decade and although still present, they play more of a minor role.

There is, though, a soldierly row of glass jars in the larder, each portly glass Kilner filled with beans and grains and curls, strings and shells of pasta. There is one each of white haricot, cannellini and chickpeas, one of orange lentils and another whose cargo of pulses is the green-blue of forest lichen. You count them off, one by one: fine and coarse polenta; couscous small and giant; fine bulgur and coarse. Some jars are full to the brim with freekeh, the roasted green wheat, others have a meagre centimetre of arborio rice or long grains of basmati. There are myriad pasta shapes – ribbons, tubes, ears, twists and knots – and dried beans the colour of parchment. They are all dinners-in-waiting.

Recipes that use these low-cost, filling starches are scattered throughout the book, but here, in 'the green pages', are some whose vegetarian or vegan qualifications mean they are better suited here.

Eagle eyes will notice I have included Parmesan in a few of the recipes. There are vegetarian versions of that and other cheeses for those whose are concerned by their presence.

# Roast vegetables

Slice a wedge of pumpkin or an aubergine or two, toss them with olive oil, thyme and a clove or two of garlic, then roast till their flesh is giving, their edges bronzed and chewy, and you have a dinner of sorts. Include a dressing of yoghurt flecked with basil or fresh mint leaves and you have a luscious one.

I have been roasting vegetables for my dinner for years and never tire of the sweet, caramelised edges and silky flesh. And not only squashes and aubergines, but peppers too, with stuffings of feta or tofu, cauliflower with miso, onions first boiled then roasted with an impromptu sauce of melted Taleggio.

Sometimes, those vegetables will be served with rice that I have steamed with peppercorns and bay or perhaps a plate of wide noodles to soak up the toasty juices from the roasting tin.

It seems extraordinary to think that the aubergine was a mystery to me until I was in my early twenties. (It appeared on the menu of a restaurant whose kitchen I worked in, in a mahogany stew with lamb, dried oregano, tomato and strips of orange peel.) So common are they now that I am rarely without. They have become one of the most oft-cooked ingredients in this kitchen – most usually grilled with a basil and lemon dressing, sometimes baked with rosemary and garlic, most deliciously perhaps as a purée with notes of thyme and smoke.

## Baked aubergines, lemon and za'atar

*Serves 2*

| | |
|---|---|
| aubergines  2, medium to large | za'atar  2 tablespoons |
| olive oil  6 tablespoons | a lemon |

Set the oven at 200°C. Remove and discard the stems from the aubergines, then peel them with a vegetable peeler. Cut them in half lengthways, then in half again. Now cut each piece into two or three fat chunks, about 4cm in length. Put the aubergines on a baking tray and douse them with the oil, making sure they are generously coated.

Roast for 30 minutes, turning them over once during cooking to encourage them to colour evenly. You want them to be silkily soft, rather than crisp. Remove the aubergines from the oven, sprinkle with the za'atar and return to the oven for 10 minutes.

Squeeze the lemon juice over the aubergines and serve.

# The ridiculously useful mashed aubergine recipe

Dear reader, I cannot tell you how often I make this. A thick, smoky mash of aubergines the colour of parchment, it is part and parcel of this kitchen. Follow the recipe below and you will have a soft, vegan-friendly cream with which to play. I like to use it under the roast aubergines opposite or spread, thickly, in a deep ivory-hued wave on toasted sourdough. It makes a silky mash in which to dip baked mushrooms or a filling for rolled flatbread (the real thing, thin, supple and toasty, not the ubiquitous cardboard slippers in plastic bags). Few things are more useful to find in your fridge than this creamy sauce when you fancy pasta for dinner. (Boil your orecchiette or trofie as usual, then toss in a generous amount of this aubergine cream, some torn basil leaves, a shot of lemon juice and a few toasted pine kernels.) A handful of chopped mint is worth thinking about too, added as you sit down to eat. Few things make this cook hungrier than the scent of smoked aubergine, lemon and mint.

Set the oven at 200°C. Slice a couple of large aubergines in half lengthways and put them cut side up in a roasting tin. Cut deep into the flesh, almost through to the skin, in a criss-cross pattern. (It will encourage the heat to go deep into the flesh.) Trickle over 3 tablespoons of olive oil. Bake for about 40 minutes, till their cut surface has blackened and they are tender right through. (Don't be shy with the blackening – it is crucial to the smoky notes of the dish. Cook them over a griddle if you prefer and have a very good smoke extractor.)

Scrape the flesh from the skin with a spoon and put it into a bowl. Mash the aubergine flesh to a coarse purée with a fork. Stir in a couple of tablespoons of lemon juice, a little salt and 3 or 4 tablespoons of olive oil till you have a sloppy, silky, fragrant cream.

Baked onions, Taleggio sauce

You could make all manner of complicated cheese sauces and use every pot, sieve and whisk in the kitchen, but I don't think they come much better than those made by simply melting soft cheese in warm cream. Okay, I have seasoned it with thyme and a little black pepper, but this is nevertheless a fine cheese sauce for spooning over soft, golden baked onions.

## Baked onions, Taleggio sauce

*Serves 4*

| | |
|---|---|
| onions  8, medium | butter  60g |
| bay leaves  3 | thyme  8 sprigs |
| black peppercorns  12 | double cream  250ml |
| olive oil  3 tablespoons | Taleggio  200g |

Bring a large, deep pan of salted water to the boil. Set the oven at 200°C. Peel the onions, keeping them whole. Add the bay leaves and peppercorns to the boiling water, then lower in the peeled onions. Leave them at a brisk simmer for about 30 minutes, until they are soft and yielding.

Lift out the softened onions with a draining spoon and place them in a baking dish. Pour the olive oil over the onions, add the butter, the leaves from half of the thyme sprigs and a little black pepper, then bake for about 40 minutes, basting once or twice as they cook.

Warm the double cream in a small saucepan over a low heat. Cut the Taleggio into small pieces, then leave to melt, without stirring, in the cream, adding the remaining sprigs of thyme and a grinding of black pepper.

Serve two onions per person together with some of the Taleggio thyme sauce.

# Carrots with orzo

There is an instant appeal to a recipe that uses ingredients that are probably already in the house. This one can be made without the dill if you wish, the other ingredients being kitchen and store-cupboard staples. No shallots? Use an onion. No orzo? Use any other tiny pasta such as the star-shaped stellette. Such recipes are standard midweek fodder in my house, but what is particularly endearing about this one is the silky, almost slippery quality of the rice-shaped pasta and the sweetness of the fried carrots.

*Serves 2*

| | |
|---|---|
| summer carrots, long and slim 400g | olive oil 2 tablespoons |
| shallots 2, medium | orzo 125g |
| butter 60g | dill, chopped 1 tablespoon |
| | parsley, chopped 2 tablespoons |

Put a deep pot of water on to boil and salt it lightly. Trim and discard the leaves and stalks from the carrots, lower into the boiling water and boil for 4 minutes until just al dente. Drain and slice the carrots in half lengthways. (Slicing in half encourages them to brown lightly and sweeten when you cook them with the shallots.)

Peel and finely chop the shallots. In a large, shallow pan, warm the butter and olive oil. When they have melted together, add the shallots and let them cook over a moderate heat for about 10 minutes, till soft.

Bring a deep pan of water to the boil, salt generously, add the orzo and cook for 8 minutes, or till tender. Meanwhile, when the shallots are ready, add the carrots to the pan, and leave over a moderate heat till they have started to brown lightly.

Drain the orzo, then toss with the carrots, shallots, dill and parsley and serve.

# Roast onions, miso and sesame

Onions, bronzed by the oven, are one of those side dishes I have previously elevated to that of a main course, either by stuffing them with goat's cheese and thyme or by serving them with a sauce, rice and a crisp leaf accompaniment. The inherent sweetness of their caramelised outer layers is a contrast to the deep, savoury quality of miso, and with a bed of brown rice becomes a most satisfying dinner. The essential point is to simmer them long enough in their bay-scented stock to be on the verge of collapse, rendering their layers soft and giving, before putting them in the oven for their final roast.

*Serves 4*

bay leaves 4
black peppercorns 6
onions 8, medium
ginger a slice the size of
   a 50p piece
sake or dry sherry 4 tablespoons

dried chilli flakes 2 good pinches
honey 2 tablespoons
light miso paste 4 lightly heaped
   tablespoons
lemon juice 3 tablespoons
sesame seeds 1 tablespoon

*For the rice:*
brown or white basmati 150g
bay leaves 3
cardamom pods 6
lemon peel 5cm strip

cucumber 1
parsley, chopped 2 tablespoons
rice or wine vinegar a few drops

Bring a deep pan of water to the boil with the bay leaves and peppercorns. Set the oven at 200°C.

Peel the onions, then lower them into the boiling water and turn the heat down to a simmer. Leave for 25–30 minutes, until the onions are almost translucent and soft enough to pierce effortlessly with a skewer. Lift the onions out with a draining spoon and place them, just touching one another, in a roasting tin or baking dish.

Peel the ginger and grate to a paste on a very sharp, fine-toothed grater. Scrape the ginger into a small bowl and stir in the sake or dry sherry, chilli

Roast onions, miso and sesame

flakes, honey and miso. Blend in the lemon juice and 4 tablespoons of warm water. Pour the resulting dressing over the onions, turning them over so they are glossily coated. Scatter the sesame seeds over the top. Bake in the oven for 40–45 minutes, occasionally basting with the juices from the baking dish.

Wash the rice in three changes of warm water, swishing the rice around with your fingertips – a strangely pleasing task. Drain the rice, tip into a small saucepan and cover with enough water to come 3cm above the rice. Add the bay and cardamom pods, cracking the pods open as you go, then drop in the piece of lemon peel.

Bring the rice to the boil, lower the heat and cover with a tight-fitting lid. Leave to simmer for 10 minutes, then remove from the heat and leave, lid untouched, for a further 10.

Peel and halve the cucumber, remove the central core and seeds, then cut the flesh into matchsticks. Toss half of the parsley leaves with the cucumber. Shake over a few drops of rice or wine vinegar.

Remove the lid from the rice and run the tines of a fork through the grains to separate them, stir the remaining parsley through the grains, then spoon on to deep plates. Place the onions on top, spooning over any sauce, then scatter with the cucumber and parsley.


A red pepper, cut in half, is a hollow in which to bake small, sweet-sour tomatoes, the juices of both mingling in the bottom with olive oil and, almost certainly, basil leaves. I tuck lumps of salty sheep's-milk feta amongst the cargo, and occasionally olives and a sprig or two of thyme. It forms a quick supper, with chewy white bread to soak up the bright, basil- and olive-scented oil. Recently, though, I have taken to using tofu instead. I like the way the tofu bakes, soaking up the aromatics and tomato juices.

I would use silken tofu for stuffing the peppers. Its light, panna cotta texture is good with the sweet flesh of the roasted peppers. You can add coriander here if you wish – it is particularly at home with the tofu, olives and tomatoes. Use it in place of, or in addition to, the chives. You'll need bread for the juices.

Baked peppers with tofu and olives

# Baked peppers with tofu and olives

*Serves 3*

red peppers  3
silken tofu  500g
cherry tomatoes  250g
olive oil  100ml

green olives  10
chives  10
parsley, chopped  2 tablespoons

Set the oven at 200°C.

Halve and deseed the peppers. Put them, cut side up, in a baking dish or roasting tin. Divide the tofu evenly between the peppers. Cut each of the cherry tomatoes in half and add them to the peppers, tucking them in with the tofu. Pour some of the olive oil into each of the peppers. Season with black pepper and a little salt.

Bake the peppers for an hour or until they are truly tender.

Stone and roughly chop the olives and put them in a small mixing bowl. Finely chop the chives and mix them with the olives. Toss the parsley with the olives and chives. Scatter over the peppers as they come from the oven and serve.

# The roast potato

Over the last thirty-odd years, I have possibly written more about the roast potato than any other recipe. I will concede, when cooked to perfection, they are without question one of my favourite things to eat.

The thought of a roast chicken, a loin of pork or leg of lamb is quite unthinkable without roast potatoes. There is almost nothing I find more delicious than a potato roasted in the fat and juices from a joint of meat. The savour of fat and caramelised meat juices that make the potatoes stick to the roasting tin, the tantalisingly salty, sticky Marmite-tinted crust that sticks the potatoes to the tin. You could give me a plate of them and keep the meat and other vegetables all to yourself and I'd be the happiest guy alive.

I have always boiled or steamed my potatoes before roasting. As they fall from the steamer or colander into the hot roasting tin, their edges fray and crisp lightly, their insides fluff up and cook to the point of collapse. Roasting them from raw gives them the hide of a rhino. The craze for dusting them with polenta or grated Parmesan never quite worked for me. It introduces a gritty quality.

## The best roast potato of all

(I am writing this at 5.20 on Christmas Day afternoon, having just prised a cold roast potato or three from the roasting tin.) They are golden and lacily crisp, the inside both waxy and, at the edges, fluffy. They have a film of goose fat on one side, the other, translucent and crisp. I eat one after another as I load the plates into the dishwasher.

Those potatoes were peeled and cut into 'roast potato-sized' pieces, then boiled in salted water for about 7 minutes or so. Drained, shaken back and forth gently in their pan to bruise the edges (it makes them fluff crisply when they hit the hot fat), then tipped into the sizzling roasting tin. They were roasted, around the bird, for a good 25 minutes at 200°C, then, once the roast was removed to rest, returned to the hot oven, cranked up to 220°C, for 20 minutes.

I do, however, like to ring the changes, and occasionally roast mine with a little ground spice, a tobacco-coloured dusting of coriander seeds, cumin and turmeric. It adds another layer of flavour. Last summer I made a raita in which to dip the hot, mildly spiced potatoes, served thoroughly chilled. A raita flashed with the gold and carmine of a summer sunset. It was served with the spiced roast potatoes as a side dish for cold and bloody roast beef but could just as easily have been a partner for grilled aubergines.

# Roast spiced potatoes, beetroot raita

This mildly spiced recipe with its yoghurt raita is crunchy with grated beetroot and tomatoes and speckled with coriander.

*Serves 4*

Maris Piper, or similar
  potatoes 1kg
onions 3, medium
groundnut oil 6 tablespoons

coriander seeds 1 teaspoon
cumin seeds 1 teaspoon
ground turmeric 1 teaspoon

*For the raita:*
raw beetroot 150g, peeled
tomatoes 2, medium
garlic 2 cloves
ginger 25g piece
nigella seeds 1 teaspoon

natural yoghurt 200ml
iced water 100ml
coriander leaves, chopped
  4 tablespoons

Bring a large pot of water to the boil and salt it generously. Cut the potatoes into large pieces, cook them in the boiling water for 10 minutes, then drain.

Set the oven at 180°C. Peel the onions and cut them into quarters from root to tip. Warm the oil in a roasting tin, then add the onions and the drained potatoes, turning them over in the oil as you go. Roast for 50 minutes or until the potatoes are golden and the onions soft.

Crush the coriander and cumin seeds to a coarse powder, then mix with the ground turmeric. Add the spice mix to the potatoes and onions and toss gently to coat. Return them to the oven for a further 10 minutes.

Make the raita: coarsely grate the peeled beetroot into a bowl. Finely dice the tomatoes and add them. Peel and finely crush the garlic and grate the ginger to a purée, then stir into the beetroot. Mix the nigella seeds together with the yoghurt and the iced water, whisking them until smooth, then stir in the vegetables and the coriander leaves. Serve, chilled, with the hot roast potatoes and onions.

# Crushed roast new potatoes with kefir, feta and dill

*Serves 2*

| | |
|---|---|
| small, waxy potatoes  450g | dill  6 bushy sprigs |
| olive oil  2 tablespoons | feta  200g |
| garlic  6 cloves | thick kefir or yoghurt |
| butter  50g | 4 tablespoons |

Set the oven at 200°C. Boil the potatoes for 15–20 minutes or so till tender. Drain them, then crack each potato by pressing down on them with the back of a spoon.

Pour the olive oil into a casserole over a moderate heat. Add the garlic cloves, still in their skins, then the butter. When the butter has melted add the cracked potatoes and let them fry for a minute or two, then bake them in the oven for 40 minutes.

When the potatoes come out, toss them around in the oil, letting them break up a bit if they wish, then tip them out into a serving dish. Finely chop the fronds and stems of the dill, crumble the feta and mix the two together. Spoon the kefir or yoghurt over the potatoes, toss the cheese mixture over and serve.

# Roast new potatoes, creamed spinach

Another recipe for roast new potatoes, this time with brilliant green, creamed spinach sauce. New potatoes will roast to a fudgy texture, like little balls of gnocchi. Score them deeply, toast-rack style, and they will crisp nicely too.

*Serves 4*

| | |
|---|---|
| new potatoes  500g | garlic  2 cloves |
| olive oil  5 tablespoons | butter  30g |
| spinach  100g | flaked almonds  2 tablespoons |
| double cream  250ml | pea shoots  a handful (optional) |
| Parmesan, grated  3 tablespoons | |

Roast new potatoes, creamed spinach

Set the oven at 200°C. Wash the potatoes, place each one flat on a chopping board, then score them deeply with a knife at 0.5cm intervals, taking care not to cut right through to the chopping board. Toss them in the olive oil, making sure it gets between the slices, then place the potatoes in a roasting tin in a single layer. Bake for 45 minutes until they are golden and fudgy. (I like to turn them over halfway through.)

Wash the spinach, put the leaves and a thin film of water into a large saucepan, cover tightly with a lid, and place over a moderate heat until they start to relax and turn bright green. Remove, refresh in a colander under cold running water, then squeeze the leaves with your hands, pressing out most of the water. Roughly chop the spinach then return to the empty pan, add the cream and grated Parmesan, and salt and pepper. Warm gently.

Peel and finely slice the garlic. Melt the butter in a shallow pan, add the garlic and cook until golden and lightly crisp. Remove and set aside. Toast the almonds in a dry pan till fragrant and lightly browned.

Spoon the spinach sauce onto plates and add the roast potatoes, almonds and crisp garlic. Scatter a few pea shoots over the top if you wish.

# Potato wedges with burrata

A contemporary version of the cheesy chip supper. Thicker wedges, baked in the oven, then eaten whilst almost too hot to hold, dunked into a mound of cool, milky cheese. The cheese will be split open to reveal the snowy curds within; a little puddle of olive oil, chopped tomatoes, capers and gherkins sit on top. The salty capers and acid snap of the cornichons work neatly with the soft cheese. It is hardly dinner, more likely something to eat whilst watching a film.

*Serves 2*

potatoes, large, yellow-fleshed 900g
groundnut oil 120ml
cherry tomatoes 100g

cornichons 12
capers 1 tablespoon
olive oil 3 tablespoons
burrata 2 large balls

Potato wedges with burrata

Set the oven at 200°C. Scrub the potatoes and cut them in half lengthways, then into long wedges. Toss the potatoes in the groundnut oil, then place them in a roasting tin in a single layer, with as much space as possible between them. Roast for about 45 minutes, turning them over halfway through. They should be crisp and deep gold.

Dice or cut the tomatoes into small pieces and put them in a bowl. Cut the cornichons in half and add to the tomatoes. Stir in the capers and the olive oil. Slit the burrata open, then spoon over the tomato salsa and its oil. Eat with the chips.

## Pumpkin, couscous, date syrup

There is a spiced butternut pie in the pie chapter of which I am exceptionally fond. I also particularly like the roast pumpkin with chickpea purée in *Greenfeast: autumn, winter*. They are recipes that take this glowing lantern a step or two further on from soup. A curious note is the way the addition of the sweet date syrup somehow deflects from the sweetness of the pumpkin.

*Serves 2*

pumpkin 1kg (unpeeled weight)
olive oil 60ml
za'atar 1 tablespoon
dried chilli flakes 1 teaspoon

couscous 65g
coriander 20g
parsley leaves 10g

*For the dressing:*
date syrup 4 teaspoons
garlic 1 clove, crushed
olive oil 5 tablespoons

half a lemon juiced
grain mustard 1 teaspoon

Set the oven at 200°C. Peel the pumpkin, remove the fibres and seeds and discard, then cut the flesh into 2cm-thick slices. Place the slices on a baking sheet. Mix together the olive oil, za'atar and dried chilli flakes, then spoon over the pumpkin. Bake for 35–40 minutes till tender and translucent.

Boil the kettle. Put the couscous in a bowl, pour over enough hot water to cover the couscous and set aside. Chop the coriander and parsley.

Meanwhile, make the dressing: mix the date syrup with the crushed garlic, olive oil, lemon juice and grain mustard.

When the couscous has soaked up the water, run a fork through it to separate the grains, then fold in the chopped parsley and coriander and a seasoning of salt and black pepper. Remove the pumpkin from the oven, place the couscous on a serving plate together with the pumpkin, then trickle over the date dressing.

## Roast parsnips and carrots with soy and honey

A dish to serve with rice. Habitually, I cook too much rice, but for this I would work on about 100g, washed three times in warm water, then cooked in a small pan, covered, with the same volume of water, 6 cracked cardamom pods, 2 cloves and a teaspoon of salt for about 12 minutes. I then leave the rice off the heat but still covered for a further 10 minutes before running a fork through.

*Serves 2, with rice*

ginger  40g piece
garlic  3 cloves
light soy sauce  50ml
dried chilli flakes  1 teaspoon
honey  3 tablespoons

parsnips  2, large
carrots  8, medium
groundnut or vegetable oil
  3 tablespoons
sesame seeds  1 tablespoon

steamed brown rice to serve

Peel the ginger and grate it finely into a bowl. Peel the garlic and crush to a paste. Make the dressing: mix together the ginger and garlic, then stir in the soy sauce, chilli flakes and honey.

Set the oven at 200°C. Put a pan of water on to boil. Peel the parsnips and scrub the carrots. Cut the carrots in half lengthways and the parsnips into short, thick pieces. Boil the parsnips for 4 minutes, then drain.

Put the carrots and the blanched parsnips into a roasting tin, pour over the oil and roast for 25 minutes. Remove briefly from the oven, pour over the dressing, scatter with sesame seeds, then return to the oven for 15 minutes. Serve with the brown rice.

Roast parsnips and carrots with soy and honey

Give me a bowl of hummus, some warm flatbread, a lemon and the olive oil bottle and I am happy. Include some half-moons of roasted pumpkin and I am even more so.

# Chickpeas with baked pumpkin

This is a useful dish to have up your sleeve. It is easy to veganise too, if you swap the butter for oil. This works hot as a substantial main, but also cold. Both the roast pumpkin and the hummus will keep in the fridge for a couple of days if necessary. I will admit to occasionally putting a few pink peppercorns (a teaspoon or so) with the parsley, for no other reason than I like the look of them. They are entirely optional, which is not something I say very often.

*Serves 6*

pumpkin 1kg, skin on
olive oil a little
garlic 4 cloves, skin on
rosemary 10 sprigs
thyme 8 bushy sprigs

butter 75g
parsley leaves 10g
pink peppercorns 1 teaspoon
   (optional)

*For the hummus:*
chickpeas 2 × 400g tins
1 small lemon juiced

olive oil 150ml

Set the oven at 200°C. Remove the seeds and fibres from the pumpkin then cut the flesh into six wedges. Lightly oil a baking tin (I line mine with kitchen foil for easier cleaning) and lay the wedges in a single layer. Tuck in the garlic cloves. Season with salt, black pepper and the sprigs of rosemary and thyme, then moisten with olive oil. Dot the butter in small lumps over the pumpkin and roast for 45 minutes until the squash is golden-brown in colour and the texture is soft and fudgy.

For the hummus, drain the chickpeas and bring them to the boil in deep water. Turn the heat down and let them simmer for 8–10 minutes till thoroughly hot.

Squeeze the roast garlic cloves out of their skin into the bowl of a food processor. Drain the chickpeas, then tip them into the food processor. Add the lemon juice and process, pouring in enough of the oil to produce a soft, spreadable cream.

Chop the parsley, then moisten with a tablespoon of olive oil.

Spoon the hummus into a serving dish, place the roasted pumpkin on top, then scatter the parsley and peppercorns, if using, all over and serve.

## Baked pumpkin, burrata and lentils

*Serves 2–3*

| | |
|---|---|
| pumpkin or squash 1kg skin on (unpeeled weight) | coriander leaves a handful |
| olive oil 3 tablespoons plus a little extra | za'atar 1 tablespoon |
| | thyme leaves 1 tablespoon |
| | thyme sprigs 10 |
| small green or brown lentils 100g | burrata 200g |

Set the oven at 200°C. Remove the seeds and fibres from the pumpkin and cut into thick slices. Place in a single layer on a baking sheet or roasting tin and pour over the 3 tablespoons of olive oil. Turn the slices over so they are coated with oil, then bake for about 20 minutes till translucent and tender.

Bring a pan of water to the boil, add the lentils and let them cook for about 20 minutes till tender. Drain and toss them with a little olive oil, a grinding of salt and black pepper and the coriander leaves.

Mix together the za'atar and the thyme leaves. Grind in a little black pepper then scatter the mixture over the pumpkin slices. Add the sprigs of thyme and return to the oven for a further 10 minutes.

Transfer the pumpkin to a serving dish and scatter with the lentils. Break the burrata into small pieces and add to the pumpkin.

Baked pumpkin, burrata and lentils

# Oven suppers

The first oven I knew was an Aga and I have one to this day. Wonderful for toasting crumpets and slow-cooked casseroles (and for warming your pyjamas on a bitterly cold winter's night) but of little use to a cookery writer whose recipes require a semblance of accuracy.

The food that came from that early oven (black and cream enamel and the size of a small family car) is carved so deeply in my memory I can smell it now – shepherd's pie, rhubarb crumble, chewy syrup flapjacks and, of course, Christmas cake. My ovens are now cold-hearted, stainless steel and clean themselves at the turn of a knob, but what comes out of them is just as reassuring. Food for a winter's night – aubergines baked with brick-red chilli sauce and a thyme-flecked breadcrumb crust, saffron-orange squashes stuffed with cheese and shredded cabbage or deep earthenware casseroles of sweet potatoes and lentils.

These are recipes that are often layered or baked 'au gratin'. They are good-natured dishes that are not reliant on being served the second they are ready. Generally inexpensive, these are very much sharing recipes whose quantities can easily be doubled up for a crowd. Many of these are in fact what you will get if you come round for supper, rather than a time-sensitive grill or something cooked on the hob.

## Baked aubergines with gochujang and tomatoes

The amount of gochujang you use is up to you – I suggest you taste as you go. Brands vary, but you can assume that the darker red the paste, the hotter it will be. The sugar I include is just a pinch, but seems to calm the more aggressive notes of the paste.

*Serves 4–6*

| | |
|---|---|
| aubergines  450g | chopped tomatoes  2 × 400g tins |
| banana shallots  400g | black-eyed or haricot beans |
| olive oil  3 tablespoons |   2 × 400g tins |
| garlic  4 cloves | thyme leaves  1 tablespoon |
| gochujang  2 level tablespoons | sugar  a pinch |

*For the crust:*

| | |
|---|---|
| white bread  100g | olive oil  3 tablespoons |
| thyme leaves  2 tablespoons | |
| lime or lemon zest, grated | |
|   1 tablespoon (1–2 limes) | |

Remove the stems from the aubergines. Slice each one in half lengthways. If you are using large aubergines, then cut each one lengthways into 1cm-thick slices. Heat a griddle pan, then cook the aubergines cut side down for 5 minutes over a moderate heat until they are showing good colour then turn them over. Cook the other side of each half/slice for a further 5 minutes, then remove to a bowl. Cover with a lid – the steam they produce will help them to soften further.

Peel, halve and roughly chop the shallots. Warm the oil in a deep, heavy-based casserole, then let the shallots cook over a low to moderate heat for 15 minutes, stirring occasionally, till soft and pale gold. While they are cooking, peel, thinly slice and stir in the garlic.

Stir in the gochujang, the tomatoes and the black-eyed beans (including the liquid from their tins). Stir in the thyme leaves, a little salt, sugar and the aubergines. Simmer for 10 minutes, then transfer to a baking dish. I use a deep one measuring 24cm × 16cm.

Set the oven at 200°C. Process the bread to coarse crumbs, either in the food processor or by hand with a coarse-toothed grater. Mix with the thyme leaves and the grated lime or lemon zest. Pour over the olive oil and toss to coat. Scatter over the surface of the aubergines, beans and tomatoes. Bake for 25–30 minutes until the crumb crust is crisp and the filling is bubbling around the edges.

Baked aubergines with gochujang and tomatoes

Cabbage comes in many forms, and for me this brassica's finest moment is when the leaves are shredded and fermented into sauerkraut. I have made my own, involving salt, a weight and a wait, but the commercial brands are usually good. I say usually because I've had a few horrors. For the record, those with the fewest ingredients are the best. Ideally just cabbage and salt. You are looking for something pure, clean and refreshingly sour. A tiny bowl containing a tangle of sauerkraut is a daily thing for me, in the way that kefir or yoghurt is. I like sour things.

Sauerkraut's uses are manifold. A mound of it will slice through the fattiness of a roast duck, the vegetable's inherent astringency making the meat seem even sweeter; a spoonful will add vigour to a Savoy cabbage sauté and it makes an interesting addition to a bowl of buttery winter gnocchi. A year ago, I introduced it to a sweet pumpkin roast, with cream and grated Gruyère. A butternut squash would have worked as well. A dinner of sweet and fudgy squash, piercingly tart cabbage, sweet onions and cream. It was hands-down one of the most delicious plates of food I ate all year.

## Squash (dumpling or butternut), sauerkraut and Gruyère

*Serves 3*

| | |
|---|---|
| squashes 3 small, orange fleshed | olive oil 3 tablespoons |
| butter 30g | parsley a small bunch |
| thyme leaves 1 teaspoon | sauerkraut 250g |
| onions 2, medium to large | double cream 150ml |
| | Gruyère 125g, grated |

Set the oven at 200°C. Cut the squashes in half and use a spoon to remove the seeds and fibres. Place the squash hollow side up in a roasting tin, then divide the butter and thyme between them. Season with salt and black pepper and bake the squashes for 45 minutes to an hour until the flesh is soft and giving.

While the squashes bake, peel and finely slice the onions. Warm the oil in a deep pan, over a moderate heat, add the onions and cook until pale gold and soft. Expect this to take a good 20 minutes, stirring regularly. Roughly chop the parsley, then stir into the softened onions. Remove from the heat and add the sauerkraut, cream and cheese.

Squash (dumpling or butternut), sauerkraut and Gruyère

Take the squash from the oven, divide the filling between the halved vegetables, then return them to the oven. Continue baking for about 20 minutes until the filling is turning gold and the cream is bubbling around the edges.

## Baked rice with squash and shallots

A rather lovely vegan-friendly way with a butternut squash, the texture somewhere between a pilaf and a risotto.

*Serves 3*

| | |
|---|---|
| small shallots 200g | thyme 6 sprigs |
| butternut squash 200g | rosemary 2 bushy sprigs |
| (peeled weight) | vegetable stock 500ml |
| red pepper 1, large | arborio rice 200g |
| olive oil 4 tablespoons | |

Set the oven at 200°C. Peel and halve the shallots. Cut the squash into large pieces (roughly 2cm cubes), then halve, deseed and thinly slice the red pepper.

Pour the olive oil into a deep-sided lidded casserole or roasting tin, then add the shallots, cut side down, the squash and the pepper. Pull the thyme leaves from their stalks and scatter into the pan, together with the leaves from the rosemary. Bake for 40 minutes till the vegetables are tender.

Pour the stock into a saucepan, bring to the boil and remove from the heat. Rain the rice over the vegetables then pour in the stock and bring to the boil. Cover with a lid and bake in the oven for a further 25 minutes.

Wednesdays were the best days to come home from school. A piece of ham simmering on the stove, a dish of cauliflower cheese in the oven. (There was mashed potato too. Vast glorious clouds of the stuff.) Forty, no fifty years on, I retain a fondness for cauliflower baked under a soft blanket of cheese sauce. The cauliflower has always reigned as one of the most beautiful things you can put in your shopping basket. A cream-coloured loaf of florets to bake or steam or roast. I notice it has become rather popular of late.

The finest cauliflowers are like crisp white clouds, their florets tightly packed, wisps of green leaves still present. When I find a sound specimen it is most likely to end its days cosseted in cream and cheese, because no vegetable takes to dairy in the way a cauliflower does. This brassica was made to be paired with cheese sauce.

## Baked cauliflower with Cheddar, mustard and onions

The contemporary way of roasting a cauliflower intensifies the flavour, though we should take care not to burn it, as the curds will turn bitter. I sometimes make it with a white onion sauce instead of cheese.

*Serves 2-3*

cauliflower  1kg, large, whole
onions  2, medium
olive oil  3 tablespoons
double cream  350ml

grain mustard  1 tablespoon
Dijon mustard  2 tablespoons
Cheddar, grated  100g

Trim the cauliflower, cutting off any dry or bruised stems. Leave any small, pointed leaves that are in good condition in place. Pour enough water into a large, deep saucepan to come halfway up the sides, lower in the cauliflower, then cover with a lid. Leave to steam for 15 minutes, then remove from the heat.

While the cauliflower steams, peel and thinly slice the onions. Set the oven at 200°C. Pour the olive oil into a shallow pan and place over a moderate heat, add the onions and let them cook till soft and translucent. Let them colour a little – they should be pale gold – then stir in the cream, a little salt and pepper and the mustards.

Stir the cheese into the cream and onions. Remove the cauliflower carefully from its water, then place it in the centre of a baking dish or roasting tin. Spoon the cream and onion sauce around and over the top of the cauliflower and bake for 20 minutes till pale gold in colour.

Baked cauliflower with Cheddar, mustard and onions

# Baked cauliflower, miso and tahini

Throughout most of my life, cauliflower has been inseparable from cheese sauce. A timeless culinary bond. Which is fine if you eat dairy produce as I do. But what if you would rather not? In this instance, a fragrant paste (warm, nutty, a little spicy) comes to the rescue made from white (shiro) miso paste and tahini. It is stirred with olive oil and spread on thick slices – steaks, you could call them – of cauliflower, speckled with sesame seeds and baked till the top is golden. (As you take them from the oven I feel they somewhat resemble Welsh rarebit.)

*Serves 4*

cauliflower 1, large
white miso paste
   4 heaped tablespoons

tahini 4 tablespoons
olive oil 120ml
sesame seeds 1 tablespoon

Set the oven at 180°C. Place the cauliflower on a chopping board and slice into six thick steaks. Lay the pieces of cauliflower snugly in a large roasting tin or baking dish.

In a small bowl mix together the white miso paste, tahini and 6 tablespoons of the olive oil. Brush the remaining olive oil over the cauliflower, then spread with half of the paste. Turn the pieces over and spread the other side, then cover the dish with foil. Bake for 1 hour.

Remove the foil and scatter the surface of the cauliflower with the sesame seeds. Baste with the juice from the roasting tin and return to the oven for 10 minutes, this time without the foil. Transfer the cauliflower to plates with a large kitchen slice.

# Baked tomatoes with ginger and coconut

There is a generous amount of sauce here that I like to ladle into the baking dish, then spoon it over the tomatoes at the table. We usually soak up the spice-flecked sauce with flatbread warmed in the oven while the tomatoes are resting.

*Serves 4*

| | |
|---|---|
| onions 2, medium | red or orange peppers 2 |
| groundnut oil 2 tablespoons | cherry tomatoes 20 |
| yellow mustard seeds 1 teaspoon | ground turmeric 1 teaspoon |
| garlic 3 cloves | plum, or vine tomatoes 8, large |
| ginger 3cm piece | coconut cream 160ml |
| chilli 1, red and medium hot | mint leaves 12 |

Peel and roughly chop the onions. Warm the groundnut oil in a deep saucepan over a moderate heat, then add the mustard seeds and let them cook for a minute or two, without letting them colour. Stir in the onions, letting them soften and giving them the occasional stir while you peel and slice the garlic, peel and finely shred the ginger and finely chop the chilli.

Stir the garlic, ginger and chilli into the onions and continue cooking until the onions are honey-coloured and translucent. Deseed and thinly slice the peppers and halve the cherry tomatoes. Add the peppers to the onions and cook over a moderate heat, with the occasional stir, until the peppers start to soften, then stir in the ground turmeric and the cherry tomatoes.

Set the oven at 200°C. Remove a slice from one side of each of the plum tomatoes (or the top if you are using large vine tomatoes), then scoop out the seeds and core from each tomato to give a deep hollow. Place the tomatoes in a baking dish. Finely chop the filling you have removed, discarding any tough cores as you go, and stir into the onions.

When the mixture has cooked down to a soft, brightly coloured mush, stir in the coconut cream, bring to the boil, season with salt, then remove from the heat.

Fill the hollowed-out tomatoes with the sauce, spooning any extra around them in the dish. Bake for 40 minutes until the tomatoes are soft and fragrant. Scatter with mint leaves and serve.

Some recipes quietly unfold, ingredient by ingredient, task by task. They are often those dishes that are cooked in layers, grain on top of vegetable, and usually take more than a few minutes of our time. Their preparation is to be relished, not rushed. A favourite, one I make time and again, and particularly for vegan guests, is a portly casserole filled with layers of lentils, spices and sweet potatoes. As you take it from the oven, it glows. The scent is sweet, a little spicy.

## Baked spicy lentils and sweet potatoes

*Serves 4*

split yellow lentils  250g
ground turmeric  1 teaspoon
vegetable stock  750ml
sweet potatoes  750g
onion  1
olive oil  2 tablespoons
ginger  60g
garlic  2 cloves

cumin seeds  half a teaspoon
green cardamom pods  10
dried chilli flakes  half a teaspoon
curry leaves  12
ground cayenne pepper
   1½ teaspoons
chopped tomatoes  1 × 400g tin
oil  a little for baking

Wash the lentils in cold water, until the water is no longer milky. Tip them into a medium-sized saucepan with the turmeric and stock and bring to the boil. Lower the heat, partially cover with a lid and simmer for 10 minutes, until most of the stock has been absorbed and the lentils are almost tender.

Peel the sweet potatoes and cut them into slices about 0.5cm in thickness. Put them in a steamer basket or colander over a pan of boiling water, covered with a lid. Steam for about 7–8 minutes until soft to the point of a knife. Remove the pan from the heat.

Peel and roughly chop the onion. Warm the olive oil in a deep pan over a moderate heat, add the onion and cook until it is soft and pale gold – a matter of 20 minutes. Peel and grate the ginger.

Peel and finely slice the garlic, then stir into the onion with the ginger and cumin seeds. Continue cooking for 2–3 minutes. Crack open the cardamom pods, extract the seeds, grind to a coarse powder then stir into the onion together with the chilli flakes, curry leaves and cayenne. Add pepper and half a teaspoon of salt, stirring for a minute or two. Set the oven at 200°C.

Crush the tomatoes and stir into the lentils over a moderate heat, then mix in the onion and remove from the heat.

Carefully lift the sweet potatoes from the steamer with a palette knife. Using a baking dish approximately 24cm in diameter, place half the lentil mixture in the base, then add half the sweet potatoes, followed by a second layer of lentils and then the remaining sweet potatoes. Brush with oil. Bake for 30–40 minutes until bubbling around the edges and lightly browned on top.

## Sweet potato and lentil 'shepherd's' pie

A big, fat, golden pie.

*Serves 6*

*For the filling:*

| | |
|---|---|
| onions  450g (2, large) | ground coriander  1 teaspoon |
| olive or vegetable oil | ground turmeric  2 teaspoons |
| 3 tablespoons | tomatoes  350g |
| carrots  150g | vegetable stock  500ml |
| garlic  2 cloves | red lentils  350g |
| chillies, red  2 | spinach  350g |
| cardamom pods  8 | lemon  1, large |
| cumin seeds  1 teaspoon | curry leaves  10 |

*For the top:*

| | |
|---|---|
| potatoes  500g | butter  50g |
| sweet potatoes  1 kg | parsley  a small bunch, chopped |

Peel and roughly chop the onions, then cook them in the oil in a deep pan over a moderate heat for 15 minutes, stirring from time to time.

Sweet potato and lentil 'shepherd's' pie

Cut the carrots into fine dice, peel and finely chop the garlic and the chillies (discard the seeds if you wish), then add all to the softening onions and continue cooking for another 10 minutes, until the onion is pale gold and translucent.

Break open the cardamom pods, extract the seeds within and grind them to a coarse powder. I use a pestle and mortar for the sheer olfactory pleasure, but an electric spice grinder will work too. Mix them with the cumin seeds and ground coriander and turmeric and stir into the onions. Cut the tomatoes into small dice and stir into the vegetables, leaving them to simmer for a further 10 minutes until the tomatoes have released their juice.

Add the stock and bring to the boil, then lower the heat to a simmer, season and leave to putter away over a low heat. Check the liquid level from time to time: you want a decent amount of juice, so add some more boiling water if needed.

Cook the lentils in deep boiling water for 20 minutes, until they are just tender, then drain. Try not to let them fall apart. Stir them into the tomato mixture.

While the lentils cook, peel the potatoes and sweet potatoes, then steam or boil until tender. This is best done separately as they cook at different times. Drain and mash them together with a vegetable masher or food mixer. Add the butter, chopped parsley, salt and pepper and set aside.

Wash the spinach leaves and put them, still wet, into a pan over a moderate heat. Cover tightly with a lid and let them cook for a minute or two until wilted. Remove the leaves, drain them and squeeze out most of the moisture.

Set the oven at 200°C. Stir the spinach into the lentils, together with the juice from the lemon and the curry leaves, then transfer to a deep baking dish, about 24cm × 28cm. Spoon the mashed vegetables on top – they will sink a little but no matter – and bake for 25 minutes.


# Spiced parsnip gratin

We should probably be grateful for the fat parsnips on offer in the shops now. Until the 1850s we would have had to put up with the skinny wild version for our sweet roasts. I would rather have a parsnip than a carrot. It has a carrot's sweetness, but a creamy subtlety too. They roast as crisply as a potato (more than you can say for a carrot) though are inclined to chewiness – which I love. Unlike the potato, there seems little point in boiling them first – you will never get a lacy crispness. What you do get, and what makes them interesting, is a deep toffee note and a fudgy-textured interior. The very best are those roasted around a joint of beef, where the deep umami notes of the beef juices marry with the sugar hit of the roots.

We can temper the sweetness with curry spices, or with cream as we layer them in the style of a potato dauphinoise. A muddle of browned onions amongst them is a thoroughly good thing.

*Serves 4-6*

| | |
|---|---|
| onions 2, medium | chilli flakes half a teaspoon |
| olive oil 3 tablespoons | garam masala half a teaspoon |
| parsnips 450g | a knob of butter |
| coriander seeds 2 teaspoons | double cream 150ml |
| cumin seeds 2 teaspoons | full-cream milk 100ml |
| ground turmeric half a teaspoon | breadcrumbs a handful |

Set the oven at 160°C. Peel and thinly slice the onions, then cook them in the oil in a deep pan until they are soft and golden – a good 30 minutes. Peel the parsnips – I'm afraid we must – and slice them thinly into discs or from stalk to tip as the mood takes you. The ideal thickness is that of a pound coin. Bring a deep pan of water to the boil and simmer the parsnips for 5-7 minutes, until there is a little tenderness. Drain them carefully (they are apt to break up).

Meanwhile, grind the coriander and cumin seeds to a powder, then add the ground turmeric and the chilli flakes and stir into the onions. Continue cooking for a couple of minutes, taking care not to burn them, until they are fragrant. Stir in the garam masala. You are toasting them, but we should go about it gently, as they burn easily. Butter a large baking dish or roasting tin. Lay the parsnips in the dish, neatly or not as you wish, layering the cooked onions amongst them. Mix the cream and milk in a dish and season with both salt and black pepper, then pour over the parsnips. Scatter with the breadcrumbs and bake for 45-50 minutes till golden.

Potato, Camembert and dill

There is the occasional recipe I keep for days when it snows. The light has already lowered by mid-afternoon, the windows are glowing on the walk home and the pavements are treacherous. Dinner is bound to be potato- or pasta-based, a meal we know in our house as 'carbacious'. There may well be dairy too. Baked potatoes with melted Gorgonzola, a baked Tunworth or Camembert in which to dip steamed potatoes, or perhaps a plate of soupy polenta with fried mushrooms and grated Parmesan.

It is on days such as these that I bring out a casserole of potatoes cooked with melted Camembert and cream. An unapologetically bolstering affair, heavy with starch, cream and cheese, that takes its inspiration from tartiflette – the ski-resort stalwart.

The warming effect is instant, the richness almost absurd and you will need gherkins or a mound of sauerkraut to mop up the deep pools of cream and cheese on your plate. A once a year 'emergency' dish I have come to regard as essential to my wellbeing.

## Potato, Camembert and dill

*Serves 4*

new potatoes 700g,
  yellow-fleshed
double cream 250ml

dill a small bunch, about 15g
Camembert or similar
  cheese 400g

Set the oven at 200°C. Cook the potatoes in boiling, lightly salted water for about 20 minutes till just tender. Drain the potatoes, then put them in a lidded baking dish. Press firmly onto each potato with the back of a spoon, lightly crushing them and opening them up.

Season the cream with salt and pepper. Chop half of the dill and stir into the cream. Slice the cheese thickly and break into large pieces.

Tuck the cheese amongst the potatoes, then pour over the dill cream. Cover with a lid and bake for 25 minutes, then remove the lid and continue baking for a further 20 minutes until the surface is appetisingly browned. Scatter with the remaining dill and serve.

# Vegetables from the grill

I have told you about my griddles – the ridged, cast-iron pans on which I brown a lamb cutlet or soften a slice of courgette. The smoky notes – primitive, basic and downright delicious – they impart to a scallop they will also lend to a spear of asparagus or a stem of broccoli.

The trick here is to press down firmly on the vegetables you are grilling to ensure a crisp crust and smart, dark stripes. Do it with a palette knife, or by placing a weight – such as a similarly sized pan – to keep the food in direct contact with the cast iron.

There will inevitably be much smoke, so check the proximity of your fire alarm. (I have had a team of burly firemen, hoses primed, on my doorstep more than once.) That smoke will bring everyone to the table with its notes of thyme and garlic. This sort of grilling differs from an oven grill by the position of the heat source and, more importantly, the fact that the food touches the grill and picks up deep notes of smoke and herbs.

A favourite lunch of mine involves little more than grilling slices of mushroom or courgette, dousing the soft, lightly charred flesh in olive oil, then dressing with lemon juice, pepper and shredded basil. I mop up the juices with bread or toss the aubergines with pasta. You can crumble feta over too if you like.

## Griddled asparagus with buttery lemon mash

Grill and hob needed here. The first bunch of asparagus of the year comes home on the top of the shopping basket, swaddled in whatever is to hand, to protect its fragile spears. Nine times out of ten, that first bunch of the season will be cooked in boiling water – better than steaming in my view – and I will invariably make a pot of hollandaise, despite its tendency to curdle as the mood takes it. I feel there is no better way to celebrate that first (often quite expensive) bunch.

Griddled asparagus with buttery lemon mash

As the season marches on towards early summer, I will treat asparagus with a little less preciousness, and will include the spears in a tart or a salad. (I never, though, make a mousse or a soup out of it, which always seems a less than respectful end for this elegant vegetable.) A tart filled with savoury custard and a grating of Parmesan remains a favourite, as do individual tarts of puff pastry, grated lemon and crème fraîche (*The Kitchen Diaries II*). The spears often end up with a soft, almost molten cheese sliding down them (Tunworth perhaps, or a spoonful of Gorgonzola dolce), but a lasting pleasure has been serving them with a sloppy mash of potatoes, seasoned with lemon and made almost sauce-like in its softness with butter and hot milk.

*Serves 2*

*For the mash:*

potatoes  (Maris Piper or Charlotte) 850g

full-cream milk  300ml

lemon  1

olive oil  5 tablespoons, plus extra for drizzling

asparagus  250g

Peel the potatoes, cut them into large pieces, then bring to the boil in a pan of salted water. Turn the heat down to a simmer and cook for about 20 minutes, until they are tender to the point of a knife.

Warm the milk in a saucepan and set aside. Grate a teaspoon of the lemon zest, then squeeze the lemon. Drain the potatoes, then put them in the bowl of a food mixer fitted with a flat paddle beater. Slowly beat the potatoes, adding the warm milk and lemon juice as you go, until you have a loose mash. Now beat in the olive oil. The mash should be creamy, with no lumps.

Brush the asparagus with olive oil, then cook for 3-4 minutes on a griddle, turning the spears occasionally, so they colour evenly.

Divide the mash between two plates, then place the asparagus to the side of the mash. Generously trickle with olive oil, then scatter with the lemon zest.

# Grilled tomatoes, cucumber and beetroot raita

We shouldn't assume that tomatoes don't benefit from a creamy dressing. I always felt such an intrusion would be wrong, but then I made a mixture of double cream, finely chopped parsley and tinned anchovies. Trickled over the sliced tomatoes it was a revelation.

The contrast of sizzling tomatoes and ice-cold raita is particularly pleasing. I use iced water to mix with the yoghurt but will often also add a few ice cubes to the dish as I bring it to the table to ensure it is thoroughly chilled.

*Serves 2*

tomatoes, assorted  600g

*For the raita:*

cucumber  300g

onions  2, small

groundnut oil  2 tablespoons

curry leaves  12

natural yoghurt  200ml

iced water  80ml

beetroot  300g

white wine vinegar  3 tablespoons

mint leaves  12

parsley leaves  a handful

Peel the cucumber, lightly shaving off the dark green skin with a vegetable peeler, then slice it in half down its length. Using a teaspoon, scrape and discard the seedy core from each half.

Coarsely grate the cucumber into a large sieve, sprinkle with a little salt and leave to drain over a bowl.

Switch the grill on. Cut the tomatoes in half and place them cut side up on a grill pan or baking sheet lined with foil. Lightly season with salt. Cook the tomatoes under the grill for 10 minutes or until their cut edges start to brown.

Meanwhile, peel and thinly slice the onions. Warm the oil in a shallow pan, add the onions and fry over a moderate heat till crisp and golden. Add the curry leaves and fry for a minute or so till they curl, then lift them out with a draining spoon and drain them on kitchen paper.

Put the yoghurt in a medium-sized mixing bowl and whisk in the iced water with a fork, cover and refrigerate. Peel the beetroot, then coarsely grate it into a small bowl. Sprinkle the white wine vinegar over the beetroot and set it aside. Finely chop the mint and parsley leaves and add them to the beetroot.

Squeeze the moisture from the grated cucumber, fold into the yoghurt with a fork, then add the beetroot, stirring briefly. (If you stir too much your raita will turn bright pink.) Tip into a serving bowl and add the fried onions and curry leaves.

Transfer the grilled tomatoes to a serving dish, then spoon over the juices from the grill pan. Serve with the cucumber and beetroot raita.

# Frying-pan suppers

My first piece of kitchen kit was a frying pan. It saw me through the years when I possessed neither grill nor oven. From that one pan came bacon sandwiches and the occasional full English, fish fingers and fried fillets of sea bass. It was also, I seem to remember, used for risotto. That pan, too heavy for its own good, now sits in the pot store, ditched in favour of shallow pans that are lighter and more agile.

I may no longer knock up a full English, but this is the pan in which I cook golden sweet potato cakes and green curry fritters, where I sizzle mustard greens or kale, and this is the one I use to make bubble and squeak.

## Sautéed potatoes, lemon and capers

A fragrant, knobbly, unwaxed lemon. Spanking fresh parsley. Tiny capers the colour of seaweed and flakes of sea salt like shaved ice.

*Serves 3–4*

potatoes  500g
olive oil  6 tablespoons
rosemary  2 large sprigs

half a lemon
capers  1 tablespoon
parsley, chopped  a handful

Scrub the potatoes thoroughly, then slice them thinly – the thickness of a pound coin would be about right. Put the slices into a mixing bowl and add the olive oil, salt, black pepper and the whole rosemary sprigs. Toss the potatoes to coat them evenly with the oil and seasoning.

Warm a large, wide frying pan over a low to moderate heat, add the potatoes and their oil, then let them cook for 15–20 minutes till the underside is pale gold. Turn the potatoes over and let the other side brown lightly. I like mine to be the hue of roast potatoes.

As the potatoes start to crisp, slice the lemon and squeeze one half over the potatoes. Scatter the capers over the top and then the chopped parsley and a flick of sea salt flakes.


As the years go by, I am drawn more to thin, crisp fried potatoes – I love plain and mass-market ready-salted crisps – and now prefer thin potato cakes to thick ones. Last year I pressed coarsely grated, waxy-fleshed potatoes into a frying pan, letting them cook to a crisp, golden cake, then covered the surface with a thin layer of cheese and herbs. The cheese oozed between the shreds of potato, the herbs wafted their aniseed and onion scents and we cut the big cheesy cake into pieces, like a pizza.

## Potato cake with Fontina and herbs

I'm not sure what I would call these cakes, or even if it matters. They could go by the name of galette or rösti, potato pancake or fritter. They were only a very short jump from a latke.

*Serves 2–3*

waxy, yellow-fleshed
  potatoes  650g
spring onions  4, thin
plain flour  2 tablespoons
nigella seeds  2 tablespoons

egg  1, beaten
groundnut or vegetable oil
  2 tablespoons
Fontina  100g
parsley, thyme, chives  25g

Potato cake with Fontina and herbs

Scrub the potatoes, or peel if you wish, then grate coarsely in long, thin shreds. I use the coarse grater of a food processor. Put the grated potatoes in a sieve over a bowl and let them drain for 20 minutes.

Trim the spring onions, discarding only the roots and tough ends of the shoots, then slice them finely. Season with salt and black pepper, then stir into a bowl with the drained potatoes and the flour, nigella seeds and beaten egg.

Warm the oil in a 22–25cm non-stick frying pan, keeping the heat no more than moderately high. Place the potato mix in the pan, spreading it out to fill the base. Don't be tempted to smooth it flat. The cake is lighter if it isn't compacted.

Let the potato cake cook for 8–10 minutes, regulating the temperature when necessary, until the base is crisp and golden. Check its progress by lifting up the edge with a palette knife or slotted slice. Carefully turn the cake over either by lifting with a large metal slice or palette knife, or by placing a plate over the top of the pan and, holding it tightly in place, carefully flipping the pan over, then sliding the cake back into the pan.

Leave to brown lightly on the underside. Finely grate the cheese over the top of the potato cake, leaving a rim around the edge. Place a lid over the pan, remove from the heat and leave for 5 minutes for the cheese to melt.

Chop the herb leaves and scatter over the cake. Cut into slices and serve.

## Chickpea cakes with spinach and lemongrass

An archivist going through my books would spot many a little cake fried in a pan. Cakes of salmon and crab, of potatoes and greens, of sweet potato and chilli. They would now find a new vegan one of chickpeas and spinach. What works for me is pushing my fork through the crisp crust – perhaps a little charred – and finding a soft, spicy centre.

A thin, crisp crust is essential here, a contrast to the soft, hummus-like texture of the cakes. Once the cakes have rested and firmed in the fridge, they should be lifted carefully into the sizzling oil using a palette knife, then left to form a thin, golden crust on the bottom before you attempt to turn them. Fiddling with them as they cook, although tempting, will result in them breaking up.

*Makes 12 cakes, serves 4*

spinach  200g
lemongrass  2 large stalks
chickpeas  2 × 400g tins
banana shallots  2, small
garlic  2 cloves
ginger  60g
chillies  2

lime  1
coriander  15g
mint  15g
Dijon mustard  2 teaspoons
breadcrumbs  120g,
   fine and dried
groundnut oil for cooking

Wash the spinach and remove any tough stalks. Put the wet leaves in a deep saucepan over a moderate heat, cover and steam for 2–3 minutes. Turn the leaves over and continue cooking until they are bright and soft. Drain thoroughly and give the leaves a firm squeeze to remove any remaining water.

Peel the outer leaves from the lemongrass and discard them. Chop the softer inner leaves, put them in an electric coffee mill or spice grinder and process to a coarse pulp. Alternatively, chop them very finely.

Drain the chickpeas and tip them into the bowl of a food processor. Peel and roughly chop the shallots. Add the lemongrass and shallots to the chickpeas. Peel the garlic, peel and coarsely grate the ginger, then add both to the chickpeas.

Finely chop the chillies, grate the zest of the lime finely, then add to the food processor. Pull the coriander and mint leaves from their stems, add to the bowl and process to a rough paste, seasoning with the mustard and about half a teaspoon of salt as you go.

Transfer the chickpea paste to a mixing bowl then combine with the spinach and breadcrumbs. Divide the mixture into twelve, shape each into a small cake the size of a digestive biscuit, and set aside to chill in the fridge for 20 minutes.

To cook, warm a shallow film of groundnut oil in a pan over a low to moderate heat. Lower the cakes into the pan, a few at a time, without crowding them. As they turn golden on the underside, gently turn with a palette knife and cook the other side. Remove carefully to warm plates.

At first taste, I dismissed the sweet potato as 'too sugary'. Despite a baked version being both crisp of crust and golden fluff within, the sweet flesh didn't work well with cheese. I wrote it off.

Years later, I took another look. Rather than trying to marry *Ipomoea batatas* with the ingredients that work naturally with a floury, white potato, I turned to those of its natural habitat. The chillies, tomatoes and spices of South America. Immediately, I warmed to its sugary character, balanced with ginger and spring onion and, above all, chilli. I had been dressing the sweet potato in the wrong clothes. Rather than butter and cheese, I learned to make a mixture of sautéed tomatoes and scarlet chillies to squash into its apricot-hued flesh.

## Sweet potato cakes, tomato sauce

From this impromptu supper came the idea for a slightly more complex dish, a deep casserole of layered sweet potato with a spiced sauce of tomatoes and lentils. A recipe born, I suppose, from lasagne and moussaka, where slow-cooked layers of starch and sauce combine to satiate our hunger and warm our souls.

*Serves 2*

| | |
|---|---|
| sweet potatoes 1kg | tarragon, chopped 1 tablespoon |
| butter 50g | egg 1 |
| crisp fine white breadcrumbs 120g | flour a little |
| | groundnut oil 3 tablespoons |
| lemon zest, finely grated 1 teaspoon | |

*For the tomato sauce:*

| | |
|---|---|
| tomatoes 500g | olive oil 3 tablespoons |
| garlic 2 cloves, crushed | basil leaves 10, medium |

Peel the sweet potatoes and cut into large chunks, then steam for about 20 minutes until tender enough to crush. Drain and mash with the butter and set aside to cool.

Put the breadcrumbs on a plate, then add the lemon zest and the chopped tarragon and combine. Crack the egg into a shallow bowl and briefly beat with a fork to mix the white and yolk.

When the mash is cool, shape into eight balls then pat them, in floury hands, into shallow round patties. Put them on a baking sheet and chill in the fridge for 30 minutes. Dip first into the beaten egg, then into the crumbs. Put them on a baking sheet and refrigerate for 30 minutes.

Warm the groundnut or vegetable oil in a non-stick frying pan, then lower the cakes into the hot oil and leave to cook, without moving them, for 4–5 minutes until the underside is crisp and golden. Carefully, using a palette knife or fish slice, turn the cakes over and lightly crisp the other side.

To make the tomato sauce: chop the tomatoes then cook them in a shallow pan with the crushed garlic in the olive oil for 15–20 minutes, crushing them with a fork as you go. Season with salt, pepper and the basil leaves, shredded. Serve with the sweet potato cakes.

## Green Thai bubble and squeak fritters

If you flick through the pages of my books, you will come, every now and again, to bubble and squeak. They are there because the dish is a sound way of using leftover potatoes. In theory the recipes exist for leftover greens too, but I find myself cooking the leaves from scratch – partly because I like the dish better with freshly cooked leaves. The dish has been with me all my life – both my mother and stepmother made it; I have cooked it professionally with pancetta and pieces of cheese folded into the middle and served it from cauldrons to hungry lunchers. There are leftover versions and some with cheese; others are made as one round cake whilst several of the recipes are rolled into patties and fried into little golden discs. Not all are vegetarian – snippets of bacon and pieces of smoked mackerel get a look-in sometimes. Like trifle, this is one of those recipes I run with, adding and subtracting ingredients as the mood, season or circumstances take me.

This time, a new version. James suggested it might be worth trying them with green curry paste and lots of fresh herbs. He wasn't wrong. I suspect I might do this every time now.

Green Thai bubble and squeak fritters

*Serves 3*

| | |
|---|---|
| potatoes 500g | green Thai curry paste |
| spring cabbage 250g | 2–3 tablespoons |
| olive oil 2 tablespoons | flour a little |
| butter 70g | oil and a little butter for frying |
| spring onions 3 | watercress or pea shoots |
| parsley, coriander, mint, | a handful |
| chopped 8 tablespoons in total | |

Peel and roughly chop the potatoes and boil in deep, lightly salted water for 15–20 minutes until tender enough to mash. Remove the core of the cabbage and discard it, then roughly chop the leaves. Warm the oil and 30g of the butter in a pan, add the cabbage and cook for 6–8 minutes till bright green, turning occasionally with kitchen tongs.

Slice the spring onions finely, discarding any tough outer green leaves as you go. Drain the potatoes thoroughly, add the remaining butter, then mash them using a food mixer or vegetable masher. Fold in the cabbage, drained of any liquid, the onions, herbs, the green curry paste and a generous grinding of salt and pepper. Roll into twelve balls or patties, dusting a little flour on your hands to stop the mixture sticking if necessary.

Heat a thin layer of oil and butter in a shallow non-stick pan then lower in the patties, letting them cook for 5–6 minutes till pale gold and lightly crisp on the underside. Turn each one over and lightly brown the other side. Divide the watercress or pea shoots between three plates and nestle the cakes amongst them.

## Cheesy greens and potatoes

I don't think I am ready to admit just how much of this I can eat at one sitting. The greens should, for once, be cooked in water, so they are fresh and clean-tasting as a contrast to the buttery potatoes. Comfort food, fork food of the highest order.

*Serves 4 (or 1, depending)*

greens, Savoy cabbage, chard,
   cavolo nero etc.  200g
butter  60g
spring onions  6

cooked potatoes  400g
cheese, Fontina, Taleggio or
   Cheddar-style  100g

Wash the greens thoroughly, then cook them in boiling, lightly salted water till just tender – we are talking no more than 4–5 minutes. Drain and set aside.

Melt the butter in a shallow pan, finely chop the spring onions, add them to the pan and let them soften over a moderate heat for about 5 minutes. Mash the potatoes – not too finely – and season generously, then add to the spring onions. Roughly chop the greens and fold into the potato.

Crumble or cut the cheese into small pieces and fold in. Lumps about 1–2cm square are about right, but let's not get too pedantic. The idea is to have gorgeous mouthfuls of melting cheese amongst the potato and greens. Fold everything together, then, just as the cheese starts to melt, serve in a warm bowl.

# Greens with gochujang

The polar opposite of the 'hug-in-a-bowl' above is a dish I make regularly when the days are cold and icy. Greens cooked in minutes with a kick in the stomach from a ridiculously hot spice paste. I use gochujang, the most accessible and user-friendly of the Korean spice pastes. This brick-red paste – actually more the colour of deep arterial blood – has only been part of my cooking since my trips to Korea became annual, but is now very much a part of this kitchen. I keep a plastic pot of it in the fridge door, with the Japanese yuzu koshō and the wasabi paste.

Whilst I would love to say this is a time-honoured recipe I picked up in a Korean village, it is not. Rather more like me playing in the kitchen with a few ingredients from the larder.

*Serves 1*

| | |
|---|---|
| greens  200g | gochujang  1 tablespoon |
| spring onions  2 | light soy sauce  3 teaspoons |
| garlic  3 cloves | sugar  a generous pinch |
| groundnut oil  2 tablespoons | sesame oil  a splash |

Wash the greens and remove and reserve any tough stems. Slice the stems finely. Roughly chop the spring onions. Peel and finely crush the garlic.

Heat a large shallow pan or wok. Pour in the oil and when it is hot, add the spring onions, sliced stems and garlic and let them cook over a moderate heat for a couple of minutes. Add the greens and continue cooking for a couple of minutes until the leaves relax. Turn them over occasionally with kitchen tongs.

Stir in the gochujang and let it sizzle for a minute or two, then add the soy and sugar. When the leaves start to relax, but are still green and bright, add the sesame oil and pile into a bowl together with the pan juices. And I know everyone says 'serve immediately', but this time I mean it.

In 2014, I wrote a story about my fondness for a Big Mac. ('My walk of shame is more like a ravenous dash.') I was expecting a certain polarity of opinion and I got it. The truth is that I find much (much) pleasure in holding a squidgy bun in my hand, the filling peeping out untidily. 'Yes, it is about the bun, the two thin beef patties and the secret sauce (oh God, the sauce) but so, so much more. It is about the soft rustle of warm paper as I slip my hand deep into the bag and slowly pull out the chunky waxed box. The almost imperceptible click as I unhook the cardboard seal of the carton and the salty rustle as I tip the fries into the lid. The wisp of stray lettuce. The warm, soft cushion of dough in my fingers. The peeking gherkin. The excited dribble of sauce between patty and bun. But more even than that. It's the gorgeous, tingling luxury of instant gratification.'

# Red lentil and bulgur burger

I am happy to spend time making my own burgers too. The lentil and bulgur recipe that James brought back from the Middle East being a case in point. It has the comforting familiarity of a soft warm bun, the deep earthy sweetness you get from slowly cooked onions and cumin, and the freshness of green herbs. It is not a Big Mac, and neither do I want it to be. It is a great fat parcel of vegan-friendly joy.

Make sure you have the fine variety of bulgur, not the coarse one, otherwise your patties will fall apart.

*Enough for 6 burgers*

| | |
|---|---|
| onions 2, medium | red split lentils 200g |
| olive oil 4 tablespoons | fine bulgur 200g |
| yellow mustard seeds 2 teaspoons | parsley 15g |
| ground cumin 2 teaspoons | coriander leaves 10g |
| mild curry powder 2 teaspoons | mint leaves 5g |
| ground turmeric 1 teaspoon | groundnut or vegetable oil for frying |
| vegetable stock 600ml | |

*For the accompaniment:*

| | |
|---|---|
| assorted cherry tomatoes 300g | soft buns 6 |
| olive oil 1 tablespoon | tomatoes and a few crisp lettuce |
| pomegranate molasses 1 tablespoon | leaves to serve |

Peel and finely chop the onions. Warm the oil in a large, deep pan for which you have a lid, add the onions and let them cook for about 10 minutes until translucent, stirring regularly. Add the mustard seeds, cumin, curry powder and turmeric to the onions and continue cooking for a further 3–4 minutes. Pour in the stock, bring to the boil, then add the lentils.

Lower the heat a little and cook the lentils for 10–15 minutes till they are soft enough to crush, then stir in the bulgur. Remove from the heat, cover with a lid and set aside.

Finely chop the parsley, coriander and mint and stir into the lentils and bulgur.

Roughly chop the tomatoes, put them in a saucepan with the olive oil and cook over a high heat for 5 minutes. Crush the tomatoes with a fork, then stir in a little pepper and the pomegranate molasses.

Make the lentil mixture into six large, round patties and set aside for 30 minutes in the fridge. Warm a thin pool of oil (about 3 tablespoons) in a shallow pan over a moderate heat, then fry the patties for about 4 minutes on each side, watching them carefully, till golden and crisp.

Split the buns, add a few salad leaves and sliced fresh tomatoes and a spoon or two of the tomato sauce, then place a patty on each.

The ubiquitous head of broccoli, like a goblin's wedding bouquet, is a problem. Yes, it is green and healthy – 'good for you' – cooks quickly and keeps well in the fridge, but it is quite the most boring of vegetables. Has no one ever noticed how utterly tasteless it is or that it is always, always, cold by the time it gets to your plate? And the window between raw and overcooked is like… thirty seconds. Better to my mind is the long-stemmed version. You can pile it on a platter, trickle it with hollandaise or fry it with chillies, garlic and ginger then hit it with soy or chilli sauce. It stays hot for longer, has more flavour and looks less lumpen on the plate. The long, tender stems are only slightly less delicious than asparagus and they will also take to being cooked slowly with olive oil, water, lemon and dried chilli flakes.

That said, most of us do, at some point, find ourselves with a head of it in the fridge. Heaven knows why, but we do. For that occasion, here is the recipe I use to make the most of it.

## Broccoli, pumpkin seeds and breadcrumbs

*Serves 2*

olive oil
white breadcrumbs  50g
parsley  10g

pumpkin seeds  3 tablespoons
vegetable stock (or water)  1 litre
broccoli  1kg

Broccoli, pumpkin seeds and breadcrumbs

Heat 3 tablespoons of olive oil in a shallow pan, add the breadcrumbs and cook, turning them regularly in the pan, till they are crisp and golden. Roughly chop the parsley and stir into the crumbs with a little salt, black pepper and the pumpkin seeds. (I like to chop them roughly, but it is up to you.) Set aside.

Bring the vegetable stock (or water) to the boil in a saucepan. Cut the broccoli into florets and slice the stalks into thin coins. Cook the broccoli florets and stalks for a few minutes till tender, then remove half of it.

Purée half of the broccoli in a blender or food processor with a ladle of the cooking stock, a little salt and pepper and a couple of tablespoons of olive oil. Divide between two warm plates. Drain the remaining broccoli and add to the purée, then scatter with the crisp breadcrumbs and seeds. Trickle over a little olive oil and serve.

A few minutes' daydreaming and I'm thinking how I would like to die. It is a toss-up between 'quietly in a deserted Japanese forest' and, probably more likely, sitting at a table, dunking thick, crisp chips into a bowl of Béarnaise sauce. Even that scenario underplays just how much I love a chip.

That said, I never, ever make them at home, preferring to leave the art of deep-frying to the professionals. (They are almost the first thing I order in a restaurant.) Yet I do sauté potatoes in shallow oil, grate and fry lacework latkes and make plump, golden potato cakes. You see, I adore fried potatoes in all their forms. So often, when I'm eating some fashionable chef's much publicised signature dish, I am really yearning for a plate of salty chips.

## Cheesy chips

For once, I deep fried. Not my favourite cooking method but I will do it for these. You will need a large, deep pan. One teaspoon of chilli flakes is probably enough, maybe two if you're a bit drunk.

*Serves 2*

large floury potatoes  2          dripping, lard or sunflower oil
  (about 850g)                         for frying  1 litre

*For the cheesy bit:*

| | |
|---|---|
| Fontina or Cheddar 150g | dried chilli flakes 1 teaspoon |
| Parmesan 60g | (maybe 2) |

Peel the potatoes and cut them into long, thick chips, putting them into cold water as you go. The water has the effect of preventing them browning while also washing away some of the starch. Drain and pat dry with a cloth or kitchen paper. Heat the dripping, lard or oil to 150°C in a large, very deep pan. Lower the chips into the hot oil – it will bubble up alarmingly – and fry for 6–7 minutes, until they are pale and soft.

Lift the chips out and leave to drain while you bring the temperature up to 185°C. Lower the chips into the hot oil again and fry for 3–4 minutes, maybe less, until they are crisp and golden. Drain on kitchen paper and dust lightly with salt.

Tip the chips onto a baking sheet in a shallow pile. Coarsely grate the Cheddar or chop the Fontina; finely grate the Parmesan. Scatter the cheeses over the chips, then the chilli flakes, then the Parmesan. Cook under a hot grill for a few minutes till the cheeses start to melt. Serve immediately.

# Hob-top suppers

I stand at the hob. A tangle of courgettes cut into wide ribbons like pappardelle is sizzling in a little olive oil. There is a bowl of pea purée – verdant, bright green – ready to be folded through them. A hob-top supper of quiet summer joy.

As I said in *Eat*, cooking on the hob 'allows us to get closer to our cooking than roasting or baking. It allows us a sniff, a peep, a stir, a taste.' We have a little more control, an instant ability to harness a fierce burst of heat to form a golden crust, the chance to lower the heat if something is cooking too quickly. We are in control of our dinner.

Pasta ribbons and plump cushions of ricotta and spinach bounce in bubbling water, courgettes simmer in spiced, silky dal, noodles cook slowly with lentils, beans and herbs. A creamy sauce simmers for cauliflower and pearls of couscous are ready to be tossed with tomatoes from the grill. There is always something going on here on the hob. It is the workhorse of this kitchen from early morning porridge to late-night miso soup.

# Cauliflower and orecchiette

One of the unexpected perks of putting together a book of my favourite recipes has been to correct previous mistakes. I don't know who made this cauliflower and pasta recipe as it was originally published, with a staggering 200g of Parmesan, but I hope they enjoyed their hit of umami. The quantity should be 100g, and even that is quite generous.

*Serves 2*

Parmesan  100g
cauliflower  1, medium
butter  30g
olive oil  3 tablespoons

orecchiette  125g
double cream  250ml
dill fronds  10g

Put a deep pan of water on to boil and salt it generously. Finely grate the Parmesan. Cut the cauliflower florets from the main stalk.

Warm the butter and oil together in a shallow pan, then fry the cauliflower florets for 5 minutes or so until lightly crisp and golden. Put the orecchiette into the boiling water and cook for about 9 minutes or until tender. Turn the cauliflower and cover with a lid. Cook for 7 minutes on low heat.

Pour the cream into the cauliflower, add the grated Parmesan and lower the heat. Drain the pasta and add it to the cauliflower and cream. Season with black pepper. Chop the dill fronds, stir into the pasta and serve.

There is a faded newspaper cutting in the attic containing a photograph of me leaning out of the window of my old flat, barely visible amongst the leaves of a prolific courgette plant. There is a tomato plant too, one of several that plummeted to the pavement in a storm. The story was of how I grew vegetables on a London windowsill. More accurately, the story could have been how passers-by narrowly missed being hit by a mad cookery writer's falling terracotta pots.

Cauliflower and orecchiette

I have grown courgettes pretty much all my working life. They thrive on my signature gardening style of smothering and neglect. I detail the varieties and how to grow them in *Tender, Volume I*, and insist they are the easiest of all vegetables to grow. I have cooked with them since 1976, when I would sauté them, sliced into thick coins, at a restaurant that served them fried in olive oil and lemon. A recipe that is still one of my favourite ways to deal with a surfeit. I add basil now, the leaves shredded and tossed in at the last minute so everyone gets a hit of its peppery scent.

The recipe is simply that of slicing two long, chubby courgettes (a good centimetre will suffice), then adding them to a shallow pan of sizzling olive oil, keeping the heat low until the courgettes are turning gold underneath. Turn them, cook the other side, then, when the courgettes are translucent, add a squeeze of lemon juice and a handful (6 leaves, maybe 8) of shredded basil. Serve immediately.

## Spiced courgettes with spinach

Summer squashes, courgettes and marrows will easily take the warm, earthy notes of cumin and turmeric. Little bursts of refreshing green flesh among the spicy sauce. The recipe here takes advantage of this, offering a frugal and delicious dinner with either rice or warm puffs of flatbread.

*Serves 4, with rice or flatbread*

onions 3, medium
groundnut or vegetable oil
   3 tablespoons
yellow mustard seeds 2 teaspoons
ground turmeric 2 teaspoons
ground cumin 2 teaspoons
cayenne pepper half a teaspoon

cherry tomatoes 350g
round summer squash or
   courgettes 600g
spinach with stalks 350g
chickpeas 1 × 400g tin

Peel the onions, halve them, then cut each half into three or four segments. Warm the oil in a large, heavy-based casserole, add the yellow mustard seeds and cook for one minute then, as they start to pop, stir in the onions, turmeric, cumin and cayenne and lower the heat. Cook for 15 minutes, partially covering the pan with a lid and stirring occasionally.

When the onions are golden and fragrant, halve the cherry tomatoes, add them to the onions and leave to cook until soft. Deseed and cut the squash into thick segments, or courgettes into thick slices, roughly the length of a wine cork. Fold them into the onions and tomatoes, together with 200ml of water, and bring to the boil. Leave the stew simmering for 15 minutes.

Wash the spinach and remove the toughest of the stalks. Put the wet leaves into a non-stick pan with a lid and cook them for a minute or two over a moderate heat, letting the leaves steam and relax. Remove them from the pan, then cool immediately under cold running water and drain.

Drain and rinse the chickpeas and stir them into the onions. Continue cooking, stirring from time to time, until the courgettes are translucent and tender. Check the seasoning – you may want to add salt. Squeeze as much water as possible from the spinach, then fold into the courgettes gently and without crushing them.


There is the most brilliant summer salad with peas, soft-leaved lettuce and bacon in *Tender, Volume I*. The raw peas are tossed with a dressing of oil, red wine vinegar and Dijon mustard. Good as it is, I use peas raw only in early summer when they are at their sweetest. The decade I grew my own (2003–2013) was frustrating for the lack of space I could give them. Two good rows of peas produced barely enough for four. So sweet were they, most never made it to the pot, the majority being wolfed in the garden straight from the pod. If you have never put raw peas into a feta salad I urge you to as soon as possible, trickling over some vivid green olive oil and a flick of chopped mint.

Nowadays, there is always a bag of peas in the freezer. No vegetable feels quite so at home with fish fingers. Most of them end up as purée, which I have such affection for. To the mashed peas, I stir in melted butter or olive oil, and sometimes a dash of white wine vinegar or a squeeze of lemon.

# Courgettes with pea sauce

Their latest incarnation in my kitchen saw them puréed with rocket and olive oil for a sauce to accompany courgettes. The squash is cut like pappardelle, using a vegetable peeler. Scattered with pea shoots, the plate shimmers with the green of early spring.

*Serves 2*

peas, frozen 150g          courgettes 2 large
rocket 30g                 pea shoots a large handful
olive oil 165ml

Cook the peas in deep boiling water, lightly salted, for 4 minutes then drain. Tip the peas into the bowl of a food processor and add the rocket leaves. Process to a loose paste with 120ml of the olive oil.

Using a vegetable peeler, remove long, thin shavings from the courgettes. You will probably be left with a central, seedy core to discard. Warm the remaining olive oil in a shallow pan, then add the courgettes and let them cook for 3–4 minutes till they are soft and translucent, stopping before they turn golden. Add the pea shoots. Heat the pea paste gently for a minute or two over a low heat.

Serve the courgettes with the pea sauce.

The list of vegetables on which I am not keen is short. Boiled carrots (although I will enthusiastically crunch them raw), mini-sweetcorns (like finding a cube of sugar in your Thai curry) and mangetout (a flaccid pea pod) is pretty much the length of it. Even then, I will eat them out of politeness. The only vegetable I refuse to eat is the green pepper. Raw, it will give me indigestion. Roasted, it flatly refuses to caramelise sweetly, choosing instead to turn bitter before finally burning to a crisp.

The scarlet (ripe) pepper, however, roasted till its skin blackens and its flesh turns to silk, is the most sensuous of vegetables. Actually, it's a fruit, but

Courgettes with pea sauce

this is cooking not botany, so vegetable it is. In this kitchen they are reserved for deepest summer, when they appear at the table roasted, skinned and scattered with cooked lentils. Almost without fail, their sweet, amber juices will be flecked with torn basil. It is difficult to think of a dish that embodies late summer more richly than a large oval platter of roasted red peppers in their juices with basil and a faint whiff of summer garlic.

We should probably forget raw peppers altogether, if only because they are so luscious when roasted or grilled. The juices from a roasted pepper make a fine backbone for a dressing – just stir in a little olive oil. What I have only just discovered is that those juices have the most extraordinary affinity with cream.

## Peppers, lentils and basil

*Serves 4*

| | |
|---|---|
| red peppers  3, large | bay leaves  3 |
| olive oil  6 tablespoons | double cream  150ml |
| small, dark green lentils  200g | basil leaves  a large handful |

Set the oven at 200°C.

Slice the peppers in half, discard the seeds and cores, then cut each half into three. Put them in a baking tray and trickle the olive oil over them. Bake for about 35 minutes, until the peppers are soft and the skins are brown in patches.

Cook the lentils with the bay leaves, in deep, unsalted boiling water for about 30 minutes, then drain in a colander.

Remove the peppers from the oven, then place the baking tray over a low to moderate heat. Stir in the drained lentils, the cream and the basil leaves, then season generously with salt and black pepper.

Lift the peppers onto a serving plate, then spoon the lentils and the creamy juices around them.

# Pappardelle with mushrooms and harissa

It is a rare day when I can't be arsed to cook. For those evenings there is the ten-minute pasta supper and a corkscrew. These are the nights when I toss wide ribbons of pappardelle with a mess of wild mushrooms and harissa sauce, or throw peas, pine kernels and Parmesan over a bowl of orecchiette.

*Serves 2*

| | |
|---|---|
| pappardelle 150g | olive oil 6 tablespoons |
| chestnut mushrooms 300g | harissa paste 3 tablespoons |
| spring onions 4 | Parmesan, grated a little |
| garlic 2 cloves | |

Put a deep pan of water on to boil. As it boils, salt generously then add the pappardelle and cook for 8 minutes.

Thinly slice the chestnut mushrooms and the spring onions. Finely mash the garlic cloves. Warm the olive oil in a large frying pan, then add the mushrooms. Let them fry for 4–5 minutes until they start to toast, then add the garlic. Let the garlic and mushrooms cook for a minute or until the garlic is fragrant, then add the spring onions and continue cooking for another couple of minutes until soft. Stir in the harissa paste.

Lightly drain the pappardelle, toss with the mushrooms and serve. Grate a little Parmesan over at the table.

# Pasta, pesto and peas

A bit of a lifesaver, this one. If you have time to make your own pesto – it takes but minutes, even with a pestle and mortar – your supper will be verdant, heady with the clove and pepper notes of crushed basil. I give two methods, a quick version and a lovingly hand-pounded one. Use whatever shape pasta you have to hand, but not ribbons or spaghetti or your peas will fall off. Orecchiette (little ears) will hold the peas neatly, like little cupped hands.

*Serves 2*

pasta  250g
peas  200g (shelled weight)
basil leaves  50g
pine kernels  1 tablespoon

garlic  a small clove, peeled
olive oil  4 tablespoons
Parmesan, grated  2 tablespoons

Cook the pasta in generously salted boiling water until tender. In a second pan, boil the peas for 3–4 minutes, then drain them.

Put the basil and a pinch of sea salt into a mortar and pound and twist to a paste with a pestle. Add the pine kernels and garlic and continue until you have a thick paste. Add the oil in a slow stream, working the mixture to a thick, luscious cream, then mix in the Parmesan and set aside or refrigerate – you will need to cover it tightly – until needed.

Quick way: put the basil leaves into a food processor with a generous pinch of salt, the olive oil, pine kernels and the garlic. Process briefly, until you have a creamy paste, then scrape into a mixing bowl with a rubber spatula and beat in the grated Parmesan.

Drain the pasta, leaving a couple of tablespoons of its cooking water behind in the pan, then return the pasta to the pan and add the drained peas. Stir in the basil sauce, toss everything gently together, then divide between two shallow bowls.

# Noodles and greens

A ten-minute walk away from my home is a Chinese supermarket. I return with bundles of cheap lemongrass and fat hands of ginger, bottles of chilli sauce and bags of vegetable dumplings for the freezer. They also sell fresh noodles.

One of my lazy-day recipes involves tossing those noodles in a hot wok with greens and a few cupboard essentials. I include it here simply for its usefulness. Use dried noodles if that is what you have, reconstituting them with boiling water, then draining them thoroughly before they hit the hot oil. Preparing the ingredients first is pretty much essential in this recipe. Once started, there is no time to chop as you cook.

*Serves 2*

| | |
|---|---|
| spring onions  6 | fresh egg noodles  150g |
| garlic  3 cloves | mild chilli sauce  1 tablespoon |
| spring greens  175g | dark soy sauce  3 teaspoons |
| groundnut oil  2 tablespoons | coriander  leaves from 4 or 5 sprigs |

Trim the spring onions, then chop the white and the lower part of the green stalk into thin rounds. Peel and finely chop the garlic. Snap the leaves from the spring greens, pile them on top of one another, roll them up, then shred them into finger-width ribbons.

Heat a wok over a high heat. Pour in the oil, swirl it round the pan, then, as it shimmers and starts to smoke, add the chopped spring onions and garlic. Move them quickly round the pan for a minute or two till they start to soften and colour, then add the noodles. As the noodles cook, drop in the shredded greens and stir or toss them around the pan as they cook for 2 minutes.

Stir in the chilli sauce and soy, add the coriander leaves and continue cooking for a minute or so till all is soft, glossy and sizzling.

While filming in Iran, we came across the soothing, hot and sour notes of ash reshteh everywhere we went. A sustaining mixture of noodles, chickpeas and kashk (a thick, deliciously sour yoghurt), the gently soporific soup-stew was the supper we ate night after night on our weeks of filming. It is difficult to tire of it; the recipe changes delightfully according to who makes it. We had subtly differing versions throughout our trip.

On returning home, I made my own versions, substituting soured cream or sometimes thick yoghurt for the kashk, and introducing other vegetables and greens, such as spinach or chard leaves, according to what was around. The softer leaves work best. One Christmas I put pieces of pumpkin into the saffron-yellow depths and served it, in vast ladles, for lunch.

# Noodles with lentils and soured cream

*Serves 4–6*

onions  4
olive oil  3 tablespoons
garlic  3 cloves
ground turmeric  2 teaspoons
chickpeas  1 × 400g tin
haricot beans  1 × 400g tin
small brown lentils  100g
vegetable stock  1 litre

butter  40g
linguine or Iranian *reshteh*
   noodles  100g
spinach  200g
parsley  30g
coriander  20g
mint  15g
soured cream  250ml

Peel the onions. Roughly chop two of them and thinly slice the others. Warm the olive oil in a large pan set over a moderate heat, add the two chopped onions and fry them for 10–15 minutes till soft and pale gold. Peel and thinly slice the garlic. Stir the garlic and ground turmeric into the onions and continue cooking for a couple of minutes.

Drain the chickpeas and haricot beans and stir them into the onions together with the lentils and stock. Bring to the boil, then lower the heat and leave to simmer for 30 minutes, stirring occasionally.

Melt the butter in a shallow pan, then add the reserved sliced onions and let them cook slowly, with the occasional stir, until they are a rich toffee brown. This will take a good half an hour.

Add the linguine or noodles to the simmering beans and lentils.

Wash the spinach, put it in a separate pan set over a moderate heat, cover with a lid and leave it for 3–4 minutes until it has wilted. Turn occasionally with kitchen tongs. Remove the spinach and put it in a colander under cold running water until cool. Wring the moisture from the spinach with your hands, then stir into the simmering stew.

Roughly chop the parsley, coriander and mint leaves and stir most of them into the stew. Fold in the soured cream, then ladle into bowls and fold in the remaining herbs and the fried onions.

There is no piece of kitchen kit I enjoy using more than my pestle and mortar. (Though don't even think of trying to part me from my bean-to-cup espresso machine.) There is something grounding about crushing roasted spices to powder or green herbs to a paste. Yes, the job is done in seconds in a food processor, but that would be to miss the heady notes of basil leaves or coriander seeds. Made of heavy clay, smooth and chalk white, its surface is now battle-scarred with turmeric yellow and brown scratches from crushing rock-hard black peppercorns.

Pesto is made in seconds at the click of a switch, but it is the old pestle and mortar I reach for first. The difference in time is only a few minutes, and the process deeply rewarding for those who take a certain joy in cooking. Few moments in the kitchen are more pleasing than when basil is being torn or crushed.

# Wild garlic and basil cream

*Makes a 500g tub*

wild garlic leaves and stems  100g

basil leaves  50g

Parmesan  50g

pine kernels  50g

olive oil  150ml

a lemon

Tear or roughly chop the garlic leaves and stems, then put them in a mortar. Add a pinch of sea salt – it helps the pestle grip the leaves – then pound and stir until you have a dark green paste. Expect this to take a while, and you might like to do it in two batches. Alternatively, grind the leaves and stems to a paste in a food processor.

Add the basil leaves and keep pounding and twisting to a paste. Grate the Parmesan finely. Put the pine kernels in a dry frying pan and toast over a moderate heat till pale gold. Watch them carefully (they burn in a heartbeat) then add them to the paste, smashing them in with your pestle, then mash them with the Parmesan and leaves.

Add the oil, working the mixture to a thick, luscious cream, then add a few drops of lemon juice and set aside or refrigerate – you will need to cover it tightly – until needed.

# A little stew of flageolet, broad beans and peas

*Serves 6*

| | |
|---|---|
| broad beans in the pod  400g (200g podded weight) | flageolet beans  1 × 400g tin |
| small leeks  200g | vegetable stock  1 litre |
| spring onions  200g | peas  200g (podded weight) |
| olive oil | parsley  a handful |
| small courgettes  200g | wild garlic and basil cream |

Remove the broad beans from their pods. You will need about 200g.

Bring a deep pan of water to the boil, salt it lightly, then add the broad beans and boil for 4–5 minutes. Check them for tenderness, then drain them in a colander. If they are small and tender you might like to leave them in their pale skins; if they are larger then I suggest popping them out of their skins with your thumb and finger – it will only take a few minutes. Set the beans aside.

Trim and slice the leeks into thick coins and wash them very, very thoroughly in a bowl of deep, cold water. (Grit has a tendency to get trapped between the layers.) Trim and thinly slice the spring onions.

Heat a couple of tablespoons of olive oil in a deep, wide pan, then add the leeks and spring onions. Place a piece of baking parchment over them – it will encourage them to soften in their own steam, without colour – and then cover with a lid. Let the leeks and onions cook for about 15 minutes, till soft and pale. (Young, thin leeks really won't take long at all.)

Cut the courgettes into small pieces. You can dice them, but I also like to cut them in half lengthways, then in half again, then into thick slices. When the leeks and spring onions are soft and still bright green, remove the greaseproof paper, add the courgettes and continue cooking. Drain and rinse the flageolet (you don't want the aquafaba in this recipe), then add them to the pan, together with the vegetable stock and, as it comes to the boil, the peas. Turn down to a simmer and leave for 5 minutes, till the peas are cooked.

Roughly chop the parsley and stir into the stew. Ladle into bowls and stir a good tablespoon or two of the wild garlic cream into each bowl.

A little stew of flageolet, broad beans and peas

# Mashed potatoes

A bowl of potatoes, steamed or boiled, then mashed with butter, is a recipe I have featured in almost every book I have written. Mashed potato is calming, almost sleepy, and is at its most blissful when used to soak up gravy or sauce.

You can make a fine enough mash with boiled, white-fleshed potatoes and butter. A potato masher or even the tines of a fork will do the trick. A food mixer fitted with a paddle attachment will do the job in half the time, though you need to watch it carefully. A few seconds too long and you have a gluey mash. Over the years I have come to the conclusion that the finest results come from using a potato ricer. I avoided buying one for years for lack of drawer space, but finally relented once I saw how ethereally light the results were. Potatoes pushed through the fine grill of a ricer are fluffy, full of air and take less butter to make a sensational mash.

Mashed potatoes are too good for winter alone. Summer recipes have involved mashing the potatoes with milk in which a couple of bay leaves have infused. A squeeze of wasabi paste into the finished mash is something I consider too. Chopped parsley and a spoonful of mustard are good when the potatoes are to go with baked field mushrooms, and I thoroughly recommend folding in a spoonful of crushed, baked garlic and a smidgeon of cream (*Tender, Volume I*).

The mashed potato recipe I love above all others was made in 2005 for the Christmas chapter of the *The Kitchen Diaries*. This luxurious version involves mashing steamed, floury potatoes with butter and a splash of hot milk, then beating in Lancashire or Wensleydale cheese with a wooden spoon until the mixture shines. The gloriously soft and sticky mash is then trickled with the hot chicken juices from the roasting tin. (Be still my beating heart.)

I work on a ratio of about a tenth butter to floury potato. Slightly less if the potatoes are of the yellow, waxy-fleshed variety. Adding olive oil, cream or milk will produce a silkier, almost sloppy mash which I especially like. You can mix other roots with the potato, such as beetroot, celeriac, carrot or Jerusalem artichoke, though the latter may need a bit more potato if it isn't to be on the soupy side.

# Roast garlic, lemon and Parmesan mash

*Serves 6*

garlic  a whole head
olive oil  3 tablespoons
thyme leaves  2 teaspoons
half a lemon

potatoes  1.5kg
butter  75g
Parmesan, grated  50g
plus a little extra

Set the oven at 200°C. Put the garlic on a piece of tin foil, pour over the olive oil, add the thyme leaves and the lemon, then bring the edges of the foil up and over the garlic and lemon and loosely scrunch the edges together to make a baggy parcel. Bake for 30 minutes till the garlic is soft. Peel the potatoes and cook them in a deep pan of boiling, lightly salted water for about 25 minutes till tender.

Drain the potatoes and mash them, either by hand or using a food mixer. It is worth taking care not to overwork the mixture (it will become gluey). Stir in the butter and keep beating till you have a smooth and creamy mash. Remove the garlic from the oven, squeeze the cloves from their skins and mash them to a rough paste with a fork. Pour the oil and thyme leaves into the garlic, squeeze in the juice from the hot lemon and mix together, then pour into the mash. Stir in the Parmesan and a generous seasoning of black pepper. (It may need a little salt.)

Spoon into a shallow baking dish – I use one about 26cm × 20cm – and furrow the top with a fork or make peaks with the tip of a round knife. Sprinkle with a little more Parmesan and bake for 30 minutes till the top is patchily golden.


# Couscous and tomatoes

There is peace in a bowl of couscous. The grains sit quietly on your fork, often hand in hand with parsley and lemon. The crumbs of dough possess the ability to soak up roasting juices, dressing and sauces. Some people are a little sniffy about the quick-cooking variety on which you have only to pour boiling water and leave till the couscous is tender, but I have no problem with it. The couscous recipe I make most often is one that imbues the grains with the juice of roasted tomatoes. We should probably not call it a grain – though I do – as it is technically tiny pearls of dried pasta. I have seen it made by hand, the dough rubbed through a fine metal sieve – a mesmerising sight, almost a lullaby.

*Serves 3-4*

assorted tomatoes  750g
garlic  3 cloves
olive oil  3 tablespoons
red onion  1, medium

cumin seeds  2 teaspoons
coriander seeds  2 teaspoons
harissa paste  1 tablespoon

*For the couscous:*
vegetable stock  500ml
quick-cooking couscous  200g

mint leaves  10g
parsley leaves  15g

Cut the larger tomatoes in half and place in a roasting tin, tucking the smaller ones between them. Peel and crush the garlic and add together with the olive oil. Peel and slice the red onion and add it to the tomatoes with a seasoning of salt and pepper. Crush the cumin and coriander seeds using a pestle and mortar or spice mill, then scatter over the tomatoes and onions. Roast at 180°C for 35-40 minutes until the tomatoes are soft and the skins lightly browned.

Bring the vegetable stock to the boil. Place the couscous in a heatproof bowl, then pour the boiling stock over, cover and leave for 15 minutes. Remove the leaves from the mint and parsley and roughly chop.

Use a fork to lightly crush the tomatoes so the juices bleed into the pan, then stir in the harissa paste. Run a fork through the couscous to separate the grains, then stir in the chopped herbs. Serve the roast tomatoes and their juices on top of the couscous.


My life as a cookery writer revolves around the seasons but just as important (to my editors) are the other celebrations that pepper the culinary calendar, such as Burns Night, Easter Sunday and Valentine's Day. One of these is Shrove Tuesday, a date I am apt to forget as I don't really like being told what to eat. (The chance of me wanting to eat roast lamb at Easter is officially zero.)

The years roll by and every Shrove Tuesday there is a new pancake recipe to come up with. The truth is that I generally forget until I spot the recipes being posted online. The year that I actually remembered featured a long-winded but thoroughly worthwhile recipe for pancakes stuffed with mushrooms and spinach. There is quite a lot of hassle here, by which I suppose I mean washing-up, but it is a deeply satisfying dinner to make.

## Herb pancakes with spinach and mushrooms

*Serves 4*

*For the pancakes:*

| | |
|---|---|
| butter  15g, plus 30g for frying | milk  350ml |
| plain flour  100g | basil and parsley  20g, |
| egg  1 large, plus an extra yolk |     total weight |

*For the filling:*

| | |
|---|---|
| butter  a thick slice | plain flour  1 tablespoon |
| spring onions  4 | crème fraîche  200ml |
| thyme leaves  3 tablespoons | lemon  zest of 1 |
| button mushrooms  400g | melted butter and grated |
| tarragon  2 large handfuls |     Parmesan to finish |
| parsley  2 large handfuls | |

For the pancakes, melt the 15g of butter in a small pan, remove from the heat and leave to cool. Sift the flour, together with a pinch of salt, into a large bowl. Put the egg, egg yolk and milk into a blender or food processor, add the basil and parsley and blitz to a pale green. Pour into the flour and add the melted butter, beating lightly to get a smooth batter. Set aside for half an hour.

Melt the 30g of butter in a small saucepan and set aside. Brush a 20–22cm non-stick frying pan or crêpe pan with a little of the melted butter. You just want a thin film on the bottom of the pan. When the butter starts to sizzle, give the batter a quick stir, then pour or ladle in enough to give a wafer-thin layer. Tip the pan backwards and forwards to cover the base evenly with batter. Let it cook for 2–3 minutes till pale gold underneath, then run a palette knife around the edge to loosen it from the pan. Slide the palette knife underneath

Herb pancakes with spinach and mushrooms

the pancake then turn it over quickly and smoothly. Leave to cook for a minute or two, then slide or lift out onto a plate.

Continue with the rest of the mixture. You should make about six pancakes. (You will only need four, so keep the other two for later. They make a nice little snack topped with grated cheese and butter then grilled.)

To make the filling, melt the butter in a deep casserole over a moderate heat. Finely chop the spring onions, discarding any of the stem that is very dark and tough, and add them to the butter. Leave the onions to soften, giving them the occasional stir, then add the thyme leaves. Slice the mushrooms as thick as a pound coin, then add to the pan and cook for 3–4 minutes, adding a little more butter or oil if necessary.

Set the oven at 200°C. Roughly chop the tarragon and parsley leaves, add them to the spring onions and mushrooms, then sprinkle in the flour. Continue cooking for a couple of minutes, stirring regularly, till the flour smells toasty, then stir in the crème fraîche, salt and pepper. Finely grate the lemon zest, adding half to the filling and reserving the rest.

Place a pancake on the work surface, fill with a quarter of the stuffing mixture, then roll up and place in an oiled or buttered baking dish. Repeat with the remaining pancakes and filling. Sprinkle a little melted butter, grated Parmesan and grated lemon zest over them, then bake for 10 minutes and serve.

## Spinach ricotta pancakes, soured cream

Ricotta cakes – light, easy and soft as a sigh. They were not around when I was growing up – we had never heard of such delights. We just had simple pancakes that I still like with sugar and lemon. They are some of my favourite things to cook, partly because they are so good-natured. I let them fluff up, then, just as the underside is starting to turn gold in colour, I slide a spatula under them one at a time and flip them over. You need to do this in one swift, confident move otherwise they will stick.

These little cakes are surprisingly good-natured despite the mixture being somewhat soufflé-like. The recipe makes six but you can make four and keep the rest of the mixture for an hour or so in the fridge. The last batch may not be quite so fluffy but they'll still be good. I try not to get the pan too hot, to give the inside a little more time to cook.

Spinach ricotta pancakes, soured cream

*Serves 2*

spinach leaves  100g  
eggs  3  
ricotta  250g  
plain flour  50g  
Parmesan, finely grated  
    2 tablespoons  

butter, melted  2 tablespoons  
basil leaves  a handful  
parsley leaves  a handful  
a little more butter for cooking  

Wash the spinach leaves, and while they are still wet, put them into a large saucepan over a moderate heat. Cover tightly with a lid and let the leaves cook, in their own steam, for a minute or two. Turn the leaves over and continue cooking, covered, for a further minute. Drain the leaves, rinse under cold water, then squeeze the water from them with your hands and set aside.

Separate the eggs, putting the whites into a bowl large enough to beat them in. Stir the ricotta into the egg yolks, then add the flour, the Parmesan and the melted butter. Chop the basil and parsley leaves, stir them in, then season with a little salt and set aside. Finely chop the spinach.

Beat the egg whites until light and fluffy, then stir into the ricotta mixture together with the chopped spinach. Melt a little butter in a non-stick frying pan over a moderate heat. When it sizzles lightly, add a sixth of the ricotta mixture and pat it lightly into a small cake, about the circumference of a digestive biscuit, with the back of a spoon. Add another one or two, according to the size of your pan. When the cakes have coloured lightly on the base, flip them over with a palette knife (do this quickly and confidently and they won't break), then let the other side become a soft, pale gold. The full cooking time shouldn't be more than a few minutes.

Repeat with the remaining mixture. Remove the cakes with a palette knife or spatula, rest briefly on kitchen paper, then transfer to a plate. Serve with soured cream if you wish.

# Salads

Not a day goes by without a salad on the table. Simple ones, like Butterhead lettuce with olive oil, red wine vinegar and capers or, in winter, curly Treviso with walnuts and a thick mustardy dressing (a classic oil and vinegar recipe, but with twice as much Dijon mustard). First salad of the day is simply leaves, in a wooden bowl, no dressing. Just green (and purple, maroon and speckled) leaves. I will often pick at it lazily as I read, before I start work.

Nothing has changed more in my kitchen than what is meant by the word salad. When I was ten, it meant lettuce, tomatoes, cucumber and beetroot with salad cream. At twenty, it denoted grated carrot and cabbage in mayonnaise; at forty it was a bowl of spinach leaves with toasted nuts and dried fruits. Two decades on it can mean baked sweet potato, quinoa, rocket and pomegranate seeds. Currently, a salad is likely to come with beetroot, steamed grains and ferments – there will be pickled red cabbage and micro-leaves. A jumble, yes, but an interesting one.

I keep my salads simple and fresh. A mixture of the cooked and the raw, but always made seasonally and thoughtfully.

It is difficult to follow the ups and downs of the avocado. To this cook and eater, avocados, sliced and laid on hot, thick toast, the firm, only-just-ripe flesh dressed with herbs, seeds and fabulously fruity olive oil, remains one of my favourite things to eat. The fashionistas of the food world – to whom we should pay little attention – have turned against this rather useful open sandwich and its delightful contrast of textures. Their loss. Avocados – and indeed bananas – live or die by their level of ripeness. An over-ripe avocado is as unpalatable to me as a squashy banana, so I watch their progress with an acute sense of concentration.

Avocado with pea shoots, sprouted seeds and sourdough

## Avocado with pea shoots, sprouted seeds and sourdough

*Makes 2 toasts*

| | |
|---|---|
| coriander leaves  20g | sprouted mung beans  40g |
| olive oil  4 tablespoons, | sprouted radish  30g |
| plus a little extra | mixed sprouted seeds  40g |
| pea shoots  2 handfuls | radishes  6 |
| avocados  2, medium | sourdough  2 thick slices |

Put the coriander leaves in a blender or food processor and pour in the 4 tablespoons of oil. Add a good pinch of salt and a few twists of pepper. Process for a few seconds to a bright green dressing, then transfer to a mixing bowl. Put the pea shoots into a bowl of iced water to crisp them up.

Peel the avocados and remove their stones, then cut the flesh into small cubes. Toss the avocado gently with the dressing. Rinse the mung beans, sprouted radish and mixed sprouted seeds in cold running water, then drain and shake dry.

Trim the radishes and slice them in half, then toss them with the avocado. Toast the bread till golden on both sides, then pour a generous amount of olive oil over each piece. Drain the pea shoots, shake them dry and pile them on top of the toast. Divide the sprouted seeds between the toasts, then spoon over the avocado and radishes and their dressing.

## Beetroot with mustard and maple syrup

My books are splattered with the magenta ink of beetroot recipes. I must have done twenty in the last decade alone (including a gorgeous beetroot cake in *Tender, Volume I*). Here's a new one – a light, sweet, crisp salad – a mixture of grated and sliced beetroot with a dressing of maple syrup and mustard. It sings.

You can, of course, grate the lot, but I like to take advantage of the beautiful candy-coloured rings of Chioggia – the striped beetroot. This salad makes a fine filling for a sandwich made with cheeses such as Ticklemore or Wensleydale with dark, treacle-coloured rye bread.

beetroot, small, mixed  1kg
cider vinegar  4 tablespoons
Dijon mustard  2 teaspoons

grain mustard  2 teaspoons
maple syrup  1 tablespoon
dill  15g

Peel the beetroot. Slice half of the beetroot very, very thinly, place them in a shallow dish, sprinkle with the cider vinegar and set aside for a good 45 minutes.

Coarsely grate the remaining beetroot. (I use the matchstick setting on the food processor.)

Make the dressing by mixing the two mustards and maple syrup with the vinegar from the beetroot. Add a pinch of salt. Finely chop the dill and stir into the dressing. Toss the grated beetroot with the mustard and dill dressing and set aside for 15 minutes.

Toss the sliced and grated beetroot together and serve.

## Grilled halloumi with pickled slaw

Preserved cabbage – thin white sauerkraut or jewel-bright pickled red – is often the answer to the question 'what shall I eat with this?'. The acidity gives an energy to whatever else is on your plate. I make a pickle for almost instant eating (though you can keep it longer if you wish) from sliced cabbage, both red and white, wine vinegar and garlic. It is ready in hours rather than weeks and is a winner with feta or halloumi. You need half of the pickled slaw for the halloumi recipe below. It will keep, in a storage jar, in the fridge.

*Serves 4*

*For the pickle:*
red cabbage  400g
white cabbage  350g
white wine vinegar  550ml

granulated or caster sugar  150g
black peppercorns  12
garlic  3 cloves, peeled

Grilled halloumi with pickled slaw

*For the dressing:*

natural yoghurt  125g

tahini  2 tablespoons

lemon  juice of 1, small

coriander leaves  10g

parsley leaves  10g (a handful)

iced water  4 tablespoons

*For the halloumi:*

halloumi  700g

olive oil  a little

Finely shred the red cabbage. Do the same with the white cabbage. Put the cabbages in a colander, place over a bowl, then sprinkle generously with salt. Massage the salt well into the shredded leaves and set aside to drain for 30 minutes. Then squeeze the leaves in your hands and pack into a couple of medium-sized storage jars or a large mixing bowl.

Pour the vinegar into a stainless-steel saucepan, add the sugar, peppercorns and the whole garlic. Add 550ml of water and bring to the boil. As soon as the sugar has dissolved, pour the hot liquor over the salted vegetables, toss thoroughly, then seal or cover and set aside overnight, or for at least 4 hours. Turn the vegetables occasionally by stirring or shaking the jar.

Mix together the yoghurt, tahini and lemon juice. Finely chop the coriander and parsley and stir into the sauce. Thin to coating consistency with the iced water.

Cut the halloumi into large pieces about 1cm thick. Brush them with olive oil. Heat a ridged griddle pan, place the halloumi on the hot griddle and cook for about 4 minutes on each side.

Put half the slaw in a bowl, drained of its marinade. Add the tahini dressing and toss together.

Serve the slaw with the halloumi, hot from the griddle.

## Red cabbage, citrus fruits and cashew nuts

Hats off to a salad with the spirit of sourness – a tangle of sauerkraut, a few slices of blood orange, grapefruit or pomelo or a dressing made with kefir or yoghurt. The acidity is dazzling with buttery lettuce leaves and is a good marriage with peppery rocket, basil or watercress. If that salad has the crunch of shredded

Red cabbage, citrus fruits and cashew nuts

beetroot, red cabbage or celeriac, then even better (you could use carrots or kohlrabi too). Broccoli and cauliflower stalks, thinly sliced, also get my vote.

A little caution is needed if the result isn't to feel cluttered (there's a lot of that about nowadays), but a handful of toasted nuts – peanuts, walnuts or cashews – adds protein and more crucially, a contrast of texture. There is no real recipe to my salads themselves (much depends on what is around on the day) but I do record the dressings. The one here with ginger, lime, soy and if you wish, coriander leaves, sounds like a lot of trouble. It isn't. Everything just needs a quick blast in the blender or food processor. That said, I find the texture of the cashew nuts most pleasing when I grind them using a pestle and mortar, leaving them as a rough, gravelly powder but... hey ho.

*Serves 4*

grapefruit  1
orange  1, large
red cabbage  250g

fennel  150g
celeriac  150g
beetroot  250g

*For the dressing:*

red wine vinegar  2 tablespoons
lime juice  3 tablespoons
olive oil  75ml
light soy sauce  1 tablespoon
ginger  35g
light muscovado sugar
   3 tablespoons

small hot chillies  2
cashews  75g, roasted and salted,
   plus a few to finish
mint leaves  20, finely shredded
coriander leaves  20

Make the dressing: put the vinegar, lime juice, olive oil and soy in a mixing bowl. Peel the ginger and grate it finely, then add to the liquids with the sugar. Finely chop the chillies (you can remove the seeds if you like a cooler dressing) and stir in. Crush the cashews to a coarse, nubbly powder with a pestle and mortar (or the end of a rolling pin), then add to the dressing with the mint leaves and the coriander leaves, torn up a little if they are particularly large. Stir the dressing and set aside.

Remove the peel and white pith from the grapefruit and orange, saving as much juice as you can. Separate the segments with a sharp knife and add them to the dressing with any juice.

Finely shred the red cabbage and fennel and add to the dressing. Peel the celeriac and beetroot, slice thinly, then cut into long, thin matchsticks. Toss with the dressing, check the seasoning and set aside for 30 minutes or more before serving. Add the reserved whole cashews just before bringing the salad to the table.

In the 1970s, when I made the move to London, the carrot salad was, as we used to say then, 'all the rage'. The shredded matchsticks of root vegetable first appeared at wholefood cafés, gracing a wedge of wholemeal quiche. (Pastry like wet cardboard, but we ate it in the name of 'healthy eating'.) Initially dazzled by the sight of the orange roots shining like a Belisha beacon amongst the endlessly brown 'good-for-you' fodder, then, bored by their ubiquity, the recipe was soon pushed aside for new delights. Last year, I dug up the recipe to give it a new lease of life, if only to help make a dent in the mountain of carrots that appeared in my weekly vegetable box. The recipe startles, with pomegranate seeds to balance the sugar content of the roots and the crunch of blue-black poppy seeds for a change of texture.

## Carrot and beetroot salad

*Serves 4 as a side dish*

| | |
|---|---|
| carrots, large maincrop 250g | mint leaves 10g |
| beetroot 150g | parsley leaves 15g |
| spring onions 4 | poppy seeds 2 teaspoons |
| pomegranate seeds 4 tablespoons, plus extra to serve | |

*For the dressing:*

| | |
|---|---|
| lemon juice 1 tablespoon | pomegranate molasses |
| olive oil 2 tablespoons | 2 tablespoons |

Peel and coarsely grate the carrot and beetroot into a mixing bowl. (Full disclosure, I only peel if absolutely necessary.)

Finely chop the spring onions and add to the carrot and beetroot, together with most of the pomegranate seeds. Finely chop the mint and parsley leaves and add them to the bowl.

Mix the salad dressing ingredients and season with a little salt and pepper. Pour over the vegetables and toss gently together. Scatter with the poppy seeds and the remaining pomegranate seeds and transfer to a serving bowl.

# A salad of lentils and red peppers

A wholesome salad with deep flavours that I use as both an accompaniment and as a principal dish in its own right. The dressing is made using the sweet roasting juices from the peppers and tomatoes. It will keep for a day or two in the fridge without coming to much harm, which is jolly useful.

*Serves 4 as a main, or 6 as a side*

*For the roast vegetables:*

| | |
|---|---|
| red peppers  2 | cherry tomatoes  250g |

*For the lentils:*

| | |
|---|---|
| carrot  1, medium | garlic  2 cloves |
| onion  1, medium | thyme  4 sprigs |
| olive oil  6 tablespoons | Puy lentils  200g |
| celery  1 stick | parsley  a small bunch |
| bay leaves  3 | |

Set the oven at 200°C. Wipe the peppers and place them in a baking dish or roasting tin, tucking the tomatoes around them. Bake for 40–50 minutes, till the peppers have browned here and there, and are soft enough to collapse with a little pressure. Transfer to a shallow dish, leaving the tomatoes in place, cover tightly with cling film and leave for 10 minutes. The skins will loosen in the peppers' steam.

Peel the skin from the peppers, dice the flesh finely and place in a large mixing bowl. Chop the tomatoes and fold into the peppers along with any roasting juices from the pan.

For the lentils, peel the carrot and cut into fine dice, then do the same with the onion. Put them in a medium-sized saucepan with 2 tablespoons of olive oil and place over a low to moderate heat. Finely dice the celery and add to the pan, together with the bay leaves and garlic cloves, peeled and squashed flat. Then add the sprigs of thyme. Leave to cook at a gentle pace, stirring regularly, until the vegetables have softened and are lightly toasted.

Add the lentils to the pan, then pour in enough water (about 500ml) to cover the lentils and vegetables by about 3cm. Bring to the boil, then lower the heat and leave to simmer for 20 minutes or until the lentils are just tender. Add salt at the end of their cooking time.

Remove the thyme sprigs and bay from the lentils, then add the chopped peppers, tomatoes and their juices. Remove the parsley leaves from their stems and roughly chop them, then stir into the lentils along with the remaining olive oil. Season with black pepper and serve at room temperature.

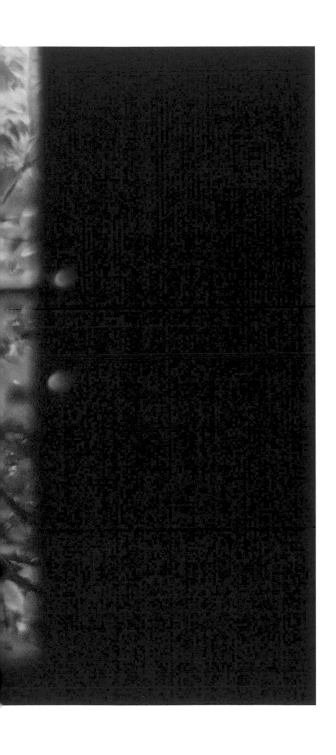

# A chicken in the pot

The early morning walk to cooking school took me through the narrow streets of the fifth arrondissement and the cafés and cobbles of the rue Mouffetard. The air thick and sweet, heavy with the smell of ripe melons. The stallholders brusque, haughty, indifferent. The ladies at the fromagerie intimidating in their white coats and with their earthenware bowls of mysterious snowy curds. The look of faux bafflement on their faces at my innocent request for 'double cream' and the dismissive flick of the wrist over their display of crème fraîche, fromage frais, fromage blanc and their muslin-wrapped strainers of cool, milky faisselle.

The poultry stall, a macabre spectacle of the feathered and the naked, the birds' fragile legs tied together in a cluster of claws, intrigued. Each breast, bonier than the ones at home, bears the legend of its provenance. Some hold a posy of herbs, of thyme and parsley, rosemary and bay. Chickens with sharp, skinny breastbones, yellow from their diet of corn. A huddle of quail on a fig leaf. Partridges, some with red legs, others with black, snuggled on a gingham cloth in a wicker basket. Next to the open cashbox, the stallholder's wooden-handled knife, a pile of brown paper and a ball of string, striped red and white like a barber's pole, was a child's blackboard, the prices drawn in chalk.

Every transaction seemed like a special occasion. Each bird held out on an open palm for inspection by the customer before being wrapped, bagged and lowered into their woven rush shopping bag. An unspoken agreement that each purchase was being handed over on the understanding it would be treated well by the cook. It was then, and only then, I realised that chickens do not all come on a Styrofoam tray and stifled by plastic. Even plucked poultry can be a thing of beauty if you take the trouble to lay it on a fig leaf. And, most crucially, that not all chickens are equal.

I now buy my chicken from my local butcher. Each one is labelled with the name of the farm from which it comes. Not a sham farm made up by a marketing company to hide the products of mass commerce, but a real one, where the birds have enjoyed access to grass and sunshine. I never buy anything that isn't free-range. I would rather go without. When I shop for chicken pieces, they will be plump thighs and breasts from such a bird. The bones will be thick and heavy. Even the most costly chicken is not *that* expensive if you strip the carcass for meat for sandwiches (with chewy bread and sprigs of watercress and basil and lemon mayonnaise) and make stock with the bones, a bunch of thyme and bay and a clove-studded onion.

# A bowl of stock

There are two sorts of chicken stock, and both are worth making. The first is the slowly simmered broth made by cooking a whole raw chicken with a handful of extra wings, an onion, cloves, a carrot, three or four bay leaves, and a bunch of thyme, parsley stalks and a short length of celery. The second, a thinner, less silkily textured affair, made by boiling up the roasted bones from the Sunday roast with aromatics and root vegetables. This latter stock lacks body but is still worth making.

The method is untroublesome, requiring no more than the occasional check as it putters on the hob. The result, a golden broth for pho or risotto, is worth every second of your time. Put a plump chicken in your largest and deepest pot, tuck around it a medium-sized yellow onion, skin on, pierced with three or four cloves; a stick of celery and its tuft of leaves; and a small bunch of thyme twigs and bay leaves. Squeeze in a stubby leek and a dozen black peppercorns. No salt. Cover the bird with plenty of cold water and bring to the boil. Skim off the froth that rises to the surface, then turn the heat down to a very low simmer. The liquid shouldn't bubble, but blip calmly. Leave for a couple of hours, then turn off the heat and leave to cool. (It is far, far too dangerous to attempt to pour the broth out whilst it is still hot.) When finally cool, pour off the liquid, retrieve the chicken and chill it for later, discard the aromatics then set the stock in the fridge. Covered, it will keep for a week. A glass bowl of amber treasure. Money in the bank.

# Roasting a chicken

The bird is out of the oven now, resting on its white earthenware dish, a plump parcel of crisp skin, soft flesh and golden juices. The hiss and crackle that accompanied its progress in the oven has calmed to the faintest whisper. The oven's heat is cranked up a notch to crisp the potatoes that have been roasting alongside. Whatever else I may have learned since roasting my first chicken, it is that roast potatoes are its only truly essential accompaniment. That, and a puddle of the amber liquor from the tin.

I roast a chicken for the succulence of its brown thigh meat; for the long, thin slices of ivory-hued breast with their rim of golden skin; and for the juices that collect in the tin that I have come to think of as the essence of the bird. But this is a dinner made just as much for the tune it sings in the oven, the gentle sizzle as it cooks, the wing tips whose edges stick toffee-like to the corners of the tin, and for the oysters, those two plump cushions of meat that hide under the carcass.

The sound of a chicken roasting is a message that says all is well. A Pied Piper beckoning us to the table. It is the sound and scent of bonhomie and a cook's love for the happiness of others. After all, you rarely roast a chicken for yourself. You roast a chicken for others to enjoy, to share, to carve, to tug and tear at and to pass around the table to your friends and loved ones. That said, I have and regularly do roast a chicken just for myself. It is the best form of self-gifting I know.

There are those who find a Sunday lunch plate piled high with meat and vegetables appealing but I have to say that way of eating is not for me. I find an overcrowded plate off-putting. More pleasurable I think is to eat the chicken and potatoes first, then mop up the delicious juices afterwards with green vegetables or, perhaps most often, a huddle of butter-soft salad leaves. The only way such a plate could be bettered is, for me at least, when there is a spoonful of creamy, nutmeg-scented bread sauce to merge with the deeply chickeny roasting juices.

There were years when my roast chicken came with short, skinny sausages and tight curls of bacon. Others when the plate was regularly flooded with flour-thickened gravy. There were the stock-cube gravy years of the 1970s and the decades during which I made a shallow cake tin of thyme and onion stuffing to eat with it. I have cooked the bird on a spit and have laid rashers of bacon lovingly across its breasts, and briefly, when I lived in the North, served my Sunday lunch with a puffy crown of Yorkshire pudding.

Over the years I have stripped the recipe back to basics and it is better for it. A good bird, the thoughtfully seasoned pan juices and a roast potato or three is more than enough.

## Roasting and resting

Mum's roasting tin was black and buckled from years of service. A thing of beauty, each splatter of burned-on fat was a snapshot of Sunday lunches past. My own roasting tin is heavier and large enough to take a plump, free-range chicken and the accompanying potatoes.

After a half-century of Sunday lunches I believe wholeheartedly that any meat is improved immeasurably by allowing it to rest before carving. Leaving the bird in the switched-off oven for 10 to 15 minutes with the door ajar is all the attention it needs, but if the roasties need a few minutes longer then I usually bring the meat out and let it snooze on a warm dish, hidden under a crinkly tent of foil. Resting, I cannot emphasise enough, is a crucial part of roasting.

## Basting

Basting, especially to a lean meat like chicken, is the key to succulent flesh. Time taken to rub the bird with fat before it goes in the oven and to regularly spoon the melted fat and meat juices over the skin during cooking is worth every minute of your time. A chicken left in the oven unattended will be fine. Roasting is, after all, the ultimate hands-off recipe. But a bird whose skin has the occasional spoonful of its roasting juices spooned over it as it cooks is likely to be a slightly more luscious affair.

You can, of course, roast a chicken with nothing but its own fat. The flesh will be tender and the flavour pure. But it will lack the crisp, burnished finish and juicy flesh of a bird cooked with fat. Butter, olive oil, dripping and pork fat

(Ibérico, from a jar) all do the job, though I regard goose fat (as in *The Kitchen Diaries III*) as the most successful for achieving bronzed skin. Best of all, it is the fat that produces the roast potatoes of my dreams.

Goose fat is expensive and I reserve it for special occasions. A jar will keep for weeks in the fridge. For 'special occasions' read special birds, those whose price makes you swallow hard at the butcher's counter. My fortnightly chicken gets a mixture of butter and olive oil. One fat flavours and burnishes, the other moistens. The olive oil prevents the butter burning.

While the chicken roasts, baste it two or three times. Briefly open the oven door, tip the tin to one side and delve into the pan juices with a large metal spoon. Pour these over the breasts and legs, then close the door. The job should be over in less than a minute; you don't want the oven to lose its heat.

## Seasoning

Salt and pepper are seasoning enough. We can, however, introduce a few aromatics without gilding the lily. Thyme is the herb I use most often here. The plant's woody stems and tough leaves survive the heat of the oven. I stuff wisps of it deep into the chest cavity and squeeze a couple of sprigs into the pinch-point between leg and breast. Some cooks suggest pushing a herb or spice butter under the skin so the flesh is moistened continuously, and it is something well worth doing, but I am clumsy enough to tear the skin occasionally, which then shrinks and the naked flesh dries out as it cooks.

Tarragon has a legendary affinity with chicken, but I was wrong to suggest it as an addition to the roasting bird in *Real Food*. The result isn't worth the price of the herbs. Instead, I would chop its aniseed-scented leaves into the pan juices once the bird is cooked. This gentler warmth will release the herb's fragrance. A squeeze of citrus juice will accentuate the aniseed notes.

A lemon is another possibility. For years I popped half a lemon inside the bird as it roasted and still do so from time to time. Mostly on a summer's day, for the citrus spirit it imbues to the meat juices.

# The roasting juices

Once the bird and its potatoes are out of the tin, we are left with a gift. A deeply savoury, shallow pool of chicken juices and a sticky, almost caramel-like goo of toasted sugars and aromatics. This is a concentrated essence that we can trickle over the meat as it is, or dilute with stock, wine or water to pour over the carved meat on the plate. Over the years I have learned not to sully this treasure with flour to make a thickened 'gravy' like my mum did but only to keep it as it is. Sometimes I stir in a glass of white vermouth or a dry and nutty sherry. Often as not, I don't even bother to do that, instead dipping pieces of bread into the pan and letting them soak up the intensely chickeny liquor. Let me tell you, I've cleaned many a roasting tin that way.

About twenty years ago I started adding a whole head of garlic, sometimes two, to the roasting tin. Once the cloves had softened and browned, I squeezed them from their skins and mashed the soft, caramelised flesh into the pan with the back of spoon. The recipe in *The Kitchen Diaries* is the one I use to this day, with its whiff of thyme and mild, sweet garlic.

Tarragon is the only soft-leaved herb I use in the gravy. About twenty large leaves is enough. This is also the only time I would add cream to the pan. Roasting juices, tarragon and cream being very much the Father, Son and Holy Ghost to a chicken.

A small glass of dry Marsala, stirred in with a wooden spoon as the juices simmer on the hob, always reminds me of Christmas. White vermouth is less sweet, summery even. Once you have let everything bubble, correct the resulting liquid with salt, fine pepper and perhaps the merest squeeze of lemon.

New thinking should probably be discouraged here, but I have recently been pleased with the inclusion of a splash of walnut-hued sherry vinegar to the juices.

# The accompaniments

Slices of breast, a handsomely burnished thigh and a puddle of thyme-freckled jus is more than I need on my plate. Did I just say 'jus'? I'm sorry. It won't happen again. But I will not refuse a roast potato or three, especially if they are sticky from being cooked around the chicken. Over the years I have served stuffing alongside the meat. In my twenties it was sage and onion from a packet, then, once I knew better, a homemade version with sausage meat, sweet onion and fresh thyme. I rarely bother now, preferring stuffing that is cooked outside the confines of the rib cage, in a separate tin, allowing it to form a crust.

If I want a stuffing swollen with the juices from the meat then I involve a few new potatoes no bigger than a bird's egg, briefly steamed, lightly cracked and cooked inside the bird. There are other starches worthy of our attention: pieces of sweet potato swollen with the hot fat from the pan; chickpeas, cooked within the bird then crushed to a rough mash. I have also eaten my Sunday roast with a buttery mash of potato and melted cheese, even pearls of giant couscous stirred into the cooking liquor to soak up the sticky brown goo from the pan. All delicious in their own way. But far from essential. That is the term I reserve for roast potatoes.

## Roast potatoes

Of course, I like them to be crisp but also, somewhat contrarily, when they are chewy and crisp on one side and slightly soggy with roasting juices on the other. I have cooked the chicken and potatoes separately, but the latter lacks the sticky sides and toasted edges of those you have had to scrape, reverently, from the chicken's roasting tin.

Over the last decade or so I have boiled my potatoes for around 10 minutes prior to roasting them. You get a softer, fluffier interior that way. And yes, they really should be cooked around the bird, so they swell with its juices. I cannot emphasise the importance of this enough.

# Bread sauce

A softly textured sauce which, when made with care and robustly seasoned, is a perfect contrast for the crisp-skinned chicken. Made with a parsimonious hand the result is pure pap and probably to be avoided. I stand by the rather luxurious recipe in *Eat* that uses both milk and double cream, lemon thyme and sage. It sounds more trouble than it is.

Hummus, the creamy chickpea purée, makes a gorgeous alternative to both potatoes and bread sauce. Especially when you make a shallow hollow in the mound with the back of a spoon, then trickle the hot roasting juices into it, along with a squeeze of lemon.

# Roast chicken with roast potatoes and roasting juices

*Serves 3-4*

| | |
|---|---|
| a free-range chicken 1.5-2kg | bay leaves 3 |
| olive oil 2 tablespoons | garlic 6 plump cloves |
| butter or goose fat 50g | potatoes 1.5kg |
| thyme 8 small sprigs | |

*For the gravy:*

| | |
|---|---|
| dry Marsala or white vermouth 4 tablespoons | stock 200ml |

*Optional:*

| | |
|---|---|
| lemon half | stuffing |

Set the oven at 200°C. Choose your heaviest roasting tin. A solid vessel is less likely to buckle when you transfer it to the hob to make the 'gravy'. Retrieve the bag of innards from inside the bird. (I can't tell you how many times I have forgotten to do that.) You can add them to the stock if the mood takes you. Place the chicken in the roasting tin and season it inside and out with sea salt and pepper. (I prefer a coarse grind.) Rub the olive oil into the breast and legs, then massage the breasts, legs and wings with the butter or goose fat.

Roast chicken with roast potatoes and roasting juices

Put half the thyme and the bay leaves inside the chicken and tuck the rest round the bird. If you are adding stuffing or lemon, do so now. Add the garlic to the pan. You will barely detect it as such, but the toasted cloves will lend a deeply pleasing, mellow sweetness to the juices. When the oven is hot enough, put the chicken in the oven. A 1.5kg chicken will take about an hour; a 2kg chicken 90 minutes. During cooking, baste the bird two or three times with the contents of the pan.

While the bird is cooking, peel the potatoes and cut them into large pieces (about 45–50g each for me, but only you know what size you like your roast potatoes to be), then bring to the boil in deep, salted water. Once the water is boiling, let them cook for 10 minutes or until they will easily take the point of a knife. Drain them in a colander, then return them to the pan and give them a quick shake from side to side to rough the edges up. They will crisp lacily if their edges are frayed and bruised. Once the chicken has been roasting for 25 minutes, add the potatoes to the roasting tin, turn them over in the fat and continue cooking.

The bird is done when its skin is puffed and golden, the flesh firm and its juices run clear when the thigh is pierced with a skewer at its thickest part. When it is ready, remove it from the oven, cover loosely with foil and keep in a warm place. If you have potatoes to brown, return them to the oven, putting the temperature up to 220°C and keeping a close eye on their progress. Watch that the pan juices don't evaporate or burn. The potatoes will take up to 10 minutes. They should, rather neatly, be ready by the time the chicken has gathered its thoughts.

## A few notes

To make the gravy: once the bird is resting under its foil, and the potatoes are out, place the roasting tin over a moderate heat and bring the juices to a bubble. Squeeze the creamy interior of the garlic into the tin and discard the papery skins, then mash them into the fat and aromatics with a spoon. Stir in 4 tablespoons of dry (secco) Marsala or white vermouth such as Noilly Prat and the stock. Now, this is the crucial bit: as the liquid starts to bubble, scrape at the tin with a wooden spatula or spoon, loosening all the jammy, crusty bits of Marmite-like goo from the tin. These are the concentrated meat juices and caramelised sugars that will enrich your gravy. They are the very essence of the roast bird. Stir as the liquid bubbles, dissolving any deliciousness from the roasting tin as you go. Season generously and, if you wish, pour through a sieve into a warm jug.

# Baking a chicken

## The wings – a feast of tiny bones and big flavours

A spiky tangle of chilli-hot chicken wings. No knives necessary. But you'll need something cold to drink. A pale, icy beer perhaps. Chilli and the chicken wing appear as a regular marriage throughout my books. When you pick up the bones to suck them the presence of chillies, fresh red or dried, makes your lips smart, and then you get a second aftershock, as you lick your fingers. I often use sugar in the recipe. Once it has caramelised in the heat of the oven the sugar makes sure the chilli sticks to your lips.

I notice I came a little late to the chicken wing. Odd, because its diminutive size and the speed with which it can be baked made it a perfect candidate for *Real Fast Food*. An early recipe of mine has me baking a tray of wings with coarse pepper, bay and lemon. You can forget the bay, it does nothing in this instance, but the lemon and lots of roughly crushed black peppercorns make a treat for the chilli-phobe and a good introduction to hot wings. The pepper is bashed with a pestle rather than finely ground in a mill and the wings are then baked with olive oil and lemon juice for 45 minutes at 200°C till the tips are blackened. It's a humble, lip-tingling feast.

Good though their citrus heat was, it seems I yearned for wings with an altogether stickier dressing. At first it came in a straightforward version, with grain mustard, runny honey, lemon and garlic. Aromatic rather than hot, I make this simple version still, though I cook them at 200°C for a good 40–50 minutes, a notch lower than I used to.

Sweet and sticky chicken-wing recipes I could clearly do, but I wanted hotter and more lip-stinging with every batch. By the time I got to *The Kitchen Diaries II* I had learned the fun to be had from marinating the wings first. It is no trouble.

The whole point of cooking wings is to render the meat and cartilage not only tender but intensely chewy. In an ideal world they will stick to the bottom of the baking tin, forming a glossy crust on the base and in places singed to a deep mahogany. The two little strips of meat will slide effortlessly from the bones; the pointed tips, supple as ballerinas' feet, will end up like dark, chewy toffee. You will suck and gnaw and winkle the last nugget of meat out with your tongue.

While I am on the wing, so to speak, I should mention that I do occasionally fry them too. Often as not dusted with salt 'n' peppered flour, shallow-fried in oil till crunchy then eaten with a pot of garlic mayonnaise, wet wipes at the ready.

Wings, I should add, are worth adding to any chicken stock, be it made with raw chicken or cooked. They enrich far more effectively than you would expect for bones of their size. You could do worse than to tuck a handful in with the roast chicken carcass next time you make a post-Sunday-lunch pan of stock.

## The stickiest wings

I have nailed down what I really want from this almost throw-away cut of meat. The glossy, tacky coating of the meat to stick to my fingers, the very tips of the wings to be both crisp and chewy, the result to be aromatic, hot to the lips and, let's be honest here, to allow me to lick my fingers with gusto. The wings are at their most delectable when they are dark brown and deeply caramelised. Serve them with plain steamed rice, which you could eat with your fingers, and follow these with ripe, dark-fleshed plums or, in winter, a ripe papaya, seeded and sliced.

*Serves 2*

garlic  a fat, juicy clove
lemongrass  2 stalks
small, hot red chillies  3
ginger  a 40g piece
vegetable oil  1 tablespoon

light soy sauce  1 tablespoon
lime juice  1 tablespoon
fish sauce  1 tablespoon
honey  3 tablespoons
large, free-range chicken wings  12

Peel the clove of garlic, crush it to a paste with a pinch of sea salt using a pestle and mortar or a knife blade, then scrape into a jam jar. Discard the outer leaves of the lemongrass and roughly chop the tender shoot within. Put the chopped lemongrass into an electric spice mill or coffee grinder and process to a paste. You can do this by hand with a pestle and mortar, though it will be coarser in texture. Add it to the jar.

Finely chop the chillies and their seeds and add to the garlic and lemongrass. Peel the ginger, then grate it finely to a purée and scrape into the jar.

Add the oil, soy sauce, lime juice and fish sauce, then spoon in the honey, tighten the lid and shake to combine to a thin, syrupy marinade. Pour into a mixing bowl, add the chicken wings and turn them over in the marinade until thinly coated, then set aside in a cool place for a good hour, or longer if you have it.

Set the oven at 200°C. Transfer the wings and their marinade to a roasting tin and bake for 25 minutes. Remove the wings from the oven, turn them with kitchen tongs, then continue baking for 10–15 minutes or until they are deep gold in colour, the tips slightly charred, and very sticky. Leave them to settle for 5 minutes before serving. Eat while they are still hot, though I should add they are an unsurpassable feast eaten from the fridge, at midnight. Oh, and you'll need something with which to wipe your fingers.

Plump thighs in a sweet sauce the colour of molasses. Pale and elegant white breast meat with an ivory-cream sauce flecked with painstakingly chopped parsley. Flicking through my archive, there is an untold number of ideas for using 'bits of a bird'.

For all the pleasure of sharing a whole roast bird with others, there is something special about having a thigh or two to oneself. Carving a whole chicken always feels like an occasion, whereas the everyday casualness of a supper of chicken pieces has an ease to it, and, I think, more of an opportunity to be a little creative.

My first published recipe for chicken thighs is one I make to this day, the meat baked on the bone with olive oil, lemon juice, thyme and fat cloves of young, purple-flushed garlic. The skin crisps temptingly, the accompanying liquor a puddle of golden, citrus-spiked roasting juices. The recipe has barely changed in three decades.

Some cuts feel more appropriate to certain treatments than others and much of this is to do with the character of the meat. The darker meat of thighs and drumsticks lends itself perfectly to spicier seasonings. The subtly flavoured white breast meat suggests a softer approach, with the use of herbs and cream rather than piquant seasonings. Robust meats deserve more robust treatment.

Sometimes, on a Monday afternoon, I will bake a batch of chicken thighs with olive oil and a halved lemon. Depending on what is to hand, a whole head of garlic will go in amongst them, or a few sprigs of rosemary or thyme. Baked until their skin is puffed and crisp and their undersides have stuck to the tin, they are then cooled and kept in the fridge to pick at.

Over the next few days, I pull the meat off the bone and toss it with Little Gem lettuce or thick-stemmed watercress, tear it into thick strips for a sandwich with Kewpie mayonnaise and lip-numbing yuzu koshō or a soothing balm of chopped parsley, dill and tarragon leaves. On many occasions, when making a sandwich seems like too much trouble (really, it sometimes gets to that point), I munch those fat, citrussy thighs straight from the tray.

At their simplest, the thighs can be tossed with a dressing of lime juice and honey, seasoned with salt and plenty of black pepper and baked till the skin is blistered and nut brown. It's a little three-ingredient wonder that is good eaten straight from the oven, with flakes of snow-white sea salt and an extra spritz of lime.

A recipe I make on a winter's evening asks for nothing more than stirring together 150ml of oyster sauce, 2 tablespoons of soy sauce and the same of light muscovado sugar, a good pinch of chilli flakes and two crushed cloves of garlic. You roast six chicken thighs at 200°C then, once their skin is starting to colour, you turn them in the glossy, molasses-brown sauce and bake for another 20 minutes.

When we were working on the recipes for *Eat* we got through a lot of thighs. Few cuts of meat fitted the premise of a book about quick midweek suppers quite as neatly. One version of which I became particularly enamoured was mostly for its nannying creaminess, and involved making a paste of olive oil, crushed garlic and dried chilli flakes which you baste over the chicken before baking. In a saucepan we heated a couple of cans of cannellini beans with some crème fraîche, seasoned with salt and pepper, then crushed them to a fluff with a potato masher. A suitable foil for the slightly spicy chicken.

If the wing and possibly the drumstick is the meat of spice and stickiness, then the thigh lends itself to softer seasonings. Late in the day, sometime around 2018, I found out just how much this plump, meaty little cut has an affinity with sherry and almonds. You brown the meat in a little oil in a large pan, tuck in new potatoes, sliced into coins, a handful of salted, roasted almonds, then, when the potatoes are lightly coloured, pour in equal amounts of Fino sherry and water and bake for half an hour. The whole chicken, sherry and almond threesome feels timeless, somehow imbuing the dish with the character of something long cooked that has taken all day. It is something I wish I had known earlier in life.

## Chicken thighs, lemon and basil

Put the chicken thighs – I suggest two large ones per person – in a heavy metal baking dish or roasting tin, pour over a generous slosh of olive oil, season them with salt and black pepper, then roast at 200°C for 40 minutes or so till the skin is golden. Remove the thighs from the dish and rest them under foil on a warm plate (they can go back in the switched-off oven).

Put the baking dish on the hob, add a generous squeeze of lemon and bring to the boil, scraping at any sticky roasted juices and goo that may be in the dish. Tear up a handful of basil leaves and add them to the juices. Return the thighs to the dish and serve immediately. A dish of green beans would be a neat accompaniment, as would a bowl of soft, green leaves.

## Baked chicken with sherry, potatoes and almonds

The recipe has moved on a little from the original, but it remains a comfort on a cold winter's night. A slice of blue cheese, a Picos de Europa perhaps, and a few dark and seedy raisins is all the 'afters' you need.

*Serves 4*

chicken thighs  6 large,
    free-range
olive oil
new potatoes  400g
salted, roasted almonds  75g

Fino sherry  200ml
bay leaves  3
green olives  12
parsley  a small bunch

Baked chicken with sherry, potatoes and almonds

Set the oven at 200°C.

Brown the chicken lightly and evenly in a little olive oil in a deepish pan over a moderate heat. Wash the potatoes and slice them into thick coins. Add the potatoes to the pan and let them colour a little, then scatter in the almonds. Continue cooking for a minute or two, till the almonds are starting to smell warm and nutty, then pour in the sherry and tuck in the bay leaves. When the steam subsides, pour in 200ml of water and bring to the boil.

Season with black pepper, cover with a lid and transfer to the oven. After 35 minutes, check the potatoes for tenderness. Add the olives. Remove the leaves from the parsley and chop roughly, then stir into the chicken juices and serve.

The eighty days of pandemic lockdown in the spring of 2020 brought with it an urgent need for dishes that served to soothe rather than excite. Most welcomed by me were those accompanied by a mildly seasoned broth that felt somehow healing. Whilst holed up in self-isolation I cooked chicken with green spring vegetables such as lettuce and young, thin leeks that took on a silky texture in the oven, with the juicy stems of the lettuce retaining a little of their crispness. Cos and Little Gem were the most suitable, the exceptionally fragile leaves of the round Butterhead variety somewhat less so. This seemed to fulfil the brief: healing flavours for troubled times. Later, I swapped the lettuce for tiny orzo pasta, which also added a silken quality to the broth. To follow, rhubarb, baked with brown sugar and served with a blue and white jug of yellow cream.

## Braised chicken with leeks, orzo, peas and parsley

*Serves 3*

olive or vegetable oil
   3 tablespoons
chicken thighs  6, large
leeks  250g
chicken or vegetable stock
   1 litre

half a lemon
peppercorns  6
orzo  200g
peas  150g (shelled or
   frozen weight)
parsley and tarragon  a small handful

Braised chicken with leeks, orzo, peas and parsley

Warm the oil in a deep, lidded pan, add the chicken pieces, skin side down and lightly seasoned, then cook until the skin is a rich, deep gold. Turn them and colour the underside similarly, then remove from the pan and set aside.

Set the oven at 200°C. Trim the leeks, discarding the roots and very tips of the leaves. Cut into short pieces about the length of a wine cork, then wash them thoroughly, removing every grain of grit trapped between their layers.

Pat the leeks dry, then fry them in the chicken pan over a moderate heat for about 5 minutes, covered with a lid, so they soften without browning. Pour in the stock and bring to the boil, stirring as you go, then add the half lemon, peppercorns and a teaspoon of salt. As the stock boils rain in the orzo and continue boiling for 3 minutes. Return the chicken to the pan, cover again and bake for 35 minutes.

Remove the lid, add the peas, then return to the oven for 5 minutes. Check the seasoning, then add the tarragon and parsley and serve in bowls, with spoons.

# And the drumstick

I have little love for the chicken drumstick. Despite having a useful handle to hold, the meat to bone ratio seems mean in comparison with the beefy thigh. Or perhaps it is just that they remind me of 1970s wedding buffets and (shudders) garden barbecues? The few recipes I have for them I use more often with thighs or breasts.

And yet, there is a certain simple pleasure in roasting a tray of drumsticks with butter, oil, salt and pepper, then giving them a quick toss with sesame seeds and a splash of mirin 5 minutes before they come out of the oven. On a winter's evening, I sometimes stir a little sherry vinegar into the juice of a freshly squeezed orange, then stir in a little melted butter and pour it over the drummers. The dish then goes in the oven with the empty orange shells tucked among them. The fug of sweet citrus and sherry warms the kitchen. It is worth mentioning that the drumstick also has a place in my kitchen baked with marmalade or tossed, Vietnamese-style, with fish sauce and mint.

Marmalade chicken

# Marmalade chicken

You put six large drumsticks in a foil-lined baking tray. In a small bowl combine 6 heaped tablespoons of orange marmalade and 3 of grain mustard. A little black pepper, no salt. Spread the marmalade over the drumsticks. Bake for 30–40 minutes at 200°C, keeping an eye on them so they don't burn. Enough for two or three.

# Chicken and cucumber salad with lime and fish sauce

Put six large drumsticks in a small roasting tin, pour over enough groundnut oil to moisten them, dot with small pieces of butter, then season with salt and pepper. Roast for about half an hour at 200°C till golden and the skin is crisp. Remove the flesh from the bones, leaving it in large, juicy pieces.

Squeeze the juice from two limes into the roasting tin and place over a moderate heat. Stir in a tablespoon of fish sauce and warm gently, scraping at any sticky bits on the dish with a wooden spoon. Return the chicken pieces to the pan.

Mix together a couple of handfuls of crisp lettuce, a handful of mint leaves, a chilled cucumber cut into pencil-thick slices and a bunch of glossy, beautifully fresh watercress. Add the chicken and toss with the juices from the baking dish.

# Chicken on the hob

Once upon a time I cooked in a castle. A proper castle, built in the eleventh century, with ramparts, cool cellars, narrow windows from which to fire arrows and a romantic, octagonal tower. It had winding stone staircases, a vineyard and a ghost, which is all you can really ask of such a building. I worked in the kitchen with three other young cooks in the long hot summer of 1976.

While the others set about making coq au vin in blackened Le Creuset casseroles and shallow earthenware dishes of gratin dauphinoise, my first job of the day was to remove the breasts from fat, heavy-boned chickens. I was under strict instructions to cut as close as possible to the bone, taking care to waste as little of the pale, lean meat as I could, and to ensure the breasts were plump and full. I baked them each evening in butter, with fronds of fennel picked from the castle's walled herb garden, then flamed them briefly in Pernod and doused the flames with cream. Forty years later I continue to scent chicken breasts with aniseed in the shape of fennel or dill. The subtlest of flavours when used with discretion that works in sympathy with such delicate flesh.

My butcher sells large chicken breasts with a neat single bone attached. They come with a hefty price tag and once in my kitchen are treated like the precious ingredients they are, baked with mild flavours that flatter such an elegant cut. If garlic is used at all, it is the fresh ivory bulbs of early summer whose white, waxy skin is flashed with mauve. An evergreen treat on my table is when the breasts are baked with olive oil and lemon, then sliced and tossed in a dressing vivid green with fresh parsley, crushed anchovy and basil.

In a high-sided, shallow pan such as a sauteuse, I melt a thick slice of butter, slice two chicken breasts into pieces as thick as my finger, then sauté them till their flat sides are golden. In goes a handful of tarragon leaves torn from the stem, and then a minute later, a carton of double cream. As the mixture of chickeny butter, herbs and cream bubbles in the pan, I introduce an essential fizz of energy with a couple of teaspoons of tarragon or white wine vinegar. There will be lettuce or a stack of neatly trimmed French beans to hand with which to wipe the sauce from our plates.


And whilst we are treating ourselves with such delicate flavours, something I have done for ever and a day is a herb and wine sauce made from the chicken's own juices. The dish couldn't be simpler. I lightly brown a couple of breasts, skin intact, in a generous slice of butter and a dash of olive oil to stop the butter burning, then let them cook over a low heat till their skin is a shade of palest nut-brown. Add in a glass of white wine or vermouth and the magic starts. As the liquid bubbles in the pan, I scrape away at the golden sediment left behind by the meat, stirring it into the liquid to form a pale and limpid juice. In goes a bulging fistful of chopped parsley, or dill or tarragon or chervil, and then the juice of half a small lemon. As you stir, the juices and herbs come together and need nothing more than a final thick slice of butter, which you beat into the pan juices with a whisk. You lift the chicken out onto warm plates and spoon the impromptu, green-flecked butter sauce over the top.

## Chicken breasts

For all my fennel-scented nostalgia, I find the meat from the breast the least interesting part of the chicken. Too lean. Too monotone in texture.

Chicken breasts lack natural fat, so we need to prepare them in a way that keeps their flesh soft. We can get over this lack of succulence by basting a chicken breast with butter and herbs as it cooks, spooning the fizzing golden fat and herbs over the skin as it slowly turns to gold. Putting a lid on the pan will help too, the meat being kept sweet and juicy by its own steam. Cooking a chicken breast is a job to take your time over, especially if it is thick, so the skin takes on a certain crispness and the flesh cooks right through to the middle.

## The goodness in the sauté pan

The point of cooking a chicken breast or thigh in a pan on the hob is not only the way the skin gilds and crisps, it is the possibilities introduced by the delicious sticky goo that collects on the pan as it cooks. This golden-brown ointment, much the same as that we know from the roasting tin, is more than caramelised sugars and cooking juices. It is concentrated chicken flavour. Its culinary soul. It enriches and adds a whole savoury depth to the pan juices or a sauce made from them. I could weep when I see someone stick the pan in the washing-up without taking advantage of the deliciousness they have in their hands.

This concentrated flavour will enrich any liquid added to it and is what I use as the backbone of a simple sauce, stirring in stock, wine or cream to make an impromptu but deeply delicious accompaniment. Which liquid I add will depend on what I am to eat the chicken breast or thigh with. My first choice, from those early days in the castle kitchen, has always been cream, as it has an affinity not only with the delicate nature of the breast meat but also with the tarragon, parsley, dill or fennel I finish it with.

Chicken breasts with mustard and Marsala

And yes, of course you can use white wine or white vermouth such as timeless Noilly Prat, but it would be remiss of me not to mention Marsala, my favourite alcohol in the kitchen and whose warm, nutty notes marry blissfully with dairy.

## Chicken breasts with mustard and Marsala

*Serves 2*

| | |
|---|---|
| chicken breasts  2, large | grain mustard  1 tablespoon |
| olive oil  2 tablespoons | cornichons  6 |
| butter  40g | capers  a teaspoon |
| dry Marsala  125ml | parsley  a small bunch |
| crème fraîche  200ml | white wine vinegar (or juice from |
| Dijon mustard  1 tablespoon | the cornichon jar)  a little |

Season the chicken with a little salt. Warm the oil in a shallow pan over a moderate heat, add the butter, and let it melt. As it starts to bubble lightly, place the chicken breasts in the pan, skin side down, and leave to cook until the skin is pale gold. Keep an eye on the heat, taking care to lower the heat as necessary to ensure the butter doesn't burn. When the underside is golden, turn the chicken over and continue cooking, partially covered with a lid, for 10 minutes.

Once the chicken is firm to the touch and golden on both sides, test it for doneness by piercing at its thickest part with a metal skewer. If the chicken's juices run clear, it is ready. Remove the chicken and set aside, covered lightly, to rest.

Pour most of the fat in the pan away, leaving just a shallow pool behind, then pour in the Marsala. Stir with a wooden spoon, turning up the heat so the liquid comes to the boil. When the Marsala has reduced to about half its volume – a matter of 2 minutes or less – stir in the crème fraîche and mustards. Lower the heat so the sauce simmers gently, then add the cornichons, cut in half down their length, the capers and a little salt and black pepper.

Remove a small handful of parsley leaves from their stalks, finely chop and stir them into the sauce. Finish with a drop of two of the vinegar, then return the chicken to the pan, spoon over the sauce and serve.

# Chicken thighs with coconut and coriander

A brilliant treatment for chicken thighs, brick red and deeply aromatic. It offers both the nip of heat so beloved of fans of this cut and the sweet, nutty quality of coconut cream. Once the meat has been removed from the bones, and you resort to fingers, this becomes a gloriously messy little dish. This is a new version of the recipe in *The Kitchen Diaries II*, without the new potatoes and with a slightly racier level of spicing, for which you'll need a bowl of steamed white rice. To follow, ripe Alphonso mangoes.

*Serves 3*

groundnut oil  2 tablespoons
chicken thighs  6, large
fresh ginger  a 60g piece
garlic  2 large cloves
small, hot red chillies  2
ground chilli  half a teaspoon

ground turmeric  half a teaspoon
ground coriander  1 teaspoon
tomatoes  450g
creamed coconut  a 90g piece
coriander or mint leaves  a handful

steamed rice to serve

Warm the oil in a large shallow pan, season the chicken thighs, then fry till golden on both sides, turning them over once so they colour evenly. Once they are ready, remove from the pan and set aside in a shallow dish.

Peel the ginger and garlic and reduce them to a pulp in a spice mill or food processor. Roughly chop the chillies, then add them to the paste and process briefly. Add to the pan in which you browned the chicken together with the ground chilli, turmeric and coriander. Keeping the heat fairly low, stir the spices and oil together. You will have a loose, aromatic, golden-orange paste. Dice the tomatoes and stir them in, then add the creamed coconut, 200ml of water and a generous pinch of salt.

When the coconut has dissolved, return the chicken to the pan, together with any juices from the dish. Set the heat at a gentle simmer, partially cover with a lid and leave for 30 minutes, with the occasional stir, till the sauce is thick enough to coat the chicken. Stir in the coriander or mint leaves, check the

Chicken thighs with coconut and coriander

chicken is thoroughly cooked, add a few twists of black pepper and bring to the table in its cooking pot, together with a bowl of steamed rice.

A simple chicken salad, eaten at a table in the garden on a summer's day, is the most quietly pleasing of events. A meal of ease and calm cooking, carrying the undemanding flavours of white meat and crisp, ice-cold salad leaves. Ideally there will be cucumber, white-tipped radishes, thin spring carrots and a bowl of mayonnaise. Maybe a tomato or two.

As much as the idea of a cold roast chicken will always bring me to the table, I have learned to appreciate the composite salad too, the meat torn from its bones before it leaves the kitchen, tossed with herbs and sprigs of salad leaves, dressed and served in a vast bowl for everyone to dig deep. To bring out such a feast divests someone of the task of carving the chicken or even passing the mayonnaise.

There are two such salads that shine out. Roast chicken and melon, and one I make with sautéed chicken, using the pan juices as part of the dressing. It is a peaceful, untroubling recipe but not one without spirit.

## Sautéed chicken salad with cider and watercress

The juices from cooking the chicken are used here not to make a sauce but a dressing. The result is a chicken salad without cream or mayonnaise. Just clear, cider-bright flavours, with chicken still warm from being cooked on its bones, hidden amid ice-cold watercress and lettuce leaves. A tart, perhaps of summer cherries or, later in the year, plums, would be a fine end to such a dinner.

*Serves 2–3*

chicken thighs  4, large
butter  40g
olive oil
garlic  half a head
apple juice  500ml
cider vinegar  1 tablespoon

mildly flavoured honey
    1 tablespoon
wholegrain mustard  1 tablespoon
watercress  100g
a Little Gem or small Cos lettuce
cucumber  half

Season the chicken pieces with a little salt. Warm the butter and oil in a sauté pan, add the chicken and brown lightly on both sides. Break the garlic into individual cloves, peel them and add them to the pan, letting them colour lightly.

Pour the apple juice into the pan and let the chicken continue to cook for 15 minutes or until the juices run clear. (Pierce the meat at its thickest point with a metal skewer; if the juices that leak out are clear, then it's ready.) Remove the chicken from the pan and pull the meat from the bones.

Bring the pan juices to the boil and continue to bubble down to half their volume, stirring the cider vinegar, honey and mustard in as you go. Squash the garlic cloves into the dressing with a fork, then season carefully with salt and a little pepper.

Wash the watercress and place it in a bowl of iced water to crisp up. Break the Little Gem or Cos into individual leaves and add to the iced water. Slice the cucumber in half lengthways, remove the seeds with a teaspoon if you wish, then slice the flesh into pencil-thick chunks.

Toss together the chicken, drained watercress and lettuce, cucumber and the dressing, sprinkle with a pinch of sea salt flakes and serve.

# Grilling chicken

You are allowed to keep a sharp knife and single piece of kitchen kit. What would it be? A question I can answer in a single heartbeat. 'My ridged, cast-iron griddle pan, if I may.' Not the large rectangular one on which I have cooked a butterflied leg of lamb or made rounds of asparagus bruschetta for six, but my tiny griddle the size of a dinner plate, with just enough room for a couple of chicken legs. A neat piece of kit, blackened by years of service to lamb chops and aubergines, this single piece of iron will allow me to make my favourite dish on earth.

A chicken leg, bones removed and skin intact, is brushed with oil and placed skin side down on the griddle. It is held firm on the bars by a heavy weight, usually an iron pan-lid, and left over a moderate flame till its skin has become translucent and its surface becomes blistered, scorched in deep black lines on the furrows of the pan. The juices run clear and bright. Amber flecked with black pepper.

The flesh is constantly basted by the skin and fat as it cooks. A halved lemon is all the accompaniment it needs. The sweet meat juices, the bitter sting of charred skin, lemon juice and sea salt is for me the finest dinner there is.

My introduction to grilled chicken came, aged twenty-one, at a restaurant, where the slab of black-etched meat came with a tarragon-cream sauce. There was a splash of herb vinegar amongst the cream and a further piquancy and heat from bottled green peppercorns. Because of that single dish I bought a griddle and it has been at my side ever since.

There is something ancient about this method of cooking. The kitchen, your apron, your hair, smell like they have been caught in a bonfire. Yet my seasonings are thoroughly contemporary. The miso paste that reminds me of the chicken served at a favourite counter in Kyoto; the tahini I stir through plain cool yoghurt that for me was the flavour of Lebanon. These are the accompaniments that take their turn to nudge up against my favourite dish. The dish I hope will be the last thing I eat before I leave this earth. (Frankly I doubt it. My last dinner is more likely to be something through a straw.)

## Boning the thighs

Boning a chicken leg is easy but even more so if you ask your butcher to do it. They will pull out the pesky tendons, the thin white threads that will make the meat curl annoyingly as it cooks. And yes of course you could do this with a flattened chicken breast, but the meat will be less succulent. From *Eat*: 'place the chicken leg, plump side down on a chopping board. Make two deep cuts with a small, sharp knife, following the two bones (you can feel exactly where they run with your fingers). Wheedle the knife in and out, slicing the flesh away from the bones until you have two clean chicken bones and a roughly rectangular piece of chicken. It may take a few goes before you can accomplish it perfectly, but a few holes is really neither here nor there.'

You can use them as they are, but they will be better if you tug out any white ribbon-like tendons. The chicken will cook more evenly if you bat it out a little with a rolling pin, or, should you have such a thing, a cutlet bat.

# Grilled chicken with za'atar and tahini

Some wonderful flavours going on here with the smoky chicken and its slightly charred skin, and the deep nutty notes of the tahini and the underlying hit of sourness from the lemons and yoghurt. I would serve warm flatbread with this. The dough soft and puffy, its dimples and folds caught black from the griddle. A salad too, of halved ice-cold radishes, ribbons of Cos lettuce and a dressing of finely chopped shallots, white wine vinegar and olive oil. To follow, a tiny square of honey-soaked baklava or perhaps a scoop of mint sorbet.

*Serves 4*

chicken thighs  4, large

*For the marinade:*

olive oil  50ml                          garlic  2 large cloves
juice of a medium lemon        za'atar  1 tablespoon

*For the yoghurt:*

thick yoghurt  200ml               tahini  4 tablespoons

*For grilling:*

lemons  2

Remove the two bones from the chicken thighs and flatten the meat out. Place on a piece of cling film or even in a plastic freezer bag, then bat the meat out a little with a rolling pin. There is no need go the full escalope, just bash it a little to flatten out the thicker parts of the thigh. It is not essential so don't worry if you don't have anything suitable, it just helps to cook the meat more evenly.

Mix together the olive oil and the lemon juice. Crush the garlic cloves then stir into the liquid with the za'atar. Place the chicken thighs in the marinade and leave for at least 40 minutes. They will come to no harm if left overnight.

When you are ready to eat, get a cast-iron griddle hot, then place the chicken pieces, shaken of excess marinade, onto the bars of the griddle and let them cook till the skin is golden. Turn and cook the other side. They are ready when the juices run clear when pierced at their thickest place with a metal skewer.

Grilled chicken with za'atar and tahini

While the chicken is cooking, put the yoghurt in a bowl and stir in the tahini. I prefer to do this lightly, leaving ribbons of the sesame paste marbling the snow-white yoghurt.

Slice the lemons in half and place them cut side down on the griddle for a few minutes till they are warm. You will get more juice from them that way. Let the chicken rest for 5 minutes, then eat with the tahini dressing and the griddled lemons.

# Chicken with miso and honey

You don't really need anything with this other than a bowl of soft, pale lettuce leaves, chilled, super-crisp cucumber cut into matchsticks and some spanking-fresh watercress. If you feel you need it, some steamed rice, seasoned with bay and black peppercorns, is rather good when it meets the sweet chicken. To follow: blood oranges, sliced and thoroughly chilled, laid in a single layer on a small and very beautiful plate.

*Serves 2*

mirin 135ml
white miso paste 4 tablespoons
honey 4 tablespoons

vegetable oil a splash
chicken thighs 4, boned

In a small saucepan, mix the mirin, miso paste, honey and vegetable oil and bring to the boil. Once the miso has dissolved (it will need a good stir), remove immediately from the heat. Place the chicken thighs on a plate, pour the marinade over them and set aside for half an hour.

There are two ways to cook this. On a heated griddle pan or under an oven grill. The first produces much smoke and leaves you with a tricky pan to clean. The second is less troublesome but lacks the smoky notes and caramelised skin you get with the first.

Method one: heat a ridged griddle pan, then place the chicken, skin side down and lightly drained of the marinade, on the pan. There will be much smoke, so keep the heat no higher than moderate and switch the fire alarm off. When the skin is golden and has dark lines scorched into it, turn it over and cook the other side. The whole cooking time will be about 15 minutes, but test it for doneness by piercing with a skewer at its thickest part. The juices should run clear. As the chicken cooks, brush it from time to time with the marinade.

Method two: get an oven grill hot. Place a piece of foil on a baking sheet. Put the boned thighs on the foil, well coated with their marinade, and cook under the hot grill, a good 20cm from the heat, for 8–10 minutes or so till deep gold, then turn and cook the other side.

# Everyday dinners

I can barely remember a day when I didn't make something to eat. It is just something I do, almost unthinkingly. On the days I go out for my evening meal – not as often as you might think – I will probably still make lunch.

Many of my everyday dinners – quick meals that can be on the table in an hour or so – have been collected in *Real Fast Food* and *Eat* and a few of those are repeated here. But there are many that have never made it into a book, even though they regularly turn up on the table. I include those, or at least those that contain meat or fish, in this chapter. (There is another for everyday recipes that are vegetarian or vegan.)

It may sound like heresy, but I genuinely don't want to spend my entire day in the kitchen. There are far too many other things to do. That said, I do want to eat something good, simple – made with a few ingredients that are comfortable in each other's presence – every day of my life. For the most part this will be simple stuff made without the need for expertise or specialist shopping. This isn't fancy hobby cooking. This is just something I knock up for supper that I think others might like to eat too.

As I get older, I eat a little less. I am not sure it has anything to do with age, just a slow realisation that I have probably always eaten a little more than I needed to. Perhaps we all do, I don't know, but it is worth a moment's thought. My main meal of the day is usually a single course. Occasionally there will be pudding. There are always salad leaves. A mixture of sweet and bitter greens eaten either with dinner or, more often, early in the evening. Frequently, they will be accompanied by a piece of cheese or cured or smoked fish (a curl of dill-edged gravlax or a gilt-skinned smoked mackerel; a roll of pickled herring or smoked cod's roe spread on thick slices of hot toast). This second meal is always light and will often finish with a piece of fruit – a mango in summer, a fig or a good peach.

Despite a turn towards plant-rich eating, there continues to be meat or fish on my table a couple of times a week. I suspect there always will be; a pork chop the size of my hand, its fat crisp and blistered; sausages – plump and herb-freckled – with a mound of soft chickpea mash at their side; or perhaps pieces of chicken cooked quickly with florets of broccoli and citrus juice. Walk into my kitchen early on a summer's evening and there might be a row of skinny lamb cutlets on the grill, chubby scallops or whiskery prawns, or very occasionally a rib-eye steak. In winter there may be a wheel of Cumberland sausage in the oven or a frying pan of lamb meatballs flecked with beetroot and dill. There may be a tangle of fettucine tossed with crab meat, coriander and cream, or a chilli and citrus-scented fishcake.

A quick daily dinner will press my buttons all the more if there are bones to chew or shells to suck. I don't ever see me giving up such primitive, visceral pleasures. Their presence may have become less frequent, but with that all the more essential and longed-for. I might even say... lusted after.


There are a couple of everyday dinners I cook over and over (and over) again. The first involves the tiniest clams I can find, the best being those the size of a broad bean. I warm a slice of butter in a shallow pan, add a splash – no more – of olive oil and clatter the little clams in. A couple of minutes (barely) over the heat till they open, then a splash of dry sherry, a twist of black pepper and then into a simple stoneware bowl. I eat them with my fingers. The juices are sponged up with bread.

The second, for when I'm feeling carnivorous, is a plate of skinny lamb cutlets – I like them cut very thin, like those you buy in Middle Eastern food halls – then I brush them with olive oil and grill them till the tips of the spindly bones are black and the fat is the colour of honey. No potatoes, no vegetables, just a deep bowl of hummus pimped with lemon juice, olive oil as green as an emerald and a sprinkle of za'atar. No knives or forks, just fingers, hot flesh, fat and thick bean purée.

# The clams

*Serves 2*

tiny clams, the smallest you
  can find  500g
butter  30g

olive oil  a splash
dry or Oloroso sherry  a splash
bread to serve

Sort through the clams, discarding any whose shells are open. Melt the butter in a wide, deep pan over a high heat and add the olive oil. Add the clams, cover and cook for 2 minutes until the shells open, then lift the lid and add the sherry. Once it has spluttered and sherry-scented steam rises up, tip the clams into dishes, then strain the liquor through a fine sieve over them.

# The cutlets

*Per person:*

lamb cutlets, very thin  4–6
hummus  200g
olive oil

za'atar
lemon  1

Get the griddle hot. Season your lamb cutlets and place them on the griddle. Put a heavy weight on top of the chops to hold them firmly on the bars of the griddle and let them brown crustily on the underside. Turn them over and continue cooking till they are brown on the underside. I like mine pink within, but you can only really gauge whether they are as you like them by slicing into one with a very sharp knife. In theory, you should let them rest a bit before serving, but I can't resist plunging them into the hummus whilst still far too hot to eat.

A trick to perk up commercial hummus. Tip the chickpea dip into a small bowl. Pour in a couple of tablespoons of fruity, peppery olive oil to every 250g, then a generous pinch – about half a teaspoon – of ground za'atar and a fat squeeze of lemon juice. Stir brusquely and finish with yet another trickle of olive oil.

# Three sausage suppers

Sausages with Cheddar roast-potato mash. Just let that sink in for a minute. Of all the world's sausages – the African merguez and Spanish chorizo; the Italian fennel-seed-studded finocchiona and the garlicky French Toulouse; the skinny, air-dried Chinese and the handsome Bury black pudding – I still regard a coil of Cumberland as one of the finest to grace a butcher's slab. A portly, freckled sausage, curled into a ring and held together with thin wooden skewers, it can be grilled, baked or fried in the piece. You should do this slowly, so it cooks evenly through, and baste it while you're at it, then bring it to the table proudly, like a crown.

You can buy Cumberland sausage as individual links too. It will still have the characteristic notes of black pepper and nutmeg but is easier to handle. That said, I will always buy a whole reel of Cumberland sausage if ever I see one. Leftover cooked sausage is a wonderful treat to find on a midnight fridge raid.

## Cumberland sausage and Cheddar roast-potato mash

*Serves 2–3*

floury potatoes 900g
banana shallots or small onions
  2, large
olive or groundnut oil 50ml
Cumberland sausage 500g,
  held together by skewers

Cheddar, such as Montgomery's
  or Keen's 75g
parsley a small handful, chopped

Set the oven at 200°C.

Peel the potatoes and cut them into large pieces. Bring to the boil in deep, salted water then lower the heat a little and let them cook for 15–20 minutes or so till tender enough to mash. Drain them and crush roughly with a fork. There is no need to work them to a purée – stop while they still have a rough, open texture.

Cumberland sausage and Cheddar roast-potato mash

Peel the shallots and halve them lengthways. Pour the oil into a roasting tin, place the shallots cut side down in the oil and roast for about 25 minutes till they are golden on the underside, then turn them over. Add the mashed potatoes to the pan and return to the oven. Put the Cumberland sausage, lightly oiled, in a small roasting tin, then bake for about 40 minutes till golden brown.

Grate the Cheddar. Remove the potatoes from the oven, scatter the cheese over the top and return to the oven for a few minutes till melted. Cut the sausage into large pieces and serve with the potatoes, shallots and cheese.

Sauerkraut held a place in my life long before the current rage for ferments. The sourness bringing vitality to anything it touches. A glass jar of plain fermented cabbage is an infinitely useful addition to the fridge, and it goes with anything from cold ham to a toasted cheese sandwich. It is also a useful accompaniment when you are short of green vegetables. When the thought, in darkest February, of yet another plate of Savoy cabbage palls, I toss in a handful of sauerkraut to bring the earthy brassica to life.

It goes without saying that a tangle of pale fermented cabbage is very much at home with a sausage, but I want to put in a plea for kielbasa, the skinny, lightly seasoned pork sausage from Poland, with which it works particularly well. Feeling lazy, I will sometimes cut the sausages into thick coins, toss them with equal-sized rounds of lightly cooked new potatoes then fry them in a large, shallow pan with a little oil. As soon as the potatoes are starting to brown, I fold in skeins of sauerkraut and a handful of coarsely chopped parsley. A fine supper for the exhausted or just plain lazy.

## Kielbasa or kabanos, sauerkraut and mushroom

Although kabanos are not generally cooked, I use them if I can't find the more coarsely textured and garlicky kielbasa. Polish sausage suits the sauerkraut well but you could use pretty much any rough-textured banger you have to hand. A one-pan supper that has graced my table on many an occasion. Thank you, Poland.

Kielbasa or kabanos, sauerkraut and mushroom

*Serves 2*

| | |
|---|---|
| floury potatoes such as Maris Piper 350g, medium-sized | olive or groundnut oil 2–3 tablespoons |
| onion 1, medium to large | sauerkraut 200g, rinsed |
| chestnut mushrooms 200g | dill 2 tablespoons, chopped |
| kielbasa or similar sausages 200g | soured cream 4 heaped tablespoons |

Peel the potatoes, cut them into quarters, then boil them in deep, salted water till tender to the point of a knife. Drain them, then slice thickly.

Peel and finely chop the onion. Slice the mushrooms and cut the sausages into thick pieces.

Warm a tablespoon of oil in a large, shallow pan – I use one measuring 28cm in diameter – then add the onion and let it soften over a moderate heat for 5 minutes. Add the sliced mushrooms, sausages and potatoes and, if necessary, a little more oil. Continue cooking till both mushrooms and potatoes are starting to turn golden brown.

Add the sauerkraut to the pan, tucking it among the mushrooms and onions. Season with salt, pepper and the chopped dill, then add the soured cream in spoonfuls – do not be tempted to stir the cream in – and serve.

# A word about chorizo

I love the gutsy, paprika-red Spanish chorizo. Both as a slicing sausage (with a diminutive, ice-cold beer, please) and as a whole cooking sausage. The latter is equally at home simmered slowly in the company of sweet onions, plump white beans and stock as it is charred over hot coals. Split and grilled it becomes a fine variation of the sausage sandwich, especially when the rust-coloured fat trickles its way through the air pockets of a hunk of ciabatta. (It is a happy supper indeed when a plate of grilled chorizo lands on the table with another of sautéed potatoes and fried onions.)

That said, chorizo can dominate, and particularly its orange fat. Frankly, I could eat the stuff with a spoon, but it is not for everyone. You can calm an especially spicy chorizo (they come in two heats, dulce and the more spicy picante) by mixing its flesh with beans or chickpeas, either in a stew or, as I found recently, with a tin of mashed chickpeas. The mixture is a happy one, particularly when rolled into balls and fried.

This fat-speckled, rust-red length of minced pork and paprika pops up in so many recipes now, but I have never found a better way to eat it than grilled till its edges brown, then stuffed into a soft roll filled with crisp, cold watercress.

High on my list of favourite smells (snow, old books, wet moss, bunches of sweet peas and a steaming basket of dim sum) is that of the inside of an Italian grocer's shop. A cool and gentle smell of fresh pasta and San Daniele ham; of mozzarella in open bowls, Parmesan and basil in bunches beautiful enough to be carried by a bride. They smell the same all over the world too, a gift to those of us who don't live in Milan.

The sausages, flecked with fennel seed and black peppercorns, the chubby sort, loosely linked to one another with fine string, are one of the reasons I have always lived within walking distance of an Italian deli. Those sausages, with their coarse meat and pearls of white fat, are a summer feast in this house. Grilled or cooked in a shallow pan till their skins are toasted, their insides on the cusp of bursting, they turn up at dinner on the garden table, often with ciabatta and jars of purple pickled cabbage. Sometimes I offer them round, with branches of rosemary from the garden, with a pile of haricot bean mash, or perhaps chickpeas, the fat from the sausages trickled over its surface.

## Grilled sausages, herbed chickpea mash

A coarsely textured sausage is appropriate here – something with large nuggets of meat and plenty of herbs. You can speed the recipe up by using frozen, bottled or tinned chickpeas, or by using a pressure cooker. If using the tinned or bottled variety, warm them in a little stock before mashing them, as in the recipe.

Grilled sausages, herbed chickpea mash

*Serves 2–3*

chickpeas  2 × 400g tins
bay leaves  4
onion  1, medium
fennel-seed sausages  6–8
olive oil  60ml

rosemary sprigs  6
parsley  25g
thyme  4 or 5 bushy sprigs
cooking water from the
　　chickpeas  120ml

Drain the chickpeas and put them in a deep saucepan, cover with water and bring to the boil. Add the bay leaves and the onion, peeled and halved. Lower the heat, partially cover with a lid, then leave to simmer for 5–10 minutes.

Cook the sausages, either under the grill or in a frying pan with a little of the oil and the rosemary. Remove the parsley and thyme leaves from their stems and roughly chop them. Drain the chickpeas, removing the bay and onion and reserving 120ml of the cooking water. Warm the rest of the olive oil in a small pan. Mash the chickpeas using a food processor or blender (taking care not to over-process). Pour in the warm oil and water, then season generously with salt, pepper, the parsley and thyme.

When the sausages are golden brown, slice them thickly. Pile the mash on a serving dish with the sausages, adding a little olive oil as you serve.

# Three ways with mince

Mince is a rare visitor to this house. I have no idea why, other than the notion that I may have, at one point in my life, cooked with it a little too often. Let's call it the moussaka-lasagne-ragù years. Mince can, of course, be delicious. The trick is always to get your pan and its thin film of oil or fat hot first, then introduce the minced meat and leave it to brown appetisingly on the underside.

If I am to eat meat at all, I want to see the full, unbutchered shape of the meat I buy, its bones and the road map of fat that runs through its flesh. The day when hanging carcasses of meat disappeared from most butcher's shops was a sad one, forcing us to separate the meat on our plate from the animal it once belonged to. I am rarely tempted by anything minced. It seems anonymous and a bit lost, somehow not part of the animal.

That said, from time to time I return home clutching a bag of minced meat. Nine times out of ten it will end up rolled into balls. (For the other time, see the pork rib ragù in the Meat feast chapter.) Meatballs, possibly the least romantic term for the kofta, keftedes, frikadellen and albondigas enjoyed by the rest of Europe, appeal more to me than the many-layered thing that is the usual use for minced meat. The summit of the meatball mountain is, for me, one made from pork, seasoned with lime leaves, ripe chillies, ginger and nam pla. Close behind is the Italian version, with minced but quite discernible pancetta, grated pecorino and oregano. Even the plainer versions, such as those passed over the marble counters in Sweden, with their tongue-prickling cucumber pickles and sweet-sour lingonberries, have much to commend them.

I often think that minced lamb is happiest in Greece. There it is given the opportunity to rub shoulders with wild marjoram, fresh mint and young garlic; it is where it can take a paddle in shallow pools of sun-scorched tomato sauces or be tucked up in bed with layers of aubergines and a duvet of white sauce. But I also believe Greek food is best eaten under the shade of a fig tree with sand between your toes.

The shaping of a meatball is entirely pleasurable: a gentle squeeze of the seasoned flesh, then a slow rolling in the palms of your hands, will produce spheres of flesh that you can shape or flatten at will. I do it with my fingers pointed upwards as if in prayer. What we are about to receive is a plate of sizzling balls rippled with a deep red of grated beetroot and fresh dill, glistening with a slick of yoghurt, more dill and capers.

It is always a mistake to start moving the meat about in the pan too soon. If you stir too much, and the heat isn't high enough, your meat will steam rather than form a deeply savoury brown crust. That is why mince is so rarely good when cooked in large quantities.

Use your widest pan – not too deep – and one that has a good solid base. Get the pan hot first, pour in the oil, and then add the mince. It should sizzle immediately. If it doesn't, then your pan isn't hot enough. Leave the meat be, without poking or stirring, until the meat on the bottom is golden brown. You can then, and only then, stir it. The best mince will be that which is not too lean and is cooked over a high heat to get some good colour. The juices that form a sticky residue on the pan are a crucial seasoning for what is to follow. They are the heart and soul of it all.

# Minced lamb with lime and coriander

Use minced pork for this if you prefer.

*Serves 2*

broccoli  350g, including stalks
spring onions  3
garlic  3 plump cloves
hot red chillies  2
groundnut oil  3 tablespoons
minced lamb  300g

a lime
fish sauce  1 tablespoon
caster sugar (or palm sugar)
  a teaspoon
coriander leaves  a handful

Remove the broccoli florets from their stems and blanch them in boiling, lightly salted water for 1 minute, then drain and set aside. Cut the stems into thin coins and do the same. (You can steam them if you prefer.) Chop the spring onions, discarding the darkest of the green shoots as you go. Peel the garlic and chop it finely, then deseed and chop the chillies. Get the oil really hot in a shallow pan (you will need one about 30cm in diameter – I sometimes use my wok), then cook the spring onions, garlic and chillies till soft but not coloured, moving them quickly round the pan as you go. It will appear there is too much oil but bear with me. Remove the seasonings and set aside.

Return the pan to the heat; there should be a little oil left in it. Add the minced lamb and let it colour appetisingly. It should go a rich golden colour. When it is brown, add the drained broccoli.

In a small bowl, mix the juice of the lime with the fish sauce and sugar. Tip into the hot pan and leave to sizzle briefly, scraping at the gooey stickings on the bottom of the pan and stirring them in as you go. Return the onions, garlic and chillies to the pan, check the seasoning and stir in the coriander.

After much trial and error, I have settled on a ratio of half meat to grain or vegetables by volume. To each amount of raw minced meat, I use the same quantity of other ingredients, be they vegetables or grain. Favourites include cooked onion – softened and browned in butter – a grain such as couscous and vegetables such as grated carrots or beetroot.

Minced lamb with lime and coriander

I sometimes feel besieged by beetroot. Since it jumped from the salad bowl to the oven a decade or so ago, this ruby-hued root seems to come at you from all angles, and never more so than in the weekly organic box delivery. Beetroot's earthy quality works neatly with lamb, especially when they come together as little patties.

# Beetroot and lamb patties

I suggest chilling the little cakes for an hour in the fridge before cooking. It isn't essential, but you will find them easier to handle if you do. You will need to put them into hot oil, then lower the heat and leave them alone until they have formed a crust on the base before attempting to turn them. Use a palette knife and turn them carefully, otherwise they will fall apart. You can bind the beetroot and lamb with an egg yolk to make a more resilient patty if you wish.

*Serves 4*

| | |
|---|---|
| bulgur, fine 75g | garlic 2 large cloves |
| beetroot, raw 250g | dill, chopped 2 tablespoons |
| minced lamb 400g | parsley a small bunch, chopped |
| onion 1, small to medium | groundnut oil a little |

Put the kettle on. Put the bulgur in a heatproof mixing bowl, pour over enough boiling water to cover, then set aside.

Peel the beetroot, grate coarsely into a large bowl and add the minced lamb. Finely chop the onion, crush the garlic and add to the beetroot with the dill, parsley and a generous grinding of salt and pepper.

Squeeze any water from the bulgur with your hands and add to the meat. Mix everything together thoroughly, then squish the mince into twelve pieces, each about the size of a golf ball. Flatten each ball a little, place on a baking tray and cover with cling film, then refrigerate for at least an hour.

Set the oven at 180°C. Warm a frying pan over a moderate heat, brush the patties with a little oil and fry till lightly coloured on both sides. Transfer to a baking dish and finish in the hot oven for 15–20 minutes then serve.

# Pork and lemon meatballs

Delectable little balls, these. You probably wouldn't mind a few wide and slithery Italian noodles on the side, or perhaps some rice. Or maybe just a plate of greens, such as sprout tops or purple sprouting broccoli.

*Serves 4*

fresh white breadcrumbs 70g
minced pork 500g
a lemon
parsley leaves a large handful,
   chopped
thyme about 6 bushy sprigs
Parmesan or pecorino, grated
   2 tablespoons

anchovy fillets 8, chopped
olive oil 2 tablespoons
butter 40g
flour a little
chicken stock 200ml

Put the breadcrumbs and pork into a mixing bowl. Grate the lemon zest and add it to the pork, then halve and squeeze the lemon. Add the lemon juice to the pork with the parsley and thyme leaves. Tip in the Parmesan, then the anchovy fillets. Season the mixture with a little salt, then more generously with black pepper. Mix thoroughly.

Make about eighteen small balls of the mixture, using a generously heaped tablespoon of pork for each one. I shape them into a rough ball, flatten them slightly, then put each one on a floured baking sheet.

Warm the oil and butter in a heavy-based non-stick pan. Roll the patties lightly in a little flour, then fry them, about eight at a time, for 4–5 minutes until they are crisply golden on each side. Lower the heat and leave to cook through to the middle – a matter of 6–8 minutes more. I tend to turn them no more than once or twice during cooking so they develop a crisp, slightly sticky exterior.

Remove the meatballs and keep warm. Tip the fat, or at least most of it, from the pan, then pour in the chicken stock. Leave to bubble for a good 2–3 minutes, scraping up and stirring in any caramelised pan stickings. Let the stock bubble down a bit, then divide the patties between four plates and spoon over the juices from the pan.

Pork with figs

# Three ways with a chop

Sunday roasts aside, from six to twelve years of age I lived on a diet of chops. They were either lamb or pork, with accompanying potatoes and peas, which I considered the only acceptable vegetables. My parents indulged me, and it was only when we moved homes that I would even consider ham, gammon, even a sausage as dinner. What sort of eight-year-old refuses a sausage?

Chops are straightforward to cook and have the advantage of a bone to gnaw. When I first ate them, pork chops came with apple sauce – still almost impossible to beat, the fruity acidity of the sauce a wonderful contrast to the sweet fattiness of the pork – and lamb chops came with a green-flecked puddle of mint sauce. A fruity accompaniment still gets my vote – the above apple, but also figs and blackberries. Lamb, those sweet little chops, are more likely to be seen at my table with a crumbling of feta cheese or a puddle of hummus. Sometimes both.

## Pork with figs

Pork and autumn fruit is always a good combination. And not just pork and apples.

*Serves 2*

| | |
|---|---|
| pork chops  2 | figs  4 |
| butter  25g | redcurrant (or apple) jelly |
| olive oil  2 tablespoons | 2 tablespoons |
| dry, sparkling cider  250ml | butter  a small knob |

*To serve:*
wide noodles (about 125g for 2) or some floury white boiled potatoes

Season two pork chops on both sides. Melt a little butter in a shallow pan and add the oil. Brown the chops, lightly seasoned with salt and pepper, on either side. The fat should colour nicely. (Make certain the chop browns on both sides before you introduce the cider. That way the pan juices will be tastier.) This will take about 10 minutes.

Remove the chops to a plate, cover and keep warm. Pour in the cider, let it bubble, then lower the heat, add the figs, cut in half, and cover with a lid. Continue cooking for about 5 minutes, then remove the lid, add the jelly and beat in the butter. Let the sauce reduce by about half and serve.

## Pork chops (or steaks) with courgettes and sauerkraut

The key is not to add too much, just a tablespoon or two of the sharp, lively pickles to each batch of fresh vegetables.

*Serves 2*

| | |
|---|---|
| pork steaks  2 × 200g | butter  30g |
| olive oil  2 tablespoons | dill  4 tablespoons |
| lemons  2 | sauerkraut  4 tablespoons, |
| courgettes  2, small | (plus 2 tablespoons of the juice) |

Rub the pork all over with a little olive oil, black pepper and salt. Cover and set aside. Finely grate the zest from one of the lemons into a mixing bowl. Halve and squeeze the juice, then add to the zest. Using a vegetable peeler, take long, flat strips from the courgettes and place in a bowl. Get the griddle pan or grill hot.

Place the meat on the griddle and cook till golden, brushing the surface with a little oil from the dish as necessary. Season with salt and more pepper. Slice the remaining lemon in half and place it cut side down next to the meat.

Remove the pork and lemon and let the pork rest. Place the courgette ribbons on the griddle and cook for 3–4 minutes, turning from time to time. Warm the butter in a pan, stir in the lemon zest and juice, and black pepper. Roughly chop the dill. When the courgettes are tender, lift them into the warmed, seasoned butter. Add the sauerkraut, 2 tablespoons of its juice, the chopped dill and mix gently.

Serve the pork with the grilled lemons, courgettes and sauerkraut.

Lamb cutlets, broad beans, soured cream

# Lamb cutlets, broad beans, soured cream

*Serves 2*

onions  2, medium
olive oil  3 tablespoons
broad beans  600g
   (weight including pods)
   or 300g frozen

lamb cutlets  6–8
thyme leaves  2 teaspoons
garlic  1 clove, peeled and crushed
soured cream  100ml
parsley  a handful

Peel the onions and slice thinly into rings. Warm the olive oil in a shallow pan, then fry the onions over a low heat for about 20–25 minutes. Stir them regularly, until they are soft, translucent and pale gold in colour.

Bring a medium-sized pan of water to the boil. While the onions are cooking, pod the broad beans, then cook them in the boiling water for about 7 minutes, depending on their size. Check them for tenderness, then drain. Pop the beans from their papery skins. I really think this is one time you shouldn't skip this.

Warm a grill or griddle pan. Lightly oil the lamb cutlets and season with salt, pepper, the thyme and garlic and cook them until their fat is golden. (I like to press them down on the griddle with a heavy weight.) Inside, the lamb should be pink and juicy.

Remove the onions from the heat and strain off any excess olive oil. Fold the soured cream and most of the broad beans through the onions, and season with black pepper and a little chopped parsley.

Divide the onions and soured cream between two warm plates, settle the cutlets next to them and serve with the remaining beans.

# Two great little curries

Curry is many things. You could write a book on the meaning of the word alone. Indeed, some have. Here, I use the word to signify a recipe that is deeply aromatic, generously spiced and fragrant. None of the recipes that follow can be considered authentic to any culture or region, they are the product of my pottering around in the kitchen with my little spice grinder. They should not be seen as anything more than that.

## Chicken with tomatoes, yoghurt and garam masala

*Serves 4*

a large chicken jointed into 8 pieces,
   or a mixture of thighs and breast
a little groundnut or vegetable oil
onions 2, medium to large
cinnamon half a stick
cloves 3

tomato passata 500g
garam masala 1 level tablespoon
natural yoghurt 100ml
coriander leaves a handful,
   roughly chopped

*For the spice paste:*
green cardamom pods 8
black peppercorns 8
garlic 4 cloves
ginger a 40g piece
ground cumin 2 teaspoons

ground coriander 2 teaspoons
ground chilli, mild or hot
   1 teaspoon
vegetable or groundnut oil
   2 tablespoons

steamed rice to serve

Season the chicken pieces. Warm a thin layer of oil – just a couple of tablespoons – in a deep casserole over a moderate heat. Add the chicken and let it colour appetisingly on all sides, turning as necessary. Lift out and set aside.

Peel and roughly chop the onions and add them to the casserole with a little oil. Then add the cinnamon and cloves. Cook over a low to moderate heat for about 15-20 minutes, stirring regularly, until the onions are soft, sweet and fragrant.

Meanwhile, make the spice paste. Crack the cardamoms with a heavy weight, remove their seeds, then put them into a blender or food processor with the peppercorns, peeled garlic, ginger (peeled and roughly chopped), cumin, coriander and ground chilli. Pour in a couple of tablespoons of oil and blitz to a stiffish paste.

Add the spice paste to the onions. Move it continually round the pan with a wooden spoon for a couple of minutes, allowing it to sizzle but not darken. Add the passata and 100ml of water and mix well. Add salt and black pepper, and then return the chicken to the pan. Bring the sauce to the boil, then immediately turn down to a gentle simmer, cover with a lid and leave to cook for 35-40 minutes until the chicken is tender. Towards the end, stir in the garam masala. Add a little water if the sauce is getting too thick.

Remove from the heat, stir in the yoghurt and the roughly chopped coriander, and serve with steamed rice.

## Mussels, coconut and noodles

A borderline Thai curry and none the worse for it.

*Serves 4*

ginger 50g
green bird's-eye chillies 2
spring onions, trimmed 3
coriander, leaves and stalks 50g
mint 15 large leaves
garlic 3 cloves
groundnut oil 5 tablespoons
ground turmeric 1½ teaspoons
green peppercorns, fresh or
    brined 16

coconut milk 2 × 400ml tins
fish sauce 2 teaspoons
lemongrass 2 large stalks
mussels 350g
rice noodles 60g
palm or caster sugar half a
    teaspoon, to taste
lime, mint and coriander to serve

Peel the ginger, cut into short lengths, then drop into the bowl of a food processor. Remove the stalks from the chillies, then add them complete with their seeds to the bowl, together with the spring onions, coriander and mint leaves. Peel the garlic, then add it to the ginger and herbs. Pour in the oil, then process for 30 seconds or till you have a smooth, wet paste. Scrape into a small bowl, cover with cling film and refrigerate till you are ready to use it. The paste will keep in good condition for a day or two.

Place a deep, medium-sized pan over a moderate heat and add the herb and spice paste, stirring it for a minute while it warms. Stir in the turmeric, peppercorns, coconut milk and fish sauce and bring to the boil. Using a rolling pin or the back of a heavy kitchen knife, smash the lemongrass so it splinters but remains together, then tuck it under the surface of the liquid. Lower the heat and leave to simmer, bubbling gently, while you cook the mussels.

Wash the mussels under running water, discarding any whose shells are chipped or that refuse to close when tapped firmly on the edge of the sink. Place a saucepan over a high flame, add the mussels in their shells, then cover tightly with a lid. Leave for 1–2 minutes, occasionally shaking the pan back and forth, then remove from the heat. Pull the mussels from their shells, but keep the small amount of liquid that has accumulated in the pan. Put a kettle on to boil.

Place the noodles in a heatproof bowl and pour over enough of the boiling water from the kettle to cover them. Add the mussels to the soup, straining their cooking liquid through a small sieve into the soup. (There will only be a small amount, but it is too flavoursome to waste.) Check the seasoning of the soup, adding fish sauce or salt and some of the palm sugar as necessary. Drain the noodles, then divide them between four deep soup bowls. Ladle over the soup and mussels, adding a generous squeeze of lime juice and, if you wish, a few extra coriander and mint leaves.

# Some quick chicken dinners

## Chicken with yuzu and broccoli

*Serves 2*

light soy sauce  2 tablespoons
mirin  2 tablespoons
sesame oil  1 tablespoon
yuzu juice  2 tablespoons
togarishi seasoning  half a
   teaspoon, plus a little extra

chicken breasts  500g
sticky (sushi) rice  150g
broccoli  150g

Put the soy sauce in a mixing bowl, add the mirin and sesame oil, the yuzu juice and the togarashi seasoning. Stir to combine. Cut the chicken breast into finger-thick strips and push down into the marinade, then set aside for a good couple of hours.

Put the sticky (sushi) rice into a saucepan and pour over enough water to cover it well, about 400ml. Add a teaspoon of salt and bring to the boil. Cover tightly with a lid, lower the heat to a simmer and leave for 10 minutes. Remove the rice from the heat and leave to rest, still tightly covered, for 10 minutes. Put a pot of water on to boil.

Warm an overhead grill and line a grill pan with kitchen foil. Put the marinated chicken strips onto the foil in a single layer, taking care not to pack them too tightly together. Grill for 8–10 minutes. Baste them occasionally with the marinade and turn once or twice. You may want to move them closer to the heat for the last few minutes.

While the chicken cooks and the rice rests, wash and trim the broccoli, then drop it into the boiling water and let it cook for 3–4 minutes until the stems are just tender to the point of a knife. Drain and finely chop the broccoli.

Stir the broccoli into the rice and divide between two bowls. When the chicken is dark and sizzling, place it on top of the rice and season with a little more togarashi.

Chicken with yuzu and broccoli

Chicken with peppers, lemon and mint

Making something to eat is one of the great joys of my life, but that doesn't mean I don't occasionally welcome a dinner where the preparation time is almost zero. I have a chicken supper that fits neatly into that scenario, where peppers roast till silky and on the verge of collapse, where their juices mingle with those of roast chicken. The sweetness is spiked with sour lemon and cool mint. A dinner that is as much about the juices on your plate as about the meat. You will need good bread to mop them up.

## Chicken with peppers, lemon and mint

*Serves 3*

| | |
|---|---|
| romano peppers 4 | chicken thighs 6 |
| orange or yellow peppers 2 | olive oil 6 tablespoons |
| cherry tomatoes 400g | preserved lemon 1 |
| garlic 4 cloves | mint leaves a small handful |

Slice the romano peppers in half lengthways, remove any seeds, then cut each half into two short lengths. Do the same with the orange or yellow peppers, then put all of them in a roasting tin. Add the cherry tomatoes, left whole. Set the oven at 200°C.

Peel the garlic cloves, flatten them with a knife and add them to the roasting tin. Place the chicken thighs, skin side up, among the peppers, pour over the olive oil and season well with salt and black pepper.

Bake for 50 minutes to an hour, until the chicken is golden brown and crisp and the peppers are soft.

Halve the preserved lemon and scrape out and discard the flesh. Chop the lemon shells into small pieces, then add to the juices in the roasting tin and continue cooking for a couple of minutes.

Put the chicken, tomatoes and peppers onto plates, then chop the mint leaves and stir them into the juices in the roasting tin. Spoon the juices over the chicken and peppers and serve.

In 1993 I published a recipe (in *Real Food*) where chicken pieces are cooked in a pan with small brown mushrooms, wine and cream. I have lost count of the number of times readers have told me it is one of their favourites. That, surely, is enough reason for its inclusion here.

# Coq au Riesling

*Serves 3*

onions  2, small
garlic  2 cloves
butter  50g
olive oil  1 tablespoon
streaky bacon or pancetta
    100g, diced

chicken thighs  6
brown mushrooms  200g
medium-dry white wine  500ml
double cream  250ml
parsley, chopped  3 tablespoons

Peel and roughly chop the onions. Peel and finely chop the garlic. Melt the butter in a heavy-based casserole and pour in the oil. Add the diced bacon or pancetta and let it colour a little, then add the onions and garlic. Let them cook for a good 20 minutes or so, stirring regularly, till they are soft and pale gold. Scoop them out of the pan into a bowl and set aside.

Add the chicken to the pan and let it colour, till golden, on both sides. You may need to add a little more oil. Add the mushrooms to the pan and continue cooking till they soften, then return the onions to the pan. Turn up the heat, pour in the wine and bring to the boil. Lower the heat and stir well to dissolve the toasty bits that have caramelised on the pan. Turn the chicken from time to time.

Remove the chicken from the pan, leaving the onions and mushrooms in place, then pour in the cream and let it bubble for a minute or so, stir in the parsley and season with salt and black pepper. Return the chicken to the pan, make sure it is hot, then serve.

# Roast chicken wings with lemon and black pepper

This is finger food at its very best. So simple you could do them with a blindfold on, these roast chicken wings are probably one of my all-time favourite things to eat. You can double the recipe easily enough for larger numbers. The trick is to roast them till they are almost stuck to the roasting tin. Don't even think of using a knife and fork here.

*Serves 2*

large chicken wings  12
a large juicy lemon
black peppercorns
  1 heaped tablespoon

olive oil  2 tablespoons
sea salt flakes  2 teaspoons

Set the oven at 200°C. Check the chicken wings for stray feathers. Put the wings into a roasting dish, halve the lemon and squeeze it over them, then cut up the lemon shells and tuck them between the chicken pieces.

Put the peppercorns in a mortar and bash them so they crack into small pieces. They should still be nubbly, rather than finely ground. Mix the peppercorns with the olive oil, then toss with the chicken and lemon. Scatter the salt flakes, without crushing them, over the chicken. Roast for 40–45 minutes, turning once. The chicken should be golden and sticky, the edges blackened here and there.

# The gory glory of steak

I spent my teenage years deep in the countryside, with few neighbours and a two-mile walk to school. There were few places to eat out. A couple of half-timbered pubs with oak settles and open fires, copper kettles and ancient Labradors dozing in the bar. A net-curtained café in a local market town with a set roast lunch and roly-poly pudding and, joy of joys, a Berni Inn. This last one, in the 1960s, felt like the biggest treat, a proper grown-up restaurant with red carpets and wooden beams where fruit juice was considered a 'starter'. We came for the steaks, which were thick and rare and came with good chips, which was all that really mattered to a thirteen-year-old.

I tend to cook steak when I am on my own, which of course makes it an even bigger treat. No chips (I make sauté potatoes instead) and always, always Béarnaise sauce. Nowadays I like my steaks thinner than of old, usually bavette or the thicker rib-eye. Never fillet, which I find uninteresting no matter who cooks it.

Generally, I tend to leave steak to the experts – professional chefs cooking sirloin, bavette and rib-eye, lovingly, confidently, day in day out. Just occasionally I cook steak at home. Truth told, it isn't that easy to get right. In fact, I would say cooking a great steak – its crust walnut-bronze, the fat crisp, deep gold outside and almost jelly-like within – is one of the most difficult things you can do in a kitchen. The quality of the meat and how it has been hung is absolutely critical, but so is how we cook it.

## Steak with creamed spinach

Of all the possible accompaniments to steak, there is only one I consider essential – Béarnaise sauce. However, I will never say no to a bowl of creamed spinach. I make one, not with a white sauce as so many do, but with crème fraîche and butter.

Use 400g of firm, pointed spinach leaves, not the tender salad variety. Discard the thickest of the stalks and wash the leaves thoroughly. Place a deep pan over a moderately high heat, add the still-wet spinach leaves and cover tightly with a lid. The leaves will wilt in their own steam. Remove the lid after a minute to check their progress. Turn the leaves over with a pair of tongs, then cover again and continue cooking for a further minute or two till silky, soft and wilted. Remove from the heat and tip into the colander. Return the empty pan to the heat, then add the drained leaves and 50g of butter. When the butter has melted, stir in 200g of crème fraîche and season with salt and black pepper. As soon as the mixture bubbles it is ready.

# The Béarnaise

The Béarnaise sauce, or at least my version of it, involves a little care on the part of the cook, if only because of its ability to separate. The trick is to make certain that it never gets too hot.

| | |
|---|---|
| shallot  a small one | egg yolks  2 |
| tarragon vinegar  3 tablespoons | Dijon mustard  a little |
| black peppercorns  6 | butter  150g, cut into small dice |
| tarragon  3 or 4 bushy stalks and their leaves | |

Peel and finely chop the shallot and put it in a small saucepan with the vinegar, peppercorns and tarragon leaves and stalks. Bring to the boil and watch it while it reduces to a tablespoon or so. Put the egg yolks and a little mustard (about half a teaspoon) into a heatproof glass bowl and place it over a pan of gently simmering water. The bowl should sit snugly in the top of the pan. Whisk the reduced vinegar into the egg yolks, holding the debris back in the pan, then slowly add the butter, a little at time, whisking between additions until it is smooth and velvety. You can turn off the heat halfway through. The sauce must never get too hot. It may need a little salt. It will keep warm, with the occasional whisk while you cook your steak.

# To cook the steak

You know how you like your steak. But this is how I do mine. I like a medium-rare rib-eye; that's the bit found at the front of the sirloin, but it has more fat than that – fat that brings flavour and succulence to the meat. I use salt at the beginning, pepper much later, a sprig of thyme and lots of butter. There is smoke, plumes of it, and it can be a bit of a juggle making the Béarnaise at the same time. And yet every time I do it – and get it right – I question why I don't do it more often.

I get a shallow pan hot, but not scorchingly so. I add the steak, lightly salted, and press it down on the pan firmly (a palette knife, even a heavy weight such as a smaller pan, is good for this) then let it cook till the fat starts to run. The meat stays in place for 5 minutes or so, then I turn the heat up a notch or two. As soon as the underside is nut-brown the steak is turned, I press it down in the pan again and once the underside is browned, I add 50g of butter and a few twists of the pepper mill. As the butter melts, I baste the frothing butter over the steak with a spoon, almost continually, for a further minute, adding the thyme sprig as I go.

Then, the crucial bit – the steak is rested for a good 5 minutes before serving with the sauce and creamed spinach.

# Seven pasta suppers

In the 1980s I seem to have lived on pasta and red wine. Penne, rigatoni and fettucine, all eaten in the British style, piled up in bowls, with as much sauce as starch, and in portions the size of Snowdonia. And with that, the inevitable side-order of zig-zag energy patterns, the peaks and troughs of hyperactivity and coma-like sleep of a badly made high-carbohydrate diet.

I don't eat much pasta now. I do cook it – lasagne, cappelletti, orzo, spaghetti, fettucine – for others though, and the popularity of the recipes I have published for it over the years seems to have endured, so I happily include the most popular in this collection. Servings are on the modest side, as I have found them in Florence, Milan and Venice. They are as far from the old-school British way of eating pasta as you could imagine.

There is an immediacy to a pasta supper that only adds to its appeal. IMHO, the quicker and humbler the pasta recipe the better. (I will concede the most worthwhile of all is probably homemade gnudi – a recipe that takes a good forty-eight hours – but I shall not bother you with that here.) The sauces that are made in roughly the time the pasta takes to cook are often the most welcome, taking just enough time to make us feel we are actually cooking, without going into full rolled-up sleeves and apron mode.

With speed in mind, there are two – published several years ago – whose simplicity never fails to delight. They are light and fresh, not a carton of cream in sight.

## Courgettes and orecchiette

*Serves 2*

| | |
|---|---|
| orecchiette 250g | garlic 2 young cloves |
| courgettes 2, medium | basil leaves about 12, |
| butter 40g plus a little more | medium to large |
| olive oil | a lemon |

Boil the orecchiette in deep, heavily salted boiling water. Dice the courgettes (1cm is about right) and cook the cubes in the butter and a splash of olive oil in a shallow pan till golden, translucent and tender. A 10-minute job. Peel and finely slice the cloves of garlic and add them to the courgettes. Let them colour lightly. Add the basil leaves to the pan, some finely grated lemon zest, a squeeze of lemon juice and a little more butter. Drain the pasta and toss with the sauce.

# And a cure for a cold, a hangover, everything really (though probably not a broken heart)

Under normal circumstances, I would cook the orzo in boiling water then drain it and add it to the stock. But utilising the starch that would normally be left behind in the cooking water is what makes this dish as comforting as a cashmere throw. Cooking the pasta in stock harnesses that starch. It gives body to the broth and a silky, healing texture which together with the umami notes of the fish sauce and the kick of chilli, mint and lemon makes this a broth to restore and invigorate.

*Serves 2*

| | |
|---|---|
| chicken stock  1 litre | mint  12 medium-sized leaves |
| orzo  100g | fish sauce  1 tablespoon |
| lemon  1 | chilli oil, to taste |

Bring the stock to the boil. Rain in the orzo and cook for 12 minutes. The little grains of pasta should be soft, not al dente.

Halve the lemon and squeeze into a small bowl. Finely shred the mint leaves and stir them in to the lemon juice together with the fish sauce and a few drops of the chilli oil. Stir the mixture into the hot stock, then ladle into deep bowls, adding more chilli oil as you feel the need.

# A creamy macaroni and tomato pasta

Creamy and sharp at the same time, I like this best with just a few spoonfuls of cream (I start with 3 tablespoons or so). Others may like a little more. The onion on top is essential to the balance of the dish.

*Serves 2*

| | |
|---|---|
| onion 1 | cinnamon half a stick |
| olive oil 2 tablespoons | bay leaves 2 |
| garlic 3 cloves | macaroni 100g |
| tomato purée 1 tablespoon | chickpeas 1 × 400g tin |
| chopped tomatoes 1 × 400g tin | double cream 50–100ml |

*To finish:*

| | |
|---|---|
| onion 1 | parsley, chopped a handful |
| chilli, hot 1 | olive oil 2 tablespoons |

Make the fried onion to finish. Peel the onion and finely slice into rings. Finely slice the chilli. Heat the oil in a shallow pan over a moderate heat, add the onion and let it cook till crisp. Add the chilli and continue cooking for a minute or two, then add the parsley and set aside.

Now for the pasta. Peel and roughly chop the onion. Heat the olive oil in a saucepan, add the onion and let it soften over a moderate heat for 10 minutes, stirring from time to time. Peel and crush the garlic, add to the onion and continue cooking. When the onion starts to turn gold in colour, add the tomato purée, chopped tomatoes and their juice, the cinnamon, bay leaves and a little pepper and salt. Leave to simmer for 15 minutes.

Bring a deep pan of water to the boil, salt it, and cook the macaroni for 9 minutes, or until tender, then drain in a colander. Drain the chickpeas and stir into the tomato sauce. Add the pasta to the sauce. Simmer for 5 minutes, then stir in the cream, a little at a time. (I usually stop at 75ml.) When all is hot and bubbling, serve in deep bowls. Scatter the crisp onion and chilli on top.

Pasta with spicy sausage, basil and mustard

Some recipes are more popular than others. Frustratingly, they are rarely those which you spent days testing and retesting, agonising over, writing and rewriting. It is more likely, in my experience anyway, to be the recipes you threw together at the last minute, to catch your deadline. Whatever, I remain exceptionally grateful.

## Pasta with spicy sausage, basil and mustard

Of all the thousands of recipes I have published over the years, it is this one, with pasta, sausages, mustard and cream, that I am told is 'the favourite'. It does indeed tick many boxes. That of comfort food, cheap supper and fast fix. Keep the heat sprightly, so the sausage browns and a sticky goo is left on the pan. Nuggets of joy.

*Serves 2*

dried pasta (any tube or shell shape) 250g
spicy pork sausages 4–6 depending on their size
olive oil
a glass of white wine 150ml

dried chilli flakes a pinch or 2
basil leaves a large handful, about 20g
grain mustard 1 tablespoon
double cream 200ml

Put a large pan of water on to boil for the pasta. Salt it generously. Split the sausages open and take out the filling. Warm a thin film of olive oil in a frying pan, just enough to lubricate the bottom. Discard the sausage skin, crumble the meat into the hot pan and fry till sizzling and cooked through, about 5 minutes over a moderately high heat. Add the pasta to the boiling water.

Pour the wine into the sausage pan and let it bubble a little, scraping at the sausage goo stuck to the bottom of the pan. Stir in the chilli flakes, roughly chop or tear the basil leaves and add those too. Add a little salt and the mustard, pour in the cream and bring slowly to a simmer. Cook for 1–2 minutes, stirring now and again.

When the pasta is tender, about 9 minutes after coming back to the boil, drain and tip into the creamy sausage sauce. Serve piping hot.

Linguine with 'nduja and tomatoes

The essential blandness of pasta makes it a sound vehicle for spices, and in particular chilli. You can add this in the form of chopped or sliced chillies in its accompanying sauce, as chilli oil after cooking or in form of a chilli paste such as harissa. (You can use the dark red Korean paste gochujang too but I usually keep that for noodles.) The other bringer of chilli heat is 'nduja, the spicy, spreadable pork sausage from Calabria. It adds a little substance too.

## Linguine with 'nduja and tomatoes

The 'nduja sauce is very spicy. If you feel the need to tone down its heat – and well you might – simply stir in more tomatoes, halved or crushed, as you serve the dish, or fold in a spoonful of yoghurt or cream. Oh, and I should mention that 'nduja burns easily, so keep the heat no higher than moderate while it warms and stir regularly to prevent it from scorching.

*Serves 4*

| | |
|---|---|
| linguine 250g | cornichons 30g |
| 'nduja 140g | capers 2 teaspoons |
| cherry tomatoes 300g | olive oil 2 tablespoons |

Bring a deep pan of water to the boil, salt it, then add the linguine and cook for 8–9 minutes, until the pasta is tender.

While the linguine cooks, make the sauce. In a shallow pan – one to which nothing will stick – warm the 'nduja over a moderate heat, stirring it regularly.

Slice the cherry tomatoes in half, then fold them into the warm 'nduja and continue cooking. Stir in the cornichons, sliced in half lengthways, and then the capers.

Leave to cook for 3–4 minutes until the tomatoes have started to give up some of their juice, then stir in the olive oil.

Drain the linguine, then toss it with the sauce, folding the sauce through the pasta.

Thinking about it now, I probably ate most of the pasta in my life when I was not exactly in the best of places. If that happens to be the definition of comfort food then so be it. Pasta hits the spot. Orecchiette, ravioli and even penne – the last being just a short leap from rubber tubing – followed my every drama, nursing me back to full health.

Of all the pastas and all the sauces that worked as medicine, none had the curative power of orzo, either in broth (see earlier) or in a seductive and soothing goo of melting Parmesan. The best of these being one with smoked pancetta, diced courgettes and onion. It tethers melted cheese and smoked bacon notes to my simplest pasta recipe.

## Orzo with courgettes and Grana Padano

I have suggested the mild and nutty Grana Padano for a change. Use Parmesan if you can't track it down.

*Serves 3–4*

orzo 300g
pancetta in one piece 150g
onion 1, large
olive oil 2 tablespoons

white wine 250ml
courgettes 4, medium
Grana Padano or Parmesan 50g,
    very coarsely grated

Bring a deep pan of water to the boil, salt generously, then rain in the orzo and boil for 9 minutes or until it is firm but tender. It should retain a certain bite. Drain.

Cut the pancetta into large dice. Peel and chop the onion. Fry the onion with the pancetta in the olive oil in a shallow, heavy-based pan over a moderate heat for 15 minutes, stirring regularly, till the onion is soft and translucent and the fat on the pancetta is pale amber. Pour in the wine, turn up the heat slightly, then bubble till reduced by half.

Cut the courgettes in half lengthways, then into thick slices, and add to the pan. Season with salt and black pepper and continue cooking for 7–10 minutes, until the courgettes are tender and pale gold. Stir in the drained orzo and the Grana Padano or Parmesan. The cheese should melt slightly, gently bringing the whole dish together.

It is quite wrong of me to lump noodles under the side heading of pasta, and I do it only out of convenience. Forgive me.

The contents of my larder have moved somewhat east since I first started writing. Mirin, gochujang, nam pla, nori, tofu, toasted sesame oil, several different soy sauces, wasabi and rice vinegar have taken residence in my fridge and on my cupboard shelves and stayed there. They are as much a part of my daily cooking as the mustards, vinegars and oils I have used for half a century. Nowadays, probably more so. I use them with no expertise, but with enthusiasm and, even now, a certain curiosity.

I include this noodle recipe because the seasoning, with nam pla and mint, remains one of my absolute favourites.

# Noodles with prawns

*Serves 2*

*For the marinade:*

fish sauce  2 tablespoons
mirin  2 tablespoons
rice vinegar  1 tablespoon
light soy sauce  1 tablespoon

lime juice  100ml (about 2 limes)
red chilli  1, medium
raw prawns  16

*For the noodles:*

cucumber  100g
mint leaves  12
coriander  a handful

angel-hair noodles  100g
groundnut oil  2 tablespoons

Combine the fish sauce, mirin, rice vinegar, soy and lime juice in a medium-sized mixing bowl. Finely chop the chilli and add to the bowl. Put the prawns into the marinade and leave for half an hour or so.

Peel the cucumber, slice in half lengthways and remove the core with a teaspoon. Cut into short lengths and then into large matchstick-sized pieces, then put them in a bowl with the mint leaves and coriander.

Put the noodles in a heatproof bowl, pour a kettle of boiling water over them and set aside while you cook the prawns.

Warm the groundnut oil in a shallow pan. When it starts to sizzle, add the prawns (reserve their marinade) and let them cook for 2 minutes. Remove the prawns, then pour in the marinade and leave it to bubble for a couple of minutes until it has reduced by about half.

Drain the noodles and add to the cucumber and herbs. Add the prawns, then the marinade, and toss everything together.

# A calming supper for one

There is no food to which I am addicted. But it's a close thing when it comes to pickles. I often start my day with a tiny dark-green dish of pale, knife-sharp sauerkraut. The snap of acidity, the wincing sourness, wakes me up. A spoonful of jewel-bright Japanese pickled radish or cucumber is an essential part of my breakfast rice (it's a weekend thing), and I find pickled ginger the best of all midnight fridge raids.

Growing up, 'pickles' meant the mahogany-brown walnuts my father loved more than he loved his son, and slices of brilliant purple beetroot. Later, I grew to love the crunch of a forkful of curly red cabbage and the astringency of a pickled onion. Especially when either is accompanied by a pork pie. I have taken to keeping a stock of Japanese pickles in the fridge. They have a short shelf-life which means I tend to feast on them as soon as the packet is open. Outside of Kyoto their supply is erratic – even the most comprehensive of Japanese stores here regularly declares them 'out of stock'. These are the pickles I crave.

A peaceful thing, the humble bowl of rice you hold in your hand brings with it a deep sense of calm and quiet happiness. I will, nevertheless, fire it up with slices of pickled ginger, some deep purple and absinthe-green pickled radish and a mouth-fizzingly salty and fruity umeboshi plum.

Sometimes I feel the need to be grounded. Usually when I have been eating too many cakes or puddings or have been out for too many restaurant meals. That is when I cook sticky rice – the round nubby sort used for sushi – and add to it shards of salmon or grilled mackerel, pickles and more often than not some crumbled sheets of nori seaweed.

# Rice, salmon, Japanese pickles

*Serves 2*

sushi rice  125g
salmon tail or fillet  250g
groundnut oil  a little
white sesame seeds  3 tablespoons

ginger  a 2cm lump
garlic  1 clove
black sesame seeds  1 teaspoon
Japanese pickled vegetables

Put the sushi rice into a bowl and cover it in warm water. Swish the rice around with your fingers then pour the water away. Repeat this process three or four times.

Transfer the rice to a small saucepan, pour in 300ml of water and bring to the boil. Cover with a lid and simmer for 10 minutes, then remove from the heat, leaving the lid in place.

Cook the salmon, seasoned and brushed with oil, under a hot oven grill for 4–5 minutes. In a dry, shallow pan, toast the golden sesame seeds for 1–2 minutes.

Peel and finely grate the ginger. Tip half the toasted sesame seeds into a mortar and crush them to a coarse paste with the peeled clove of garlic, half a teaspoon of sea salt and the grated ginger. Add the black sesame seeds to the reserved toasted seeds. Lift the lid off the rice and fold the sesame and ginger paste and the whole sesame seeds through it with a fork or chopsticks.

Divide the rice between two bowls. Break the warm fish into large pieces and add it to the rice, together with a few pickled vegetables as you wish.

A piece of fish, a hot grill and I'm happy. Barely a week goes by when there isn't a fillet of mackerel, a slice of halibut or a soldierly row of whiskery prawns on my grill. It is perhaps the simplest supper of all. That grill needs to be one to which the fish doesn't stick, and it may need a sprig of thyme or a brush with olive oil or butter but that is all. Once cooked and on the plate, the sizzling seafood will get no more than half a lemon or a sprinkling of citrus soy (ponzu), a pea-sized smear of wasabi or just a dab of basil butter. It's as straightforward as that.

Grilled scallops, basil butter

Few of my fish recipes involve much cooking. They are simple affairs, as far away from classic French fish-wine-and-cream style cookery as you can get. It is my belief that the less time you spend making a fish dinner the better will be the result.

# Four fish suppers

## Grilled scallops, basil butter

The classic dish of scallops in cheese sauce with a ring of mashed potato (often served in a scallop shell) has never done it for me. I don't see the point of paying a price for something only to smother it in blandness. Far better, surely, to cook it with respect. In my house, scallops are cooked on the griddle, brushed with a little butter, a fizz of green herbs, a squeeze of lemon. That is it.

*Serves 2*

butter 45g, at room temperature
basil leaves 15g
a lemon

scallops 12, small to medium
olive oil a little

Cream the butter in a bowl with a wooden spoon till soft. Using a pestle and mortar, mash the basil to a paste with a pinch of salt. Stir the basil into the butter, then add a few drops of lemon juice and set aside.

Soften the basil butter in a small pan over a low heat, then remove from the heat as soon as it is melted. Heat a griddle pan, brush the scallops with a little oil, then place them on the hot griddle pan. Press them gently down with a palette knife, so they colour nicely, then turn them over. They will need no more than 1–2 minutes on either side. Brush with some of the butter and serve.

'Set aside in a cold place for at least four hours' is not an instruction you expect to find in a chapter called 'Everyday Dinners'. But where else do you put a useful recipe for a cheap fish that can be left in the fridge for a few days, a dish to come home to, to eat with tiny boiled potatoes and a plate of treacly rye bread.

I met my first prawns in the late 1960s, in one of their infamous cocktails, a single particularly fine specimen hanging over the edge of the glass, as if trying to escape. Such sweet and succulent seafood deserved better than to be tossed with wisps of lettuce and a cloying sauce. It was years later that we became properly acquainted – in Vicenza this time – offered sizzling from the grill, hot and lemony, complete with heads and shells to tear off and suck.

It isn't easy to find large, sustainably fished prawns. When I can, I make the most of them. A pile of them, shell-on and tossed on the grill, or in a shallow pan with butter, is hardly a cheap feast, but in my book worth every penny. I include them here not because they make a regular appearance in my kitchen but because they are one of the most delicious suppers I can think of. There will be cold beer, good bread and a fat lemon.

My first thought has long been to cook them under a hot oven grill, snuggled together in a single layer, brushed with melted butter and Parmesan and served with more of both. Other times, I will drop them into a pan of butter with liquorice-black garlic and a shower of dill fronds.

## Prawns, black garlic and dill butter

A fabulously messy dish – knives and forks are redundant here. You'll need something to wipe your fingers on, too, and an extra plate for the discarded shells.

*Serves 2*

black garlic  3 cloves
butter  50g, softened
raw prawns  8–12, large

dill  a generous handful
lemon  1

Prawns, black garlic and dill butter

Remove the black garlic cloves from their skins, then mash them to a coarse purée using a pestle and mortar and a pinch of salt. Cream the butter with a wooden spoon or using a food mixer, beating in the garlic as you go.

Melt the butter in a shallow pan over a moderately high heat. As the butter starts to froth, lower in the prawns, whole and still in their shells, and leave them for 4–5 minutes, occasionally spooning the butter over them. Turn the prawns with kitchen tongs and let them cook briefly on the other side.

Roughly chop the dill. Halve the lemon. When the prawns are pink, and their shells tinged with gold, add the chopped dill to the pan, spoon the butter over them once more, then squeeze in half of the lemon.

Serve the prawns and garlic butter immediately with the remaining half of lemon, letting everyone peel away the shells, dipping the prawns in the butter on their plates.


There is a counter I visit in Kyoto to lunch on tempura. Almost exclusively vegetable in content – taro root, burdock, asparagus, shiitake, aubergine, fiddlehead ferns and some greens I am unfamiliar with – but at the end you are often presented with a single crumbed prawn. I have made these at home now, each prawn encased in a crisp shrapnel of panko crumbs with a dish of yuzu-scented soy sauce – ponzu – in which to dip them.

## Fried prawns, ponzu sauce

*Serves 2 as a main*

raw prawns  450g, shell-on
panko crumbs  6 heaped
   tablespoons
eggs  2

groundnut or vegetable oil
   for deep frying
ponzu sauce to serve

Remove the heads and shells from the prawns. Rinse the tails briefly in cold running water and pat dry.

Tip the crumbs on to a plate and spread evenly. Break the eggs into a shallow bowl and beat lightly to mix the yolks and whites.

Heat the oil in a deep pan. Dunk the prawns in the beaten egg, then into the crumbs. Press down to coat the prawns, then turn and coat the other side.

Dip the crumbed prawns into the hot oil and fry till golden – a matter of 2–3 minutes – then remove and drain on kitchen paper. Serve with small bowls of ponzu sauce for dipping.

## Hake with chorizo, Manzanilla and Judión beans

*Serves 4*

onions  3, medium
olive oil  6 tablespoons,
 plus extra for frying the hake
chorizo, cooking type  300g
thyme  6 bushy sprigs
tomatoes  750g, small

Judión or butter beans  425g,
 bottled or tinned
hake  1.2kg, cut into 4 steaks
Manzanilla or similar dry sherry
 150ml

Peel the onions, cut them in half and roughly chop them. Warm the oil in a metal roasting tin over a moderate heat, then add the onions and let them cook, stirring regularly, until they are soft and translucent. Set the oven at 200°C.

Slice the chorizo into pieces the length of a wine cork, add them to the onions together with the whole sprigs of thyme and let the sausage colour lightly. Slice the tomatoes in half, then stir them through the onions together with the drained and rinsed beans.

In a separate shallow, non-stick pan, warm the extra oil and, when it is hot, lower in a couple of the fish steaks. Let them colour lightly on the underside without cooking them right through, then turn and do the same on the other side. As each piece of fish becomes ready, transfer to the roasting tin, tucking them among the tomatoes and onions. Repeat with the remaining two pieces of fish. Once they are done, pour off any oil from the frying pan, return to the heat and pour in the Manzanilla, letting it bubble as you scrape at the sticky bits with a wooden spatula. Tip over the fish.

Place in the oven and bake for 35 minutes until the fish is done. Serve the fish, chorizo, onions, beans and tomatoes on deep, warm plates, spooning over the juices as you go.

# A couple of fishcakes

There was a time when I suspect I knew every restaurant fishcake in London. For me, they were a lunch thing (though strangely never dinner), and something I generally preferred others to make. But there is something calming about 10 minutes' rolling fishcakes in the kitchen, and I like frying them, gently in hot butter and olive oil, basting them as they cook. Sometimes, I make them smaller, like little golden croquettes, and plunge them into deep, bubbling oil.

There are two here: a round potato-based affair with a lovely old-fashioned, parsley-freckled sauce and a new recipe for hot crab and harissa balls that I find deeply addictive.

## Dill and haddock fishcakes, parsley sauce

*Makes 16, enough for 4 people*

| | |
|---|---|
| potatoes  500g, floury and white-fleshed | black peppercorns  8 |
| haddock or cod fillet  500g | dill fronds  20g |
| milk  400ml | breadcrumbs  100g, fine and fresh |
| water  200ml | eggs  2 |
| parsley stalks  6 | olive or groundnut oil  a little to cook |
| bay leaves  3 | |

*For the parsley sauce:*

| | |
|---|---|
| butter  40g | parsley  40g |
| plain flour  40g | double cream  150ml |

Peel the potatoes and cut them into large pieces, lower them into a deep pan of boiling water and let them cook for 20–25 minutes. They are done when they are tender enough to pierce effortlessly with a skewer. Drain the potatoes and leave for 5 minutes.

Put the fish into a pan, pour in the milk and water and add the parsley, bay leaves and peppercorns. Bring the liquid to the boil, lower the heat and leave to simmer for 10 minutes, or until the fish is lightly cooked. You should be able to pull the flakes apart with relative ease. Set the fish aside.

Mash the potato. It should be smooth but not gluey. Finely chop the dill and add to the potato. Remove the fish from the milk, break into large flakes, then combine lightly with the potato. Take care not to crush the fish.

Roll the fish and potato mixture into sixteen balls of approximately equal size, place on a tray and refrigerate for half an hour.

Melt the butter in a medium-sized saucepan, add the flour and stir together, cooking lightly over a moderate heat for 4–5 minutes, stirring almost constantly. Pour in the reserved milk from cooking the fish, discarding the aromatics as you go. Bring to the boil, then lower the heat, stirring until you have a smooth sauce.

Chop the parsley. Pour in the cream, add the parsley and correct the seasoning. Cover to stop a skin forming and set aside.

Scatter the breadcrumbs on a plate. Break the eggs into a small mixing bowl and beat lightly. Remove the fishcakes from the fridge and drop them, one at time, first into the beaten egg and then the breadcrumbs. Place the crumbed balls on a tray. Warm a shallow layer of oil in a non-stick frying pan, add the cakes without crowding the pan and let them colour evenly, moving them around the pan as necessary. Remove, drain briefly on kitchen paper and serve with the parsley sauce.

# Crab and harissa croquettes

If I have time, I will often prepare a crab myself, cracking the shell and tugging out the flesh with a skewer. It's a deliciously messy job for a Saturday morning. That said, for fritters and these golden-shelled croquettes, it is worth considering the ready-picked fresh crab sold in tubs. I suggest the crisp panko crumbs too, available in supermarkets and Japanese shops, for their ease and lightness. You can use fresh breadcrumbs, dried in the oven until crisp, if you prefer.

*Serves 4*

white crab meat  450g

panko crumbs  125g

spring onions  3

parsley leaves  7g (a handful)

coriander leaves  7g (a handful)

eggs  2

grain mustard  1 tablespoon

harissa  2 teaspoons

mayonnaise  120g

You will also need oil for deep-frying and lemons or limes to serve.

Put the crab and panko crumbs into a large mixing bowl. Trim and finely slice the spring onions, then chop the parsley and coriander leaves. Add all three to the crab and mix gently.

In a second bowl, break the eggs and beat lightly to mix yolks and whites, then blend in the mustard, harissa and mayonnaise. Stir into the crab, gently combining crab, crumbs and seasoning.

Shape the crab mixture into twenty balls, each weighing approximately 45g, rolling them lightly in your hands, floured if necessary. Let the balls settle for 20 minutes in the fridge.

Pour enough oil into a pan in which to deep-fry the croquettes and heat to 180°C on a kitchen thermometer. Place one of the croquettes on a draining spoon and lower into the oil – it should crackle immediately – followed by five or more of the others, taking care not to crowd the pan.

Keep an eye on the heat – you need it to remain fairly static. Fry the croquettes for 2–3 minutes until golden, lift out and drain on kitchen paper, then repeat with further batches until the mixture is finished. Serve hot, with halves of lemon or lime.

Crab and harissa croquettes

# Meat feast

Sometimes, you want to feast. I don't mean roasting a pig on a spit. It simply means you want to pass a piled-up platter of food around the table, tear at your dinner with your hands, suck bones and snap crackling. You want guests at your side, armed with tales and scandal, and everyone to have had slightly too much to drink. Feasting is about how you eat as much as it is about what is on your plate. It is rarely about greed or ostentatiousness, large numbers or outrageous behaviour (though it certainly can be) but is about unbridled generosity and sense of spirit.

There are feasts I particularly relish, from a cheap and sticky tangle of chicken wings to a messy orgy of pork bones and spicy sauce. (For me, pork will always be the ultimate feasting meat.) In my own collection there are feasts of meatballs, ribs, wings, cheeks and a leg of roast lamb. There is a duck dinner simmering. These are by no means vast meals for twelve or more; instead, they live up to their name simply with the bonhomie they bring to the table. They all celebrate meat, its blood, fat and bones. And so they should. (There are vegetarian and vegan feasts elsewhere in this collection.)

The carnivore's feast need not be about money. (The cheapest involves little more than a big bag of chicken wings or a dish of well-seasoned meatballs or a platter of sticky ribs.) The rule is only that it must be served in copious amounts, an untidy muddle of flesh and bones, meat juices, tracklements and sympathetic accompaniments. If there are to be side dishes of roast potatoes or noodles, pickles and mustards, then we should bring them all to the table at once. A plethora, a cornucopia of good things.

If such a dinner is to live up to its name, then it should probably be as much of a hands-on event as possible. Nothing should arrive at the table plated, but instead offered in our largest dishes and platters. This is the sort of event where diners get messy, where a meal is enjoyed with a certain abandon, with food passed around and across the table. The moment when the table comes joyously to life.

The cheapest meat feast of all – a mass of chicken wings and hot sauce – is one of my favourites. If you can find a butcher who doesn't trim his wing tips – the bony points at the very end of the wing – then go for them. They are the best bit, but sadly – or perhaps that should say inevitably – removed by the supermarkets. The pointed tips caramelise in the heat of the oven, turning to toffee. Their extremities may even catch a little – chewy, charred, chilli-hot bones – few things can be quite so delicious.

The unspoken rule with chicken wings is that there must be plenty. (And in the unlikely event of making too many, they are a thoroughly good thing to find, cold, in your fridge the next day.) I use a large, wide roasting tin so the heat can properly get at each wing. Overlapping, they will fail to toast satisfyingly. No one wants a pallid wing. You will need no knives or forks, only something on which to wipe your fingers.

## The chicken wing feast

If you are scaling up to feed a crowd, then increase the amount of chillies and gochujang with caution. If you are doubling you are unlikely to need 8 tablespoons of the chilli paste, but probably only about 6. Taste as you go.

*Serves 4*

| | |
|---|---|
| chicken wings, large, plump, tips on  1.5kg | garlic  4 cloves |
| olive oil  4 tablespoons | small tomatoes  500g |
| thyme  6 bushy sprigs | red chillies, hot  3 |
| | gochujang  3–4 tablespoons |

Set the oven at 200°C. Put the chicken wings in a roasting tin – I use a high-sided baking sheet measuring 30cm × 40cm – pour over the olive oil and season with salt and black pepper. Pull the leaves from the thyme and scatter over the chicken, then tuck the whole, unpeeled garlic cloves amongst them. Turn the wings over with your hands so they are nicely dressed with the oil and seasonings, then bake for 45 minutes or till deep gold in colour and crisp.

Lift the chicken out of the roasting tin and keep warm. Squeeze the soft garlic cloves from their skins into the roasting tin, then add the tomatoes,

The chicken wing feast

halving them as you go. Roughly chop a red chilli and stir in, then place the tin over a moderate heat and leave to bubble for 5 minutes, adding a little more oil if necessary, until the tomatoes are starting to soften.

Stir a tablespoon of gochujang into the tomatoes with a wooden spatula, then pour in 150ml of boiling water, scraping at the surface of the roasting tin as you go. Just as the tomatoes are starting to soften and the juices are bubbling, crush them roughly with a potato masher, then return the wings to the pan, check the seasoning, continue cooking for a couple of minutes and serve.

# The small family feast

Slowly does it. In a perfect world, I would make this a day before I needed it, leaving it to mellow overnight in its pan. (Ragù is always better for a night's sleep.) But even ladled onto pasta or soft polenta the day it is made, this is a splendid alternative to the traditional minced beef ragù. The soul of a ragù is in the browning of the meat and onion. Take your time when softening both – the onions need to be a deep golden brown, glossy to the eye and sticky to the touch before you add the rest of the ingredients.

## Sausages and sauce

*Serves 4*

olive oil  4 tablespoons
thick Italian sausages  8 (850g)
red wine  250ml
onions  3, medium
garlic  4 cloves

thyme  4 bushy sprigs
rosemary  4 bushy sprigs
bay leaves  3
fennel seeds  1 teaspoon
plum tomatoes  2 × 400g tins

*For the polenta:*
water  500ml
milk  500ml
fine, quick-cooking polenta  125g

double cream  100ml
butter  50g
Parmesan  50g, grated

Sausages and sauce

Warm 2 tablespoons of the olive oil in a large frying pan over a moderate heat, tear the sausages into small pieces and add to the oil. Leave to brown and lightly crisp, turning from time to time. The crucial point here is to let each piece of sausage meat brown before you move it, so you encourage a build-up of sticky (and very tasty) goo on the bottom of the pan. Lift the sausage meat out into a bowl, turn up the heat under the pan, then pour in the red wine. As the wine starts to bubble, scrape away at the bottom of the pan with a wooden spatula – stirring the sticky goo from the sausages into the wine. After a couple of minutes of bubbling, remove from the heat.

Peel and roughly chop the onions. Warm the remaining oil in a large, deep-sided saucepan or enamelled cast-iron casserole. Keeping the heat no more than moderately high, let the onions cook till translucent and starting to soften, stirring regularly. As they start to turn pale gold, peel, finely slice and add the garlic. Add the thyme and rosemary sprigs, the bay leaves and fennel seeds. Grind in a little black pepper, lower the heat and continue cooking till the onions are pale brown and very soft. Don't hurry this. You should be able to crush them easily between finger and thumb.

Stir in the sausage meat and the red wine, then add the tomatoes and their juice and bring to the boil. Lower the heat to a very low simmer – the liquid should blip and bubble lazily. Partially cover with a lid and leave to cook for a good hour to 75 minutes. The occasional stir will stop it sticking to the pan. Should the liquid level drop, add a little water or stock.

For the polenta: put half a litre each of water and milk on to boil in a deep, high-sided pan. As it boils rain in the polenta. Season very generously with salt and bring to the boil. Warm the double cream in a small pan. As the polenta thickens, pour in the warmed double cream, add the butter, then stir in the grated Parmesan.

# A humble feast

My gran's house, 1964. Coal dust from the open fires, the freezing-cold outside loo and the slow and peaceful bubble of a ham cooking on the black leaded kitchen range. Even now, half a century later, I think of her whenever I boil a piece of ham, its fat slowly turning to quivering jelly, the meat puttering away in an aromatic bath of water with onion and carrot, bay leaves and peppercorns – I'm pretty sure she popped a clove or three in there too. She may not have had a bean but she certainly kept a spice rack. It's a favourite dinner I cook all too rarely, despite every mouthful coming with deep affection and a ladle's worth of memories.

My gran, Lily was her name, served her ham in thin slices with some of its broth and, always, a dish of pickled beetroot. Not a cheap cut of meat, but good value. Which is probably what she needed as a working single mother of five children. I offer my recipe in a similar way, but with a tangle of pickled cabbage whose crunchy, sweet-sour addition I prefer to her beloved beetroot, and a bowl of fried Jerusalem artichokes, first steamed for softness then fried with parsley and lemon to crisp the edges. I can't imagine my gran ever saw (or heard) a Jerusalem artichoke, but they do seem to have something of an affinity with ham.

Neither would she have upended a bottle of cider into the poaching liquid, but it's something I do regularly and sometimes include an apple too. Both sweeten the cooking liquor, which thankfully is no longer salty as it was in years gone by. (The days of soaking your ham for twenty-four hours before cooking it are, it seems, over.) I always add a ladle of it – scented with juniper, onion and bay – to each plate.

# Ham with juniper and cider

I buy a piece of unsmoked ham, about 1kg in weight, tied and ready for the pot. It feeds four but leaves little for later, so it might be worth buying a bigger piece and increasing the cooking time accordingly.

*Serves 4*

a piece of boiling ham  1kg
onion  1, large
apples  2, medium
carrots  4, small
celery  1 stick

parsley stalks  a handful
bay leaves  3
black peppercorns  8
juniper berries  6
cider, still  1 litre

Place the ham in a large, deep saucepan. Peel and halve the onion, slice the apples in half, trim and scrub the carrots, cut the celery in half and add to the pan. Add the parsley stalks, bay leaves, black peppercorns and juniper berries, then pour in the cider and a litre of water. The ham may not be entirely submerged in liquid – no matter – it will partially cook in its own steam, and you can turn it over during cooking.

Bring the ham to the boil, then lower the heat to a gentle simmer, partially cover with a lid and leave to cook for 1 hour. Turn the ham halfway through cooking. Remove from the heat and set aside to rest for 10–15 minutes while you fry the artichokes.

Remove the ham from its liquor and slice thinly. Serve with the artichokes below and the red cabbage and spoonfuls of its own apple-scented cooking liquor.

Ham with juniper and cider

# Artichokes with lemon and parsley

*Serves 4*

Jerusalem artichokes  500g
butter  30g
olive oil  2 tablespoons

parsley leaves  25g
  (a good handful)
a lemon

Peel the artichokes as best you can (they are knobbly and not the easiest of things to peel) then place them in a steamer basket or colander over a pan of hot water, cover tightly with a lid and steam for 10-15 minutes till tender to the point of a knife. Remove from the heat and halve each artichoke lengthways.

Warm the butter and oil in a shallow pan over a moderate heat. As it starts to bubble, add the artichokes, cut side down, and leave for 5-6 minutes to brown lightly. Meanwhile, chop the parsley and finely grate the lemon zest. Turn the artichokes onto their backs, let them cook for a few minutes longer, then add the parsley and lemon, and a grinding of salt and black pepper.

# Pickled red cabbage and ginger

This makes more than you will need for the ham, but it feels pointless making a small quantity when it is so useful to have around. The glowing accompaniment comes out in our house with everything from bread and cheese to sushi. While this recipe has the traditional additions of mustard seeds and allspice, I introduce an element of heat with finely sliced ginger root.

*Makes 2 × 750ml jars*

cider vinegar  480ml
malt vinegar  180ml
water  480ml
black peppercorns  15
allspice berries  12
mustard seeds  2 teaspoons

chilli flakes  half a teaspoon
sugar  2 tablespoons
sea salt flakes  2 tablespoons
ginger  65g
shallots  4, small
red cabbage  600g

Sterilize your storage jars. Bring the kettle to the boil, then pour into the storage jars and leave for 2 minutes before carefully emptying.

Put the cider and malt vinegars, water, peppercorns, allspice, mustard seeds, chilli flakes, sugar and salt into a stainless-steel saucepan and bring to the boil. Peel and finely slice the ginger (you should almost be able to see through it) and the shallots, then add them to the pan and boil for 2 minutes.

Shred the red cabbage – I like mine roughly the width of a pencil, but some like their cabbage sliced more finely – and place it in a heatproof mixing bowl. Pour the hot pickling liquor over the vegetables, then toss everything together. Ladle into the storage jars, seal and allow to cool. They will keep for several weeks in the fridge.

# A feast of bones, beans and broth

Bones are synonymous with feasting. All that goodness and savour, the way their presence turns a meal into something altogether more memorable – a celebration. Whether it is a twee little lamb cutlet or a chunky beef rib, I will always pick them up, chew and suck, winkling the last little nuggets and meat juices from every crack and crevice.

When I buy pork steaks, I ask for them to be cut through the leg, so they have a central bone to send succulence through the cooking liquor. But thick pork rib steaks are just as suitable and sometimes easier to track down. The presence of a deeply flavoured liquor, meat juices only a step away from soup, is feast enough. The very presence of fork, knife and spoon will turn a single dish into a feast. The broth first, then the meat and stock-saturated beans and then, lastly, the bones.

Pork with sherry and Judión beans

# Pork with sherry and Judión beans

You will need a wide, deep pan for this. Butter beans will work here too.

*Serves 3*

| | |
|---|---|
| onions 4, smallish | chicken stock 1 litre |
| olive oil 3 tablespoons | rosemary 4 sprigs |
| pork rib chops 4 × 250g, | Judión beans 1 × 400g jar |
|    thick and on the bone |    (or butter beans) |
| Oloroso sherry 200ml | |

*To finish:*

| | |
|---|---|
| blanched almonds 40g | lemon 1 |
| garlic 2 cloves, chopped | parsley, finely chopped |
| olive oil 2 tablespoons |    6 tablespoons |

Peel the onions and cut them in half. Warm the olive oil in a large casserole, then add the onions and cook over a moderate heat until their cut sides are deep golden brown. Remove the onions and set aside.

Season the pork with salt and pepper, then brown on all sides in the oil left in the onion pan. (Add a little more oil if necessary.) Take your time and brown the meat evenly. Take the pork out of the pan. Pour the sherry into the pan, scrape at the stickings and stir them into the sherry. Let the liquid reduce by half.

Return the pork and onions to the pan, then add the stock and bring to the boil. Add the rosemary, cover with a lid and leave over a low heat for 90 minutes. Drain the beans and rinse, then add to the casserole. Remove the lid and simmer for a further 30 minutes.

Chop the almonds finely and toast them in a dry, shallow pan, then add the chopped garlic and olive oil. When the garlic is golden, finely grate the lemon zest, add to the finely chopped parsley with the garlic and transfer to a bowl. Scatter over the pork and serve.

The most useful recipes for feasting, especially those of an impromptu variety, are surely those you can easily 'scale up'. (Not all recipes can easily be doubled, trebled or quadrupled as we please.) Most of the recipes in this chapter work as dinner for two or, should you wish, a whole lot more. This way with meatballs is useful for when our dinner for four suddenly becomes supper for twenty.

# A feast for four or forty

You can buy plain, unseasoned sausage meat and season it yourself, but I prefer to use my favourite butcher's sausages - a plump, peppery breakfast recipe - and take the meat out of its skins myself. It's a straightforward enough job. If you prefer to use loose sausage meat, then I suggest you add a little interest with plenty of black pepper and perhaps some fennel seeds or ground juniper.

## Sausage and bacon frikadelle, onion and mustard

*Serves 4*

*For the frikadelle:*

pork sausages, herby,
   well-seasoned 450g
smoked streaky bacon 150g

parsley, chopped 2 teaspoons
olive oil 2 tablespoons

*For the sauce:*

onions 400g
olive oil 3 tablespoons
coriander seeds 1 teaspoon
juniper berries 6

bay leaves 2
grain mustard 1 tablespoon
double cream 100ml

*For the cabbage:*

red cabbage 500g
olive oil 2 tablespoons
cloves 4

cider vinegar 4 tablespoons
redcurrant jelly 2 tablespoons

Sausage and bacon frikadelle, onion and mustard

Slit the sausage skins and remove the meat. Put the meat into a mixing bowl and discard the skins. Finely dice the bacon and add to the sausage meat, then mix in the parsley and check the seasoning.

Roll the mixture into table-tennis sized balls, each weighing roughly 45g. You should have twelve to sixteen balls. Set them apart on a baking sheet and refrigerate for 15 minutes.

Warm the olive oil in a frying pan over a moderate heat, add the frikadelle and let them brown appetisingly, turning them over from time to time. Transfer to a baking dish or roasting tin and keep the frying pan for the sauce. Set the oven at 200°C.

Peel and finely slice the onions. Warm the olive oil in the pan in which you fried the frikadelle and add the onions. Lower the heat, partially cover them with a lid and let them cook for 15–20 minutes until soft and pale gold. Add the coriander seeds, juniper berries and bay leaves. An occasional stir will help the onions to cook evenly. Put the frikadelle in the oven and bake for 15 minutes until cooked right through. (If you need to keep them warm while you finish the dish, switch off the oven, cover them with a piece of foil and leave them be.)

Prepare the cabbage. Cut the cabbage in half and shred finely. Heat the olive oil in a deep saucepan or casserole, add the cabbage and cloves and cover with a lid. Continue cooking for 5 minutes, giving it the occasional stir, then add the vinegar and replace the lid. Leave to cook for 2 minutes, then stir in the fruit jelly and add a little salt and black pepper. The cabbage will soften in the steam.

Stir the mustard and cream into the onions and let it bubble briefly, adding a little salt and a few grinds of pepper. Transfer the cabbage to a serving bowl, put the frikadelle on top, then spoon over the onion sauce and serve.

# A feast of ribs – a bone on which to chew

Dinner becomes a feast once we get to lick our fingers. The sucking of digits, hot with spice and sticky with sauce, is an essential part of such a meal. The messier my dinner guests end up, the happier I am.

Few dishes beg to be eaten, or at least finished, with our fingers like that of a plate of ribs. Beef or pork, barbecued or roasted, sticky with honey or molasses, what matters is that you cannot do them justice with knife and fork.

My most memorable feasts have involved ribs. Mostly pork and almost always with a sauce that was both sticky and hot. The point of such seasoning is that the honey or treacle sticks to your lips; the chilli makes them tingle and smart.

## Pork ribs with kimchi and cucumber

*Serves 4*

fennel seeds  1 tablespoon
bay leaves  3
black peppercorns  12
a rack of pork ribs,
   skin removed  1kg

date syrup  2 tablespoons
pomegranate molasses
   2 tablespoons

*For the kimchi slaw:*
cucumber  150g
radishes  250g

kimchi  250g

Put the kettle on. Set the oven at 160°C. Lightly crush the fennel seeds with a pestle and mortar and put them in a roasting tin with the bay leaves and peppercorns. Pour enough freshly boiled water into the tin to come halfway up the sides and place a metal rack for the pork to sit on over the roasting tin.

Pork ribs

Season the ribs with salt, then place on the rack and cover the tin and pork tightly with foil. Place in the oven and bake for 2½ hours until the meat is tender (it should pull easily from its bones).

For the kimchi slaw, peel the cucumber and cut into slim matchstick-sized pieces. Slice the radishes into thin rounds, then add both to the kimchi and set aside for at least an hour.

Mix the date syrup and pomegranate molasses. Remove the roasting tin from the oven, take off the foil, lift off the rack and pour away the water. Turn the oven up to 220°C. Line the roasting tin with foil, then replace the rack and pork in the tin and brush the meat generously with the syrup.

Return the meat to the oven, uncovered, and bake for about 10 minutes, then brush it – again generously – with more of the syrup. Return to the oven for a further 10 minutes or until the meat is dark, sticky and glossy. (I sometimes brush it and put it back a third time.) Remove the meat from the tin and leave to rest for 10 minutes before cutting into the ribs and serving with the slaw.

# The duck feast

Sometimes, a dinner becomes special simply because everything comes together so perfectly. Such as when crisp-skinned duck legs share a plate with plump ivory beans and pink, pickled onions as sharp as a surgeon's knife. Crisp yet soft, sweet yet teasingly sharp, this duck-'n'-beans dinner is a meal, both frugal and luxurious, where everything seems in harmony.

The cannellini beans, cooked from dried, plumped up to the size of sugared almonds in a simple stock with shallot, celery and bay leaves. Drained, then baked in the same roasting tin as the duck and its fat, the dish moistened with a ladle of the beans' milky, aromatic cooking liquor. The beans, their insides swollen with stock and fat, will crisp up a little in the roasting tin.

Nudging against the duck comes a fresh, acid-sweet pickle of carrots, red onion and watermelon radish. (You could use mooli or even French breakfast radish.) You can mop up the juice from your plates – a tantalising puddle of warm duck fat, cider vinegar, rosemary and salt – with winter leaves of deep red and mottled pink, dressing them with a mustard vinaigrette.

Duck with cannellini

# Duck with cannellini

I use legs because their skin crisps more satisfyingly than that of the breasts and their flesh is infinitely more succulent and, curiously, cheaper. If they come wrapped in plastic, as is often the case, remove it, dry the skin with kitchen paper and let them come to room temperature before cooking. They will be all the crisper for it.

*Serves 4*

*For the beans:*
dried cannellini beans  500g
celery  1 stick
thyme  6 sprigs

black peppercorns  8
bay leaves  4
shallot  1, large

*For the duck:*
olive oil  120ml
garlic  7 cloves
black peppercorns  10

duck legs  4
rosemary  8 sprigs

Soak the dried beans in a bowl of deep, cold water overnight. The following day, drain the beans, put them into a large, deep saucepan and cover them with water. Add the celery stick, broken in half, the thyme, peppercorns, bay and the shallot, halved. Bring to the boil, lower the heat and partially cover with a lid. Leave the beans to simmer for 45 minutes to 1 hour or until they are tender enough to crush between finger and thumb.

For the duck, first season the olive oil with salt and pepper. Peel the garlic and put three of the cloves in a mortar or wooden bowl with a good pinch of sea salt and the peppercorns. Smash the garlic, salt and peppercorns to a paste with a pestle or the end of a rolling pin, then stir in the olive oil. Set the oven at 200°C.

Rub the duck legs all over with the seasoned oil and set aside in a cool place for half an hour. Drain the beans, reserving a good ladleful of the cooking liquor. Brown the duck legs in a roasting tin over a moderate heat, turning them now and again, until each side is golden brown. Turn the legs plump side up.

Spoon the drained beans around the duck legs, tuck in the rosemary sprigs and the reserved garlic cloves, then pour in the reserved ladleful of bean cooking liquor.

Bake the duck for about 45–50 minutes, turning the beans over once during cooking. Serve the duck and beans with the pickle below.

## Mixed vegetable pickle

I have been making these vivid pink pickles once a week, eating them with chalky white goat's cheese, tossing them into leafy salads and serving them alongside grilled pork chops. The pickling liquor makes a cracking base for a dressing with a little groundnut oil and a dash of sesame. I splash the pink juice over steamed rice, too. The pickles will keep, crisp and bright, in a covered bowl or lidded glass jar, for several days.

*Serves 4*

small gherkins (cornichons) 50g
gherkin pickling liquor 150ml
carrots 150g
red onions 2, medium
watermelon radish 1, medium
cider vinegar 150ml

white wine vinegar 125ml
black peppercorns 15
white peppercorns half
  a teaspoon
sea salt 1 teaspoon
sugar half a teaspoon

Cut the cornichons in half lengthways, reserving 150ml of the pickling liquor from the jar. Peel the carrots, slice them very thinly, then add them to the cornichons. Peel the red onions, then slice into very thin rounds. Separate the rings and add to the carrots.

Peel and very finely slice the radish, then cut each slice into quarters. Add to the carrots and onions and set aside.

Put the reserved pickling liquor, cider and wine vinegars, black and white peppercorns, the salt and sugar into a small stainless-steel saucepan and bring to the boil. Pour over the sliced vegetables and cover with a plate. Refrigerate for 4 hours, preferably overnight.

# A celebration of meatballs

There is much happiness to be had from a plate of meatballs, a long-simmered sauce and a mound of fluffy mash. We need to rest homemade meatballs in the fridge before we attempt to cook them, as we should rissoles, patties and other little cakes that seem destined to fall apart in the pan. And once they are in the pan, which should be hot and shallow and with enough patina to prevent anything sticking, it is crucial not to tinker, prod and poke.

Leave them be, sizzling merrily, giving them time to form the essential sticky crust that will help them hold together. Then, as you turn them to brown the other side, hold the meatballs in place on the palette knife with your finger and flip them over quickly before they have time to even consider falling apart.

You could, I suppose, introduce a binder, such as beaten egg yolk, to hold the minced meat or fish together, but that is too often detectable in the finished dish, so a good half-hour's rest in the fridge and a small amount of care during the initial browning is probably a better idea. I mention this only because it is a question I am often asked as someone surveys their meatballs collapsing before their eyes. It is often a sign that the mince was too coarse – but is better than the sort of meatball you could throw at a wall.

Test the consistency of the mixture by squeezing a lump of meat and aromatics together in your hand and rolling it into a ball. It should just hold together when you put it on the table. If it doesn't, you need a finer mince.

## Braised pork meatballs with rib ragù sauce

Use any leftover sauce for pasta the next day. You will need a very large pan for this. If you serve this with mashed parsnip or swede, work on about 1.2kg of roots and a good knob of butter.

Braised pork meatballs with rib ragù sauce

*Serves 4*

| | |
|---|---|
| olive oil  3 tablespoons, plus a little extra | garlic  2 cloves |
| small pork ribs (baby back)  6 (about 500g) | thyme  8 sprigs |
| | chestnut mushrooms  300g |
| | flour  3 tablespoons |
| onions  450g | chicken stock  1.5 litres |
| carrots  450g | smoked streaky bacon  400g |
| celery  200g | minced pork  900g |

Warm the 3 tablespoons of olive oil in a large, deep casserole, add the pork ribs and brown them on all sides, remove from the pan and set aside. Peel, halve and roughly chop the onions. Scrub the carrots, cut into small dice, then add to the onions. You may need to add a little more oil. Chop the celery into similar-sized pieces. Peel and finely slice the garlic. Pull the leaves from the thyme sprigs and chop. Add the vegetables to the pan, stir in half the thyme and cook for about 15 minutes over a moderate heat, stirring in any meat juices from the ribs as you go. Set the oven at 180°C.

Finely slice the mushrooms, add to the vegetables and cook for a couple of minutes. Add the flour, stir and let it cook for a couple of minutes then pour in the stock and season with salt and black pepper. When the sauce has come to the boil, return the ribs to the pan, cover with a lid and place in the oven. Leave for an hour, stirring occasionally.

Cut the bacon into small pieces and fry till crisp. Add the minced pork to the reserved thyme then add the bacon and season with salt and pepper. Combine the ingredients and roll into twelve large balls, flattening the top. Refrigerate for a minimum of 30 minutes. (If you fail to do this, they will fall apart.)

Warm a little more oil in the pan in which you cooked the bacon, add the chilled meatballs and lightly brown them all over.

Remove the sauce from the oven and pull the ribs to pieces with a couple of forks. Discard the bones. The meat and bones should pull apart easily. Lower the browned meatballs into the sauce, cover and return to the oven for 35 minutes. Serve the meatballs with copious amounts of the sauce and, if you like, mashed swede, parsnip or potato.

# The leg of lamb dinner

When I was a kid, roast lamb – leg or shoulder – was a feast. A once-a-month celebration of sizzling fat and rose-pink meat, clear, jewel-bright roasting juices and, it being the 1960s, a short, fat jug of mint sauce. Lamb has long been the food of celebration. I have seen whole animals cooked on a spit, popping and crackling over the flames, in the Middle East, Greece and Morocco. The copious fat, especially on an older animal, lends much smoke to the event, the smell of roasting meat adding an air of anticipation and of revelry ahead.

Now that less meat is eaten, a roast leg or shoulder of lamb arrives at the table to more delight than ever. I roasted maybe two legs and three shoulders of lamb during the whole of last year. They became rare and much thought-about events – as I feel meat-eating should be. And as much as the traditional seasonings of garlic and rosemary hit the spot, I do think the flavours of the Middle East – za'atar, mint, cumin and pomegranate – possess an exceptional affinity with this meat. I will find any excuse to roast a potato, but it is now the grains of the Middle East – the smoked wheat, couscous and millets – that I want to soak up the roasting juices.

## Roast lamb with za'atar and broad bean mograbiah

There is a moment, when you stir the hot juices from the roast into the dill- and bean-flecked grain, that make this one of my favourite ways to eat lamb. Its success will depend mostly on whether the meat is cooked to your liking and my timing is for a rare-ish finish. Tweak the timings to suit your own taste. If you have any left over, the meat can be torn into short pieces and folded through the couscous for lunch.

*Serves 6*

garlic  3 cloves
olive oil  4 tablespoons
za'atar  3 tablespoons

lemons  the juice of 2
small leg of lamb  1.5kg

Roast lamb with za'atar and broad bean mograbiah

*For the mograbiah:*
mograbiah  300g
broad beans  300g
olive oil  4 tablespoons

radishes  100g, sliced into rounds
dill  a handful

Peel the garlic cloves and crush in a blender or a mortar with a little salt and the olive oil and za'atar, then blend in the lemon juice. Place the lamb in a roasting tin and pierce it all over with a stainless-steel skewer. Spoon half of the marinade over the lamb, then set aside for an hour or two.

Set the oven at 180°C. Roast the lamb in the oven for about 1 hour 15 minutes to 1 hour 30 minutes depending on how rare you like your meat. Baste three or four times during cooking. Halfway through the cooking time pour over the remaining marinade.

Boil the mograbiah in lightly salted water for 20 minutes then drain. Boil the broad beans in salted water for 8–10 minutes depending on their size, then drain them and briefly refresh under cold running water. Pop the beans from their papery skins with your thumb and forefinger. Fold the beans and olive oil through the mograbiah. Thinly slice the radishes, chop the dill, then fold into the salad.

Remove the lamb from the oven and leave to rest for 20 minutes before carving and serving with the broad bean mograbiah.

Ten years ago, James introduced me to a recipe that has become, in our house, the most hungrily anticipated feast of all. Fideuà, a Valencian pasta dish, is cooked in the style of a paella, using a mixture of shellfish and tiny macaroni-type pasta. (Any very fine tubular pasta will work, such as stortini bucati, if you can get it.) Good though this mixture of pasta, tomatoes, clams and mussels is, the real celebration is turning a spoonful over to reveal the gloriously smoky, sticky crust that has formed underneath. This essential detail – it feels like winning a prize – will only form if we resist the temptation to fiddle, to poke and stir. It is that, as much as the seafood itself, that is the true feast.

James's fideuà – a feast of fish

# James's fideuà – a feast of fish

*Serves 4*

onion 1, medium
squid 2, cleaned
olive oil 3 tablespoons
garlic 4 cloves
tomatoes 600g
sweet smoked paprika
  2 tablespoons
saffron a generous pinch
  (optional)

pasta, small, macaroni-type
  such as stortini bucati 500g
chicken or fish stock 1 litre
large prawns, uncooked 12
clams 250g
mussels 12

Peel the onion and cut into small dice. Remove the tentacles from one of the squid. Cut the body sac into small dice and set aside. Cut the second squid into wide strips, removing and reserving the tentacles as you go.

Place a shallow pan over a moderate heat and pour in 2 tablespoons of the olive oil. When the oil is hot, add the diced squid and cook quickly, letting it sizzle and colour lightly on both sides.

Peel the garlic and slice each clove very finely, then add to the pan, still set over a moderate heat, together with a little more oil if needed. Chop the tomatoes, fairly finely, add them and all their juice to the pan, and cook for 2 minutes. Stir in the paprika, saffron (if using) and pasta. Let the pasta toast for a minute, then pour on the stock, season with salt, bring to the boil and leave to cook for 8 minutes, or until two-thirds of the liquid has evaporated. At this point do not stir again until a fine crust has formed on the base.

While the pasta cooks, warm the remaining tablespoon of oil in a shallow pan, add the reserved raw squid and the prawns and cook for 2 minutes, till lightly browned. Remove immediately.

Place the clams and mussels and the squid and prawns over the surface of the pasta, then make a loose dome of kitchen foil over the pan and leave everything to steam for 2–3 minutes, till the mussels and clams have opened. Serve immediately.

# Sometimes, you just want pie

A pie is easy to fall in love with. The golden crust, the soft and giving filling, the way the pastry and its contents converge on the plate. Few forkfuls of food are more delicious than the one that marries luscious juices with a pastry crust. I say pastry, but it could just as easily be potato mashed into buttery clouds or sliced like golden coins and arranged like tiles on a roof. And when I say potato, of course, I can also mean mashed pumpkin, a latticework of grated carrot and parsnip or the spice-speckled rice of a biryani.

Your pie may be of rabbit or chicken, or broccoli or salmon. It may be of cheese or of ham or haddock and mussels. What matters is that the crust and filling are as one. The pie whose pastry is perched on the filling like a hat is the pie from hell. The two must meet and merge. The filling needs to soak into the pastry here and there. A layer of puff or shortcrust sodden with meat juices is a thoroughly splendid affair. I remain unconvinced that the pastry underneath the filling needs to be crisp as it does in a tart. Soggy means saturated and that can be a very good thing.

It is difficult to know where to start this particular story. You see, dear reader, there have been many, many pies. From the meat pie my father would take from the oven on a Friday evening, its crown of puff pastry risen above the lumps of meat and dark Fray Bentos gravy, to the mother of all apple pies I make in a cake tin, its sides so deep you can cut it like a cake (*Tender, Volume II*).

As a child I loved the smooth toppings. The pillow-soft potato top of the shepherd's pies that came in aluminium trays at school or in foil dishes from the supermarket. Fifty years later, like Murray Mints and wine gums, I am craving them again. Soothing pies. No knife needed.

Sometimes I would come home from school to find a chicken pie in the Aga. The shallow disc of pastry and pale gravy was not homemade, but a favourite nevertheless. I make a version of it to this day. There is something deeply pleasing about chicken gravy and shortcrust pastry. It is a recipe I go to town on, roasting the chicken first, taking my time with a slowly stirred sauce.

Proper cooking. As so often with such recipes, there is more to it than what is on the plate. Such a pie comes with a side order of fond memories.

As much as I admire the soft thud of steak and kidney pudding sliding slowly from its crackle-glazed pudding basin, it is too much stodge, even for the most icy of days. I have tried to remember why I have such a soft spot for something I have made only once or twice. Perhaps it is just because my last attempt stood up, textbook-style, when I expected it to collapse.

All the pies I make today are modern interpretations of old classics. A little lighter, the filling spicier or softer in texture. But all well known. Every pie I eat now has evolved from a pie of my childhood, and if the fillings are new, they are not that new. I'm not sure anyone should get too clever with a pie.

# The pillow pie

My favourite pie to make is the one resembling a small pillow. No tins or pie plates needed, no baking blind, no risk of a soggy bottom. Just a sheet of puff pastry filled, sealed and baked. First came the mushroom version, a sticky mixture of softened onions, crème fraîche and mushrooms wrapped in puff pastry. The recipe appeared in *Appetite*. Later versions included broccoli and Gorgonzola and a heaven-sent carb fest that involved stuffing the pastry with slices of cooked potato, cream and cheese.

As fond as I am of a homemade fish pie, most of them take an entire morning to make. File under faff. I make a simpler version by wrapping smoked mackerel and crème fraîche in puff pastry. One of those straightforward recipes that seems to please all comers, including the cook.

Smoked mackerel pie

# Smoked mackerel pie

I am not sure whether this is a pie or a pasty, or whether such a point even matters. What is important is that you have a fish pie on the table within the hour. Despite the ease of execution, this mixture of smoked fish, cream and pastry remains one of my favourite pastries to eat. I often serve it with a salad of shredded fennel and parsley leaves tossed in lemon juice and olive oil.

*Serves 2, generously*

smoked mackerel  500g
  (prepared, boned weight)
crème fraîche  200ml
grain mustard  2 teaspoons

parsley leaves  a handful
tarragon leaves  1 tablespoon
puff pastry  a 325g sheet
a little beaten egg for glazing

Set the oven at 200°C. Put the mackerel in a bowl, then add the crème fraîche, grain mustard, a little salt and some black pepper. Chop the parsley leaves and the tarragon and add them to the smoked mackerel.

Gently toss the mixture together and set aside. Cut the sheet of puff pastry in half, then roll each into a rectangle about 24cm × 17cm. Place one on a parchment-lined baking sheet, then pile the mackerel on top, shaping it into a shallow block and leaving a couple of centimetres of bare pastry around the edge.

Brush the pastry edge with beaten egg, then lay the second piece of pastry on top. Press the sides to seal, pushing down firmly to prevent any leaks. Brush the top with the remaining beaten egg and score lines across the surface.

Bake for 40 minutes until crisp and golden.

We can get a little more adventurous. A waterlogged autumn day in 2012 and we were in need of a pie whose filling glowed. A pie to brighten and warm a day spent almost entirely sweeping up wet leaves from the garden beds and paths. I had a recipe up my sleeve for a butternut squash pie, savoury yet sweet, a hint of cinnamon, the filling swaddled in crisp and flaky pastry. The butternut filling was steamed till soft, tossed with the ground spice and wrapped in a sheet of puff pastry. We ate the shallow golden pastry with a crisp slaw of red cabbage and sultanas and poured glasses of sparkling cider.

This first of the autumn squash pies was the simplest. Over the years they have taken happily to a little embellishment. Soft cheese, a thread of thyme leaves, dried chilli flakes and a tangle of caramelised onions have at times found their way into the recipe. All of them worthy additions.

The latest incarnation of this recipe brings with it a spike of heat amongst the sweet amber softness of the butternut or pumpkin. The seasoning of ginger, garlic, chillies, turmeric, curry leaves and mustard seeds owes much of its character to dal. The spices, cooked with a little tomato, coat the squash lightly. On the side this time, a bowl of yoghurt into which I stirred mint leaves, finely chopped spring onion and diced cucumber.

## Spiced butternut pie

*Serves 4*

pumpkin or butternut  1.3kg,
   peeled and seeded weight
groundnut or vegetable oil
   5 tablespoons
butter  30g
garlic  2 large cloves
ginger  a 3cm piece
tomatoes  150g

ground turmeric  1 teaspoon
cumin seeds  1 teaspoon
yellow mustard seeds  1 teaspoon
dried chilli flakes  1 teaspoon
curry leaves  10
puff pastry  a 325g sheet
egg  1, lightly beaten

Set the oven at 200°C. Cut the pumpkin or butternut into small pieces, roughly 2cm square. (The shape is immaterial, as they are going to be crushed later, but being an equal size will help them to cook evenly.) Steam for 15–20 minutes, until the flesh is tender enough for a skewer to slide effortlessly through.

Tip the pumpkin pieces into a roasting tin or baking dish, pour over 3 tablespoons of the oil and add the butter in small pieces. Grind over plenty of salt and pepper and toss the pumpkin gently so the pieces are coated with oil. Roast for 40–50 minutes, until the flesh is soft and lightly golden on all sides. Using a fork or potato masher, crush the cooked pumpkin to a rough mash. (Take care not to process to a purée.)

Peel and crush the garlic and peel and grate the ginger. Warm the remaining oil in a medium-sized saucepan, stir in the garlic and ginger and sauté over a moderate heat for a couple of minutes.

Roughly chop the tomatoes and stir into the paste just as it turns gold in colour, then introduce the ground turmeric, cumin, mustard seeds, chilli flakes and curry leaves and a half-teaspoon of salt. Simmer, partially covered by a lid, for about 10 minutes or until the tomatoes have collapsed. If there is any liquid present, turn up the heat and let it evaporate.

Stir the crushed pumpkin into the spice paste, remove from the heat and set aside to cool. (Don't skip this, it needs time to firm up.)

Cut the pastry in half, then roll out each piece to a rectangle measuring roughly 23cm × 35cm. Lay one piece on a parchment-lined baking sheet. Pile the filling on top of the pastry, leaving a 2cm rim of bare pastry around the edge. Brush the edges of the pastry with some of the beaten egg. Lay the second piece of pastry over the top and press firmly around the edges to seal. (You could pinch the pastry together at this point if you wish, or use any trimmings to make some sort of decoration for the top.) Make two or three small slits on the surface. This will prevent the pastry from splitting as it cooks.

Brush the pie all over with more of the beaten egg, then bake for 25–30 minutes, until the pastry is crisp and golden. Leave for 5–10 minutes to settle, then slice and serve.


# The pastry-topped pie


Then there is the sort of pie you spend all day over. Such a day, when the weather is inclement and you have the radio on, is a day well spent. After you have softened the onions and made the sauce and the pastry and done the rolling and the baking, you are left with a sense of quiet contentment. And a lot of washing-up. I love these days, when all that matters is one beautiful dish to put on the table for your friends and your family. A pie to be admired for its deep sides and golden pastry and the fact it hasn't, for once, leaked in the oven.

There is no point in pretending this is anything but serious cooking, proper cooking, the sort of cooking that you wish you could do more often. If only you had the time. I have made pies since I was a kid, though mostly apple or plum or gooseberry. My savoury pie output has been confined to puff pastry pillow pies rather that something moulded in a cake tin. That changed with the success of a deep chicken pie. A smaller, more manageable version is included here, because it is a simply glorious pie, though still not one you can rush off after work. This is a pie to be proud of.

# Chicken and leek pie

The original version of this, made for my column in the *Observer*, had prunes in, an addition that added a treacly richness to the filling. Sadly, I fear their inclusion put some people off, so I have removed them for this collection.

*Serves 4*

*For the filling:*
chicken stock  750ml
chicken thighs  750g,
   skin removed
celery  1 stick, roughly chopped
carrots  4, medium,
   roughly chopped
onion  1, peeled and chopped
olive oil  5 tablespoons

leeks  5, medium
thyme  10 sprigs
plain flour  4 heaped
   tablespoons
egg  1, beaten
fennel seeds  1 teaspoon
   to sprinkle

*For the pastry:*
butter  120g
plain flour  200g

a little iced water

Chicken and leek pie

You will need a springform cake tin 20cm in diameter.

Bring the stock to the boil in a large saucepan. Put the chicken thighs into the stock, lower the heat and let them simmer for 25–30 minutes until tender.

Put the celery, carrots and onion in a large pan with the oil and cook over a moderate heat for 10 minutes, stirring occasionally. Slice the leeks into pieces 2cm thick, then wash well under running water. Add the leeks and thyme sprigs to the other vegetables and cook for 7–10 minutes. Sprinkle over the flour and cook for 2 minutes until all is nicely toasted.

Lift the chicken out of the stock and remove the meat from the bones. Cut each thigh into four pieces.

Pour the stock over the vegetables and bring to the boil, stirring occasionally. Stir in the chicken and let the sauce bubble for a few minutes to the consistency of good thick gravy. Check the seasoning. Remove from the heat and leave to cool.

Meanwhile, for the pastry, cut the butter into small pieces then rub into the flour with your fingertips. You can use a food processor if you prefer. Carefully introduce enough cold water to give a soft but rollable dough (about 3 tablespoons). Shape the pastry into a ball, wrap in parchment and refrigerate for 30 minutes.

Set the oven at 200°C. Place a baking sheet in the oven.

On a floured board, roll two-thirds of the pastry into a disc large enough to line the base and sides of the cake tin with a little overhang. Press the pastry into the tin carefully, taking great care it doesn't tear. There should be absolutely no holes or cracks. Transfer the cooled filling to the tin.

Roll out the remaining pastry to make a lid. Brush the edges of the pastry in the tin with beaten egg, then lower the pastry lid into place and press the edges tightly together to seal. Brush the surface with more egg, scatter with the fennel seeds, pierce a hole in the centre of the lid with the handle of a wooden spoon and bake for about 40 minutes until golden. Remove from the oven and leave to rest for 15 minutes before gently releasing the spring clip of the tin and serving.

# A vegetable pie

My vegetable pie, thick with sliced potatoes and cream, came about in 2020. With one of the highest Covid infection rates in the world, we were locked in our homes, hearing tragic news of the escalating pandemic, worrying for our families, our jobs, our futures. I needed to bring to the table food that would console and delight, soothe and give hope. A plate of food to lift our hearts.

Pie ticked every box. There was a bag of flour left in the larder; butter and vegetables to use up. The local grocer, who had his shelves stripped of pasta and bread, still had cream and garlic. There was thyme in the garden.

I think we all needed pie. Pastry made by hand and teased up the sides of a cake tin. A filling sliced and stirred and piled generously into the pastry case. A single thing to be shared with others like a cake or a pot of tea.

## Spinach and Stichelton pie

By all means use Stilton here, or perhaps a sharp and fruity Cheddar.

*Serves 4*

*For the pastry:*

| | |
|---|---|
| butter  150g | a little iced water |
| plain flour  250g | |

*For the filling:*

| | |
|---|---|
| onions  3, medium | spinach leaves  400g |
| butter  40g | Stichelton, Stilton or Cheddar, |
| thyme leaves  2 teaspoons | a nice fruity, sharp one  250g |
| parsley, chopped  3 tablespoons | a little beaten egg |

You will need a 20cm, loose-bottomed, straight-sided sandwich tin.

Make the pastry: rub the butter, in small pieces, into the flour. (You can do this in seconds using a food processor or do it more slowly by hand.) Stir in

Spinach and Stichelton pie

enough iced water to give a firm dough. Roll into a fat cylinder, wrap in baking parchment and refrigerate for a good 30 minutes.

Peel and thinly slice the onions. Melt the butter in a deep pan, add the onions and let them soften over a low to moderate heat for a good 20 minutes, taking care they barely colour (a little gold amongst the translucency is a good thing, but don't let them brown). When they have been cooking for 10 minutes, add the thyme leaves and chopped parsley, a little salt and some black pepper. When the onions are fully soft, remove them from the heat and allow to cool.

Wash the spinach leaves and, while they are still wet, put them in a saucepan over a moderate heat, cover tightly with a lid, and let them cook in their own steam for 2–3 minutes. Lift the lid and turn them over with kitchen tongs, then cover again and continue steaming for a further minute or two till they are wilted. As soon as the leaves have wilted, but are still bright green, remove them from the heat and plunge into iced water. Wring them out firmly but gently – you don't want to crush them – get as much water as you can out of them otherwise your filling will be wet – then set aside.

Set the oven at 180°C and place a baking sheet in the oven to get hot. (You will place the tart on top of this one – it will help crisp the pastry.) Roll out two-thirds of the pastry and use to line the base and sides of the tin. Make certain there are no tears or cracks.

Coarsely grate the cheese. Put half the onions into the pastry case, add half the spinach and then, sprinkled over the top, half the cheese. Layer in the remaining onions followed by the rest of the spinach and cheese. Roll out the remaining pastry. Brush the edge of the pastry in the pie case with beaten egg, then lower the top into place, trim and press tightly to seal.

Brush the pastry lid with beaten egg, pierce a hole or two in the lid of the pie, then bake for 40–45 minutes till golden. Let the pie settle for 20 minutes or so before carefully removing from the tin and slicing.

# The potato-topped pie

I have heard it said that a pie isn't worthy of the name unless it has pastry on top. I disagree. A cloud of potato is a sublime way to enclose a rich, stew-like mess of seafood, minced lamb with onions and thyme or perhaps chicken in cream sauce. The very outer crust of the potato should be crisp. The potato forked into furrows like a tractor ploughing a field or brought up into cumulus-like puffs so the edges catch in the heat. I often finish such a crust under a hot grill. The inside should be soft and fluffy, which is best achieved by passing the cooked potatoes through a ricer. A small-holed ricer is, as I'm sure you know, the very devil to wash, but the difference is worth every minute of your time.

The best of the potato pies is one I no longer eat. An awesome mass of bubbling mushrooms, garlic and Gruyère under a lid of Parmesan-crusted potato mash, it is the most rib-sticking of suppers imaginable. A pie so rich and filling you feel a stone heavier from simply looking at it. I can't quite face food like that any more, but the recipe is in *Real Food* if you're interested. You'll need your appetite.

Potatoes make an appropriate hat for a fish pie. The cream, herb and fish sauce bleeding deliciously into the velvety potatoes. Anyone who has ever embarked on the task of preparing a fish pie will know it is not for the faint-hearted cook. There is also always mountains of washing-up. And yet of all those you could make, the fish pie is often the most popular, especially when the weather is below freezing and there is smoked fish involved.

## Smoked haddock and mussel pie

Smoked haddock is my go-to fish for a pie. The price is reasonable, the flesh reassuringly firm and the smoky notes of the fish are blissful with the mashed potato. If you make the filling in a shallow casserole, you can pile the mashed potatoes on top and save yourself some washing-up.

*Serves 6*

floury potatoes  1kg
butter  100g, plus extra
   for the topping
haddock  500g
smoked haddock  750g
milk  700ml

bay leaves  3
black peppercorns  6
mussels  500g
flour  60g
tarragon leaves, chopped,
   2 tablespoons

You will need a deep-sided baking dish about 30cm × 22cm.

Peel the potatoes and cook them till tender in deep, lightly salted water. They will probably take about 20 minutes, but check them every few minutes. When you can easily slide a skewer into them, remove from the heat, drain them, then beat till smooth with 50g of the butter, seasoning as you go.

Put the haddock and smoked haddock in a large pan, then add the milk, bay leaves, peppercorns – lightly crushed – and bring almost to the boil. You may find the milk doesn't quite cover the fish, but it will cook in the steam. Lower the heat, partially cover with a lid and leave to simmer, very gently, for about 7 minutes, until the fish is almost cooked. The skin should come off easily. Turn off the heat but leave the lid on.

Check the mussels, discarding any that are cracked or refuse to close when tapped on the side of the sink. Put them into a deep saucepan with 200ml of water, then cover with a tight-fitting lid and bring to the boil. Leave the mussels cooking for 2 minutes, then lift the lid and check their progress. As soon as the shells have opened, they are done. Remove them from the heat and pull the mussels from their shells. Reserve the cooking liquor, pouring it through a sieve to remove any grit.

Set the oven at 200°C. Remove the fish from the milk and peel the flesh from the skin. Remove any bones. Break the fish into large pieces and put them in a bowl. Melt the remaining 50g of butter in a medium-sized saucepan – I use a 20cm deep pan – stir in the flour with a wooden spoon and let it cook for a couple of minutes until thick. Now gradually ladle in 600ml of the milk in which you cooked the fish, discarding the bay leaves, and stir in 100ml of the mussel cooking liquor. Keep stirring until the sauce comes to the boil, then lower the heat and let it simmer gently – stirring regularly and beating out any lumps as you go – over a low heat for 5 minutes. Add the tarragon to the sauce, then add the skinned fish and the mussels and season lightly – you are unlikely to need salt.

Transfer the filling to a baking dish, pile the mashed potato on top, making furrows with a fork or leaving it rough, as you wish, dot with a little butter, then bake for 30–35 minutes till the potato is golden and the filling is bubbling around the edge.

The original version of my favourite vegetable pie (made in the early days of my cookery writing life) was nice enough, but always felt a little worthy. A dish reminiscent of the much-missed Cranks restaurant in Marshall Street. Too brown, too wholemeal, a touch on the dry side.

This updated version is a lot more interesting. The refresh came about because of the need to find substantial cold-weather food for when you don't want to eat meat. A sort of shepherd's pie for a shepherd who doesn't want to eat his flock. This one is soft and generous.

I am not going to deny this dinner is a good hour and a half's hands-on work. It is a pie of many parts. There is something so life-affirming here and I make it in a dish I can bring to the table, to pile onto everyone's plate in steaming clouds. I sometimes wonder if there isn't a touch of the feeder in me.

## A big pie for a winter's day

This good-natured, resolutely old-fashioned and earthy recipe will take whichever lentils and vegetables you have lying around. Use brown, yellow or green lentils in the filling; spinach or chard for the greens; and mashed potatoes, swede, sweet potatoes or parsnip for the crust.

A big pie for a winter's day

*Serves 6*

*For the filling:*

onions  450g (2, medium)

olive or vegetable oil
   3 tablespoons

carrots  150g

celery  1 stick

garlic  3 cloves

bay leaves  3

thyme  6 bushy sprigs

parsley  4 bushy sprigs

tomatoes  500g

vegetable stock  500ml

lentils, brown or green  350g

spinach  350g

balsamic vinegar  1–2 tablespoons

*For the top:*

parsnips  1.5kg

butter  50g

thyme  a few sprigs

Peel and roughly chop the onions, then cook them in the oil in a deep pan over a moderate heat for 15 minutes, stirring from time to time.

Cut the carrots and celery into fine dice, peel and finely chop the garlic, then add all to the softening onions and continue cooking for 10 minutes, until the onion is golden and translucent.

Add the bay leaves to the pan. Remove the leaves from the thyme and parsley, then stir into the vegetables.

Cut the tomatoes into small dice and stir into the vegetables, leaving them to simmer for a further 10 minutes until the tomatoes have released their juice. Pour in the vegetable stock, bring to the boil, then lower the heat to a simmer, season and leave the vegetables to putter away over a low heat for about 15 minutes. Check the liquid level from time to time: you want a decent amount of juice, so add some more hot stock if needed.

Meanwhile, cook the lentils in deep boiling water for 20 minutes, until they are just tender, then drain and add them to the vegetable sauce.

Peel the parsnips, then steam until tender. Mash with a vegetable masher or food mixer. Add the butter, salt and pepper and set aside.

Wash the spinach leaves and put them, still wet, into a pan over a moderate heat. Cover tightly with a lid and let them cook for 1–2 minutes until wilted. Remove the leaves, drain them and squeeze out most of the moisture.

Set the oven at 200°C. Stir the spinach into the lentil sauce, then stir in a tablespoon of balsamic vinegar, taste and add more if necessary. It should add a mellow note to the sauce. Transfer to a deep baking dish, about 24cm × 28cm. Spoon the mashed parsnips on top, scatter the thyme sprigs over and bake for 20–25 minutes.

And of course there are sweet pies whose sugar-crusted pastry emerges from the oven cracked and stained with veins of crimson juice. Plums and damsons, apples and mincemeat, and the apricot which I think of as the zenith of pie fillings.

# Sweet pies

There was only ever one true pie. The pie for which I waited all year, happy to get my arms and legs bloodied by bramble thorns and my knees bruised from climbing the lichen-covered apple tree at the bottom of the garden. Blackberry and apple pie said 'home' like no other food. A deep dish of treasure in which to sink a tarnished serving spoon, through crisp pastry that sparkled with sugar like a frosty morning, the fluff of pale apples with ribbons of deep purple juice with the wild berries from the lane.

It was the simplest of pies, a shortcrust pastry crown on a deep, crackle-glazed Mason's pie dish of stewed apples and blackberries. A smell of baked apples and pastry to come home to after school. We made custard from a packet but I always preferred cream, thick and white from a tin. To this day I am not sure there is any pie I would rather eat.

But this is more than pie. This is 'back-to-school pie' and the return of a sense of order. It is the falling leaves and the first fires, apple-picking and Harvest Festival pie. If ever there was a food laden with the honey-hued glow of nostalgia, this is it. I am no flag-waving Anglophile, far from it, but this is something we do well, if not better than anyone. Sweet fruit pie. It is something to be celebrated.

# Blackberry and apple pie

My first published recipe for this (in *Real Food*) was for a single-crust pie. With the greedy benefit of hindsight I feel the pie needed more pastry. I have reworked the recipe to include a bottom crust. This second crust will always be softer because of the juice that escapes from the fruit as it bakes, but I prevent it from being soggy by baking the pie on a hot cast-iron baking sheet. I cannot tell you what a difference it makes to the texture of the bottom crust.

There is a debate as to whether it is necessary to simmer the apples before they go into the pie. I fall on the side of pre-cooking, a trick that renders the fruit fluffy, golden and translucent. If I were cooking an apple tart, I would want the apple slices to keep their shape and so I use a sweet apple and forgo any pre-cooking. But this is pie, where the filling should be soft and cloud-like, marbled with the juice of the blackberries. If you don't fancy the idea of lard, just replace it with butter. And can I please put in a plea for gooseberry pie too. You could use them in place of the apples and blackberries – you will need 850g of them, cooked briefly with 150g of sugar and a couple of tablespoons of water, then spooned into the pie tin in place of the apples.

All pie plates vary slightly in size. For the sake of accuracy, my pie plate is cast iron and measures 20cm across the bottom and 27cm across the top from rim to rim.

*Serves 6*

*For the pastry:*

| | |
|---|---|
| plain flour  300g | egg yolk  1 |
| butter  75g, cold from the fridge | iced water |
| lard  75g, cold from the fridge | a little milk for brushing |

*For the filling:*

| | |
|---|---|
| Bramley or similar sharp apples  750g | caster sugar, to taste |
| | blackberries  250g |
| butter  25g | |

*To finish:*
a beaten egg and caster sugar for sprinkling

Blackberry and apple pie

You will need a 24cm metal pie dish with a wide rim.

Put the flour into a large mixing bowl with a pinch of salt. Cut the butter and lard into small dice and rub in with your fingertips and thumbs. You can do it in a food processor but I'm not sure it's worth it. Pastry this simple is a pleasure to make by hand. When the fats and flour resemble coarse fresh breadcrumbs, add the egg yolk, lightly beaten, and a little iced water to bring it to a rollable dough. Start with a tablespoon, adding it gingerly (too much is difficult to correct) and draw the dough from the sides to form a ball. You are looking for a dough that is firm enough to roll but soft enough to demand careful lifting. Set aside in the fridge, covered with a tea towel, for 30 minutes.

Set the oven at 180°C. Place a baking sheet in the oven to get hot (you will cook the pie on top of this). Peel, core and quarter the apples, then cut them into thick slices. You should have about 650g. Melt the butter in a saucepan, then add the apples with a sprinkling of sugar. Taste them to gauge their sweetness. I like my apples fairly tart, so add just a light sprinkling of sugar. The sweeter of tooth may wish to add anything up to a tablespoon of sugar per apple. Let the apples cook over a moderate heat, covered, for 8–10 minutes until they are soft but not fluffy. Gently stir in the blackberries.

Cut the pastry in half and roll out one half to approximately the thickness of a pound coin, to fit the dish with a good overhang. Lower the pastry into the dish and press it firmly to the rim. Spoon the fruit on top of the pastry, doming it lightly in the centre.

Roll out the remaining pastry. Brush the rim of the tart tin with water (or milk or some beaten egg), then lower the rolled-out pastry over the fruit. Press the edges firmly together around the rim, then crimp them with your thumb and forefinger or a fork to firmly seal. Brush with the beaten egg and sprinkle lightly with sugar.

Slide the pie dish onto the hot baking sheet and bake for 50 minutes to an hour till golden brown. Allow the pie to settle for 15–20 minutes before serving.


In 1988, I wrote a story about the joys of pie. I wanted to include a recipe that required no culinary skill whatsoever. Entry-level pie. 'Easy as pie' pie. Rather than push the dough tenderly into a tart tin, then roll a lid and crimp and seal the edges, I simply piled the fruit in the middle of the rolled-out pastry and folded the edges loosely over the fruit. I had no idea if it would work. My fear being that the pastry would unfurl and the fruit come spilling out. To my surprise, the crust stayed in place and the pie was a success. (I notice the idea seems to have somewhat 'done the rounds'.)

## Plum and blackcurrant free-form pie

There aren't many fruits that don't work in an open-topped pie such as this. Apples, cut into thin slices, gooseberries, plums, blueberries and apricots are prime contenders. Rhubarb tends to produce a little too much juice, but nevertheless tastes wonderful. I sometimes dust it with a little icing sugar too and serve with a jug of thick double cream to pour over at the table.

*Serves 6*

*For the pastry:*

| | |
|---|---|
| plain flour 280g | icing sugar 2 tablespoons |
| cold butter 140g | egg yolk 1 |

*For the filling:*

| | |
|---|---|
| plums, ripe 600g | caster sugar 100g |
| blackcurrants or blackberries 250g | egg 1 |

Make the pastry by putting the flour into the bowl of a food processor, adding the butter, cut into small cubes, then reducing to coarse crumbs. If you prefer, rub the cubes of butter into the flour with your fingertips. Stop when they look like fresh, coarse breadcrumbs. Add the icing sugar, then the egg yolk and enough water to produce a firm, rollable dough. I start with one tablespoon, then add a second (and occasionally a third). Remove the dough from the bowl, pat into a ball, then wrap in baking parchment and refrigerate for 30 minutes.

Slice the plums in half and discard their stones. Put them in a bowl. Remove the blackcurrants from their stems and add to the plums. If you are using blackberries, add them to the plums. Add the sugar to the bowl and gently toss everything together until the fruit is coated lightly with the sugar.

Set the oven at 200°C. Put a baking a sheet in the oven. Cover a second baking sheet with baking parchment. On a lightly floured board, roll the pastry

Plum and blackcurrant free-form pie

out to measure roughly 32cm in diameter. Don't feel the need to be particularly neat or accurate about this – the pie's charm is in its free-form wobbliness. Place the pastry on the parchment-lined baking sheet.

Pile the fruit in the middle of the pastry, leaving a wide rim around it. Pull the edges of the pastry up and partially over the fruit, leaving much of the fruit uncovered. Break the egg into a small bowl or cup and beat lightly with a fork, then brush over the exposed pastry edges. Place the pie, on its baking sheet, on top of the hot baking sheet in the oven and bake for 45 minutes till golden.

I must backtrack a while for this next recipe. It is 1978 and I am working in the Lake District, in the sort of country house hotel that has stone putti on the terrace and puts a tiny vase of primroses on the morning tea tray.

Dinner was a set menu affair with no choice until dessert. Then came the tough choice between apricot fool or raspberry meringue, an ice cream of local honey or a deep fruit pie. The pastry with which the apple, plum or blackberry pies was made was exceptionally soft and crumbly, more like thin shortbread than sweet pastry. The pastry received its tender character from having been made with almost equal butter to self-raising flour and icing sugar. Such a formula makes the pastry difficult, nigh impossible to roll without 24 hours in the fridge. My version of this pastry still has a high ratio of fat and still uses self-raising flour but is infinitely more manageable. The result is as soft and tender as pie pastry can be.

There is so much talk of 'cotton wool' apricots, or those that refuse to ripen, and yet I find little evidence of this. Perhaps I am spoilt by the Turkish greengrocers on my doorstep. Many of them manage to locate a decent supply. Perhaps they have an affinity to the fruit that struggles in this climate. The trick seems to be to leave them at warm room temperature until properly ripe, taking care they do not touch one another. Choosing those of a dark colour with rust freckles seems as good a starting point as any. Like greengages, they are one of those fruits that shine most brightly when warm and sweetened by a little sugar.

# Apricot pan pie

The pastry here is exceptionally soft, so that it hugs the shape of the fruit, giving the impression of a cluster of apricot dumplings. I included lemon zest in the pastry, which persuaded the fruit to come out of its characteristic shyness. My favourite pie pastry is a little fragile to handle. I get around this by kneading the dough, briefly and tenderly, on a lightly floured wooden board before rolling.

*Serves 6*

*For the pastry:*

| | |
|---|---|
| cold butter 200g | lemon grated zest of 1 small |
| icing sugar 100g | self-raising flour 350g |
| egg 1 | milk and sugar a little to finish |

*For the filling:*

| | |
|---|---|
| apricots 750g, ripe ones | orange grated zest of 1 small |
| caster sugar 2 tablespoons | cornflour 1 heaped tablespoon |

Cream the butter and sugar until light and fluffy. Mix in the egg, then the lemon zest. Sift in the flour and fold into the butter and sugar mixture. Form the dough into a ball and knead lightly on a floured surface, then cut in half. Wrap in baking parchment and rest in the fridge for 30 minutes. Use half of the dough to line the pie plate. Place this, and the remaining half, back in the fridge.

Set the oven at 180°C. Halve the apricots and remove their stones. Put the apricots in a bowl, toss with the sugar, orange zest and cornflour, then spoon into the pie tin.

Roll the reserved pastry to fit the top. Brush the pastry rim in the pie plate with milk, then lower on the second piece of pastry. Seal the edges, pinching them together, then brush the pie with milk and dust with sugar.

Pierce a small hole in the centre to let the steam out. Bake for 45 minutes or so until the crust is pale gold. Leave to settle for 10–15 minutes before serving.

# A slice of tart

If I make a tart for you, you will know I love you. It takes an hour to make the dough, line and bake the pastry case, then another to make the filling, bake it again and then to let it cool. Making a tart is both a fiddle and a joy. You need to set aside a couple of hours, have a pastry board and rolling pin, some baking beans and own a suitable metal tart tin with a removable base. That said, I struggle to think of a single recipe that fills me with more satisfaction.

I make tarts with shortcrust pastry, puff pastry and occasionally a shortbread base. Fillings follow the ebb and flow of the season. Asparagus in the spring; mushrooms in the autumn. For Christmas there may be prawns or butternut squash. Sweet ones too. A pale lemon tart in spring, hazelnuts or figs in autumn. At Christmas there will be almond and mincemeat.

At cooking school, we learned to fill our pastry cases with restraint. Soft, caramel-sweet onions with a piquant goat's cheese. Spinach and sautéed mushrooms. Lardons of bacon and cubes of Gruyère. Savoury tarts fail when too many ingredients are introduced. A cluttered tart, with too little custard to hold it together, will fall apart on the plate.

The custard is a delicate and silky being. The eggs, cream, nutmeg and herbs make something you want to savour. The custard should never be reduced to the thing that supports your other ingredients. Even though it does. Give your ingredients room to breathe.

I noticed very quickly how adding watery ingredients such as tomatoes or courgettes to a tart can destroy the texture of the custard. A courgette tart can be worth making if you grate and salt your courgettes first, squeezing out the moisture with your fist, then combining with mint or tarragon and perhaps some snippets of crisp bacon. Before you add onions, it is worth cooking them slowly in a shallow pan, letting them soften till sweet and jammy. It will take three times longer than anyone tells you, 30–40 minutes at least. Winter onions, which are quite dry, will take less time than the juicier summer onions, having less water to bubble away. Marry such sweetness with sharp or piquant flavours – salty cheeses, pickled gherkins or sauerkraut.

For several years in the early 1980s, I made tarts for a food shop. An early morning job, the dishes were lined with shortcrust pastry and baked blind, the dough kept in shape by baking parchment and baking beans. We filled them with a seasoned custard and whatever herbs and vegetables felt right for the time of year. Grated courgette and feta in the summer, and in autumn as the leaves turned to gold we filled the pastry cases to the brim with mushrooms, pancetta and Parmesan.

I didn't know then that the crispest pastry comes from using a metal tin, not a white china flan case. Neither had I learned that they are even crisper if you put a metal baking sheet in the oven to get hot and bake them on that.

There is little less appetising than an underfilled tart. The best-looking are those whose custard quivers perilously close to the rim, giving your tart depth and generosity. Mine were sold by the slice and as whole tarts (we called them quiches in those days), and they worked well eaten cold too. But the best were those we served warm, when the filling had been given time to settle.

The early tarts I made were given their savour with grated farmhouse Cheddar. They were good, but with that came a fatty quality that was too rich for the egg and cream custard. There were attempts with crumbled Stilton and Gorgonzola, Fontina and Camembert, but it was those made with finely grated Parmesan, pecorino or Grana Padano that won me over. The hard cheeses lent a clean, unfatty, umami savour and texture that I love.

## Mushroom and dill tart

*Serves 6*

*For the pastry:*
butter 90g
plain flour 150g

egg yolk 1
Parmesan 40g, finely grated

*For the filling:*
double cream 400ml
Parmesan rind about 10cm piece
small mushrooms 300g

olive oil 3 tablespoons
dill 15g
eggs 3, large

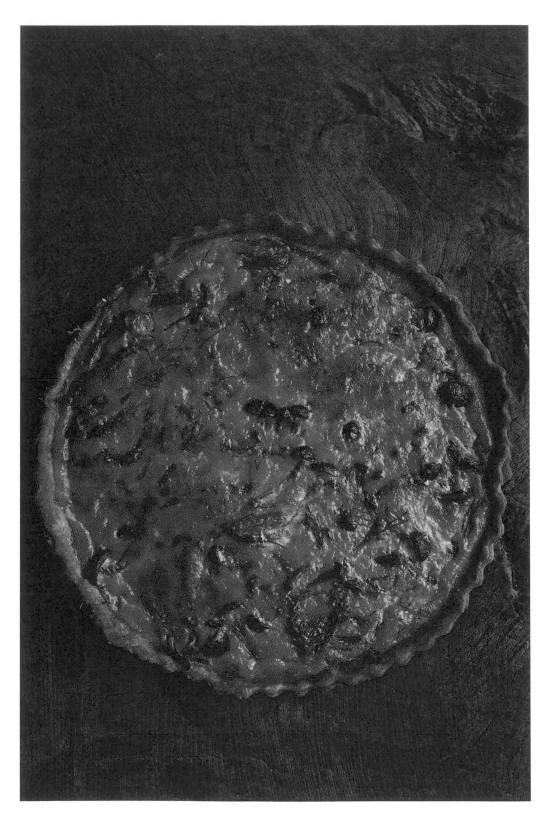

Mushroom and dill tart

You will need a 22cm tart tin with a removable base.

Cut the butter into cubes and rub it into the flour with your fingertips until it resembles coarse, fresh breadcrumbs. Mix in the egg yolk, lightly beaten, and the Parmesan, bringing the ingredients together into a firm ball of dough, adding a tablespoon or two of cold water if necessary. You can do this in seconds using a food processor.

Tip the dough onto a lightly floured board and knead for thirty seconds or so (no longer), shaping it into a ball as you go. Wrap in cling film or baking parchment and chill in the fridge for 30 minutes.

While the dough chills, make the filling. Pour the cream into a medium-sized saucepan, add the Parmesan rind and bring to the boil. Watch carefully, removing the cream from the heat immediately when it starts to boil, then cover with a lid and set aside. Cut the mushrooms into small pieces. In a small frying pan, warm the oil then fry the mushrooms for 4–5 minutes, until slightly sticky. Chop the dill, fronds and thin stalks, toss with the mushrooms and set aside.

Remove the dough from the fridge and tenderly roll into a disc large enough to line the tart tin. Press the pastry into the corners, patching it where necessary. Make certain there are no tears or holes. Chill for another 20 minutes, allowing the pastry to relax. Set the oven at 190°C and place an upturned baking sheet on the middle shelf to heat up.

Tuck a sheet of baking parchment or foil in the tart tin, fill with baking beans and slide into the preheated oven on top of the warm baking sheet. Bake for 25 minutes, then carefully remove the foil and beans and return to the oven for a further 5 minutes until dry to the touch. Lower the heat to 180°C. Break the eggs into a bowl and beat gently, then add the cream (removing the Parmesan rind). Season with salt and pepper, add the fried mushrooms, then spoon into the tart tin and bake for 25 minutes until lightly set, the pastry golden.

There are days when I want the lightness of puff pastry rather than the richness of shortcrust. I could make my own, but rarely do. The frozen ready-rolled pastry made with butter is both time-saving and, in my book, perfectly acceptable. Puff pastry works well where a soft cheese and perhaps some crème fraîche or cream cheese is used instead of an egg custard filling.

The puff pastry rises around the edge creating a deep hollow for a cargo of goat's cheese, slices of fried aubergine, tomatoes or short tips of asparagus.

# Asparagus tarts

*Makes 6 round tarts*

| | |
|---|---|
| asparagus spears  8 | crème fraîche  100ml |
| puff pastry  250g | thyme leaves  1 teaspoon |
| egg  1, beaten | Parmesan, finely grated  50g |
| goat's cheese  150g | |

Set the oven at 200°C. Put an upturned baking sheet in the oven. Bring a medium pan of water to the boil. Trim the asparagus, then cut each spear into three short lengths. Drop the asparagus into the pan and let it boil for 3 minutes, lift out with a draining spoon and lower into a bowl of iced water.

Roll the pastry out to a rectangle measuring 38cm by 25cm. Cut out six discs of pastry approximately 12cm in diameter. Place the discs on a lined baking sheet. Using the tip of a knife, or a cookie cutter, score a smaller circle 1cm in from the edges of each piece of pastry. Brush a little beaten egg around the outside of each piece of pastry.

Drain the asparagus on kitchen paper. Crush the goat's cheese with a fork and fold in the crème fraîche, thyme and half the Parmesan. Divide the mixture between the six discs of pastry and put four asparagus pieces on each. Scatter over the remaining Parmesan. Put the baking sheet on top of the preheated sheet already in the oven and bake for 25–30 minutes, until the tarts are golden. Eat immediately.

Rarely are tarts seen alone. We tend to bring them to the table in the company of other small dishes for a summer lunch: radishes on a dish of ice; a coarse, piggy terrine; a bowl of leaves and herbs; or a wedge of cheese. And yet they can be a main dish, if the filling is substantial and it is served with generosity.

In the spring of 2018, I made a tart that would pass as a principal dish. Satisfying enough to be offered as you might a pie, with a single green vegetable on the side. The result was a saffron-hued butternut and bacon tart, served with nothing more than a big blue and white bowl of peas at its side. The recipe hit the spot and I have been making it ever since.

Other ideas followed. A pastry case crammed with salmon and cream cheese, another with shredded salami and gherkins. The content is generally more seafood, meat or vegetables than custard. The tart cranked up a notch.

## Butternut and bacon tart

In theory, there is little need to peel the butternut squash, but I do here. The skin, however tender, seems at odds with the gentle texture of the tart filling. Add as much water as you need to make the pastry easy to roll, but it is worth remembering that the less water you put in the less likely it is to shrink in the oven.

*Serves 4*

*For the pastry:*

| | |
|---|---|
| butter 90g | Parmesan, grated 4 tablespoons |
| plain flour 150g | water 1–2 tablespoons |
| egg yolk 1 | |

*For the filling:*

| | |
|---|---|
| butternut squash 500g | double cream 250ml |
| smoked streaky bacon 200g | milk 50ml |
| olive oil 1 tablespoon | parsley, chopped a small handful |
| eggs 2 | |

*To finish:*
Parmesan, grated 2 tablespoons

You will need a 22cm tart tin with a removable base.

Make the pastry: cut the butter into small dice and rub into the flour with your fingertips until it has the texture of soft, fresh breadcrumbs. Alternatively, reduce to fine crumbs in a food processor. Add the egg yolk, the Parmesan and the water, a tablespoon at a time, stopping when you have a firm, even-textured dough. Set the oven at 190°C.

Peel the squash, halve lengthways and discard the fibres and seeds (you should be left with about 350g). Then cut the flesh into short wedges, each weighing roughly 35g. Place the pieces in a steamer basket and cook over

Butternut and bacon tart

boiling water for 8–10 minutes until soft. Cut the bacon into pieces the size of a postage stamp then fry in the oil in a shallow pan until the fat is translucent and just starting to crisp. Remove from the heat.

Beat the eggs, cream and milk, season, then add the chopped parsley. Place the tart tin on a baking tray and line with the pastry, making certain you have pushed the dough deep into the edges and that there are no tears or cracks. Chill for 20 minutes in the fridge.

Line the pastry case with baking parchment and baking beans, then bake for 20 minutes. Remove the beans and return the pastry case to the oven for 3–5 minutes or until the pastry is dry to the touch.

Lower the heat to 180°C. Place the pieces of squash in the pastry shell, then scatter over the crisped bacon. Pour in the custard and dust the surface with the grated Parmesan. Bake for 30 minutes or until the custard is just set. Remove from the oven and leave to cool until just warm (when tarts such as this are at their most delicious).

By definition a pie has some sort of top crust – pastry, potato, crumbs, meringue, whatever. A tart, on the other hand, is generally open-topped. There are anomalies, such as pecan and pumpkin pie (neither of which has a top crust) and Bakewell tart, whose filling is covered with thin white icing, and Linzertorte with its woven lattice of pastry. To add to the mix, there are some pies I prefer to refer to as a tart. They are thin – mostly – such as the one I made on a winter's day during the pandemic, when the cupboard was almost bare. A tart with a top (pedants can look away now), its filling made from nothing but softened leeks and crumbled Cheddar under a dome of buttery puff pastry.

## A tart of leeks and Cheddar

*Serves 6*

leeks 1kg
butter 70g
puff pastry 450g

Cheddar, a full-flavoured
　farmhouse type 200g
egg 1, beaten

A tart of leeks and Cheddar

Trim the leeks, removing their roots and the darker green section of the leaves. Thinly slice the white and pale green of the leeks, then wash them very thoroughly in cold water (leeks have a habit of holding on to grit between their layers).

Melt the butter in a heavy-bottomed pan over a low to moderate heat (if you use a thin pan the leeks will burn). Tip the leeks into the pan. Cut a circle of baking parchment slightly larger than the diameter of the pan and place it on top of the leeks and cover with a lid. Leave them to cook for about 25 minutes till they are soft and pale; they should not colour. The leeks will soften in their own steam.

When the leeks are cooked, move them from the pan to a shallow bowl using a slotted spoon – you don't want the filling to be wet. Leave to cool. Set the oven at 220°C. Put a baking sheet in the oven to get hot.

Roll out half of the pastry and cut out a 24cm disc, then do the same with the other half. Line a second baking sheet with baking parchment. Place one piece of pastry on the lined baking sheet, then spoon the cooled leeks over most of the pastry, leaving a 2cm rim of pastry around the edge. Crumble the cheese over the leeks, then brush the pastry rim with beaten egg. Lower the second disc of pastry over the top and press the edges very firmly together to seal.

Brush the pastry with the remaining beaten egg, cut a small slit in the top – it lets the steam out and stops the pastry splitting – then place the baking sheet on top of the one already in the oven. Bake for 20–25 minutes till golden.

All of which brings me to my favourite savoury tart. It made its first appearance in *Appetite* and I make it to this day.

## A thin, simple cheese and onion tart

*Serves 4 as a light lunch, 12 as nibbles*

onions  6 small to medium, 1kg
butter  a thick slice, about 50g
olive oil  2 tablespoons
puff pastry  320g

Taleggio or similar semi-soft
  cheese  120g
thyme  enough leaves to make
  a little pile on your palm

A thin, simple cheese and onion tart

Peel the onions, cut them in half from stem to root, then into thick segments – about eight to each onion half. Put them in a shallow pan with the butter and oil and leave over a low to moderate heat until they are soft. Let them take their time. They need to be translucent, golden and sticky but not brown. This only comes with slow cooking and it is pointless to try and hurry it. The actual timing will depend on the type of onion (some contain more water than others), but you can expect them to take a good 30 minutes or longer. Stir them regularly and cover them with a lid if they are colouring too soon.

Set the oven at 200°C. Roll the pastry into a rectangle 35cm × 25cm. Score a border 2cm in from the edge.

Tip the onions on to the pastry, pushing them almost, but not quite, to the border. Brush the rim with some of the onion butter. Slice the cheese thinly, then break it into small pieces, tucking it amongst the onions. Scatter over the thyme. Bake until the pastry is golden and puffed and the cheese is melting, 15–20 minutes. Cut into four or twelve rectangles to serve.


# Sweet tarts


Almond and apricot, prune, plum, lemon, treacle – there is rarely a tart that doesn't tempt this eater.

At home, I make both shallow tarts with a frangipane and fruit filling (plum, greengage, cherry or blackcurrant) and puff pastry tarts (raspberry, strawberry, apricot). The latter are rarely filled with the traditional crème pâtissière, but more likely something brighter-tasting such as ricotta, mascarpone or whipped cream.

The first and simplest tart I make is laughably straightforward. You take a ready-rolled sheet of puff pastry, bake it, cool it and fill it with cream, then cover it with raspberries. Job done. It fills the need for crisp pastry and soft fruit.

One along from that is the thin, individual apricot tart, its surface sticky with jam and flakes of pastry that stick to your lips.

In late summer and autumn, there is an urge for a tart that is straight from the oven, the skins bursting with juice, the top shining and sticky with fruit glaze. For this I have always used stone fruits, especially plums and nectarines. From *Tender, Volume I*:

'At the height of summer, we often eat around the zinc table in the garden. Whilst everyone is wiping the roasting juices from their plates with a few soft salad leaves I take the opportunity to slip a tray of paper-thin apricot tarts into the oven. A certain amount of prep is required: the apricots need to be cooked and left sleeping in their syrup; the pastry has to be cut, the oven on. It is a rather wonderful moment, bringing to the table a tray of warm, slim pastries, their crusts holding a handful of melting apricots.'

As a rule, tarts are filed under 'serious cooking'. There is pastry to be made; baking blind to be done; fillings to be mixed; a glaze of some sort. Recipes that take hours rather than minutes.

Enter frozen puff pastry and tinned apricots. Commercial puff pastry is pretty good, especially (for which read 'only') if it is made with butter. Apricots survive the canning process better than most fruits – they can often be better than the fresh fruits you so carefully poach in sugar syrup. Tarts made using such everyday shortcuts still possess the crisp, buttery pastry and melting fruits you would get if you spent hours making your own puff pastry and preparing your own fruit.

## Quick apricot tarts

*Makes 4 tarts*

apricots, fresh 10,
   tinned or poached in syrup 20
caster sugar 3 tablespoons

puff pastry 320g
apricot jam 4 heaped tablespoons

If you are using fresh apricots, halve and stone them, then put them in a small saucepan, add the sugar and enough water to just cover the fruit and bring to the boil. Lower the heat and simmer for about 10 minutes till the fruit is soft and tender. The apricots must be so soft you could crush them between your fingers. Drain them.

If you are using tinned apricots, drain them in a sieve over a bowl.

Set the oven at 220°C. Place a baking sheet in the oven to get hot.

Quick apricot tarts

Roll out the pastry to a rectangle 30cm × 23cm. (That is pretty much the size of a roll of ready-made puff pastry.) Using a 12cm-diameter template (a saucer or small plate or large cookie cutter), cut four rounds of pastry.

Place each on a lightly floured baking sheet (lined with baking parchment if you wish). Score a wide rim around the outside of each one about 1cm in from the edge – I use a 10cm cutter for this – taking care not to cut right through the pastry.

Place the apricots on the pastry, four or five halves to each tart, steering clear of the rim. Slide the baking sheet on top of the hot baking sheet in the oven and bake for 10–12 minutes, till the pastry is puffed and golden.

Warm the apricot jam in a small saucepan. Remove the tarts from the oven and brush the jam over the tarts, covering both fruit and pastry, then return to the oven for 3–4 minutes till the edges have browned and the glaze is just starting to caramelise. Let the tarts settle for 10 minutes before eating. (Only so you don't scald your mouth!)


The thick custard filling of classic French patisserie isn't really my thing. (That said, I am partial to a vanilla slice.) I prefer a filling that is cleaner and fresher-tasting. Enter ricotta. If I can get ricotta fior di latte then I will use it unadorned, its sweetly milky curds like an old-fashioned milk ice cream. If not, then I will use whatever I can get and stir it gently with a little cream. The pale, fresh cream can be flavoured with citrus zest or orange flower water. A dusting of icing sugar if you must.

One winter, when the blood oranges were in season, I laid them on top of mounds of ricotta, trickling rivulets of liquid honey and thyme leaves over the white clouds and blood-red orange slices. There was sweetness and nutty crumbs of shortbread, but also a breath of the Mediterranean, of orange groves, beehives and wild thyme. And not a tart case or baking bean in sight.

There is a certain quiet delight in revisiting a classic. We will probably never know who was the first to tuck apricots, plums or greengages into a frangipane tart, a sweet almond cocoon for the fruit. I do think a little bowl of crème fraîche will be welcome.

# Plum frangipane tart

*Serves 8*

*For the pastry:*

| | |
|---|---|
| flour 200g | egg yolk 1 |
| butter 100g | water a little |

*For the filling:*

| | |
|---|---|
| butter 100g | ground almonds 125g |
| caster sugar 125g | plain flour 60g |
| eggs 2 | small plums 400g |

You will also need a round 22cm tart tin at least 3.5cm deep with a removable base and beans for baking blind.

Put the flour and butter, cut into small pieces, into the bowl of a food processor. Add a pinch of salt and blitz to fine breadcrumbs. If you prefer, rub the butter into the flour with your fingertips. Add the egg yolk and enough water to bring the dough to a firm ball. The less you add the better, as too much will cause your pastry case to shrink in the oven.

Pat the pastry into a flat round on a floured surface, then roll out until it is large enough to line the tart tin. Lower the pastry into the tin. Push the dough right into the edges where the rim joins the base, without stretching the pastry. Make certain there are no holes or tears. Trim the overhanging pastry and place in the fridge to chill for about 30 minutes.

Set the oven at 190°C. Put a baking sheet in the oven to warm. Line the pastry case with baking parchment and baking beans and slide the tin on to the hot baking sheet. Bake for 20 minutes, then remove from the oven and carefully lift the beans out. Return the pastry case to the oven for 5 minutes or so, until the surface is dry to the touch. Remove from the oven and set aside. Turn the oven down to 160°C and return the baking sheet to the oven.

Make the filling: using a food mixer, cream the butter and sugar together till pale and fluffy. Lower the speed, then mix in the eggs and slowly fold in the ground almonds and flour. Spoon the almond filling into the cooked pastry case, smoothing it lightly with the back of the spoon.

Cut the plums in half and remove their stones. Place the plums on top of the almond filling, neatly or randomly as the mood takes you. Slide the tart tin on to the hot baking sheet and bake for 40 minutes till the filling is well risen and golden brown. Remove the tart from the oven and allow to cool slightly before serving.

One afternoon in high summer 2015 I had a fancy for a warm almond and berry tart, whose filling owed something to the old-fashioned macaroons of my childhood. In other words, crisp outside and chewy within. A filling that was lighter and less cake-like than the classic frangipane, and whose nutty richness would be softened with tart, bright-tasting currants. Would such a recipe work, I wondered?

I had a go. If the whole thing failed, I could always dump it in a glass dish, cover it with whipped cream and declare it a blackcurrant and almond surprise. To my gratification and surprise, it not only worked but was everything I had hoped it might be. (This isn't, let me assure you, how everything works. All too often what seems like a brilliant idea refuses point blank to work or turns out to have been done before. This worked.)

It is a useful tart in that it will keep for a day or two without becoming soggy (as so many tarts do) and works as either dessert or a teatime cake. I like a wave of thick crème fraîche or even vanilla ice cream on the side.

## Blackcurrant macaroon tart

*Serves 8*

*For the pastry:*
butter 100g
caster sugar 100g
egg yolks 2

plain flour 250g
baking powder 1 teaspoon
water 2 tablespoons

Blackcurrant macaroon tart

*For the filling:*

| | |
|---|---|
| ground almonds 200g | blackcurrants 300g |
| icing sugar 200g | egg whites 3 |
| plain flour 2 heaped tablespoons | cream to serve |

You will also need a 24cm tart tin with a removable base.

To make the pastry crust, cream the butter and caster sugar together in a food mixer or by hand until the mixture is light and fluffy, then add the egg yolks. Combine the flour and baking powder, then fold into the batter with the water to give a soft dough. Tip the dough on to a lightly floured work surface, knead gently for less than a minute, then roll into a ball, wrap in baking parchment and refrigerate for a minimum of 30 minutes.

Roll the pastry out on a lightly floured board and use to line the tart tin, pushing it up the sides and into the edges. Trim overhanging pastry. Leave no holes or tears. Chill the pastry case in the fridge for 30 minutes.

Set the oven at 190°C. Place an empty baking sheet or pizza stone in the oven.

When the oven is hot and the pastry chilled, fill the tart case with baking parchment and baking beans and bake for 20 minutes. Then remove the beans and paper and return to the oven for 5 minutes or till dry to the touch and pale biscuit-coloured. Remove the tart case from the oven and lower the temperature to 170°C.

To make the filling: mix together the ground almonds, icing sugar and flour. Remove the stalks from the currants. In a mixing bowl, beat the egg whites till almost stiff. Fold the whites into the almond and sugar mixture with a metal spoon. Stir in the blackcurrants without overmixing.

Spoon the filling into the pastry case and spread roughly level. Place the tart on top of the baking sheet or pizza stone on a middle shelf and bake for 40–45 minutes, covering it with foil if it seems to be colouring too quickly. When the filling is pale gold and lightly firm to the touch, remove and set aside to cool. Dust with icing sugar and serve not cold or hot, but warm, with cream on the side.

Sometimes, a dessert can bring a little peace into our lives. A plate of food without the sharpness, spice or searing colours. A dessert that whispers as your fork slides through. I'm thinking here of a custard tart or vanilla slice, a bowl of syllabub or spoonful of rice pudding. It is with this in mind that I made a tart of ricotta and cream, vanilla and eggs. A gentle tart, soft, creamy, unchallenging. A tart to smooth jangled nerves and ruffled feathers and a dairy lover's sweet dream.

This tart charms with its simplicity. That said, there is no harm in something on the side. A little bowl of apricot, plum or blackcurrant preserves; a dish of baked rhubarb; a trickle of passion fruit juice and seeds; or a plate of painstakingly sliced and trimmed blood orange segments will all be welcome.

## Ricotta orange tart

*Serves 8*

*For the pastry:*

| | |
|---|---|
| plain flour 180g | egg yolk 1 |
| butter 90g | a little iced water |
| icing sugar 1 heaped tablespoon | |

*For the filling:*

| | |
|---|---|
| ricotta 500g | eggs 1, large, plus an extra yolk |
| caster sugar 70g | vanilla extract 1 teaspoon |
| orange 1, medium | cornflour 1 level tablespoon |

*To finish:*

| | |
|---|---|
| double cream 125ml | icing sugar |
| soured cream 150g | |

You will also need a 20cm loose-bottomed tart tin.

To make the pastry: put the flour and butter into a food processor and blitz to fine crumbs. Alternatively, make it by hand by rubbing the butter, cut into small dice, into the flour with your fingertips. It should resemble fine, fresh breadcrumbs. Add the icing sugar and egg yolk, then the iced water – a tablespoon should be enough, but be prepared to add a little more if necessary.

Ricotta orange tart

You want a firm dough that will roll without crumbling. Tip the dough onto a lightly floured board, bring together in a ball, then wrap in baking parchment and refrigerate for 30 minutes. (And please don't skip this, otherwise your pastry will shrink as it bakes.)

Set the oven at 190°C and place a baking sheet in the oven. You will bake the tart on top of it; the extra heat it gives will ensure a crisp base. Remove the pastry from the fridge, roll it out into a disc large enough to fit the tart tin and come up the sides, then lower it into the tin. Press the dough gently into the edges and up the sides. Trim the top of the tart, cutting the pastry level with the top of the tin.

Gently press a piece of baking parchment or kitchen foil into the tin on top of the pastry and up the sides with a generous overhang (it makes it easier to remove if you have some spare to grab hold of). Fill it to the brim with baking beans (I use old coffee beans; they've been going for ever) then place on the hot baking sheet and bake for 15 minutes.

Remove the paper or foil and beans then return the tin to the oven for 5-7 minutes until the base of the pastry feels dry to the touch. Remove and lower the heat to 160°C.

Mix the filling: put the ricotta and sugar in the bowl of a food mixer. Zest the orange. Add the egg and egg yolk, the vanilla and orange zest and mix briefly. Add the cornflour, mix again, then transfer to the pastry case, smoothing flat with a rubber spatula. Return to the oven and bake for 25 minutes.

The filling will appear not quite set in the middle. It will wobble a little when lightly shaken. That is as it should be. Leave to cool, then refrigerate for an hour.

Beat the double cream till almost thick; it should sit in soft folds, like an unmade bed, rather than stand in peaks. Fold the soured cream in gently with a fork then spoon on top of the tart, pushing it gently over to cover the surface. Return to the fridge for an hour.

To serve, dust with sifted icing sugar. Your tart needs no decoration. Its beauty is in its simplicity and the contrast between soured cream and sweet filling.

The thick, nutty crunch of a pecan pie. The tooth-juddering sweetness of treacle tart. The lusciously cloying decadence of a tart of dark chocolate. These are recipes whose popularity is universal. What interests me are nutty tarts, those whose filling is made with roasted almonds or hazelnuts. Something to make on afternoons when I have been working outside, when someone far away is burning leaves, the garden damp and smelling faintly of mushrooms. A grey day turning slowly to gold. I come indoors, light the fire and can think only of baking. Something sweet and nutty perhaps. A cake or a tart. This time, I make a shortcrust pastry case and fill it with a mixture of ground and halved hazelnuts, a sort of frangipane with roasted nuts. As it bakes it reminds me of the marzipan tart I made thirty years ago at the castle, its fudgy almond paste filling hidden under a lattice of short pastry. A tender tart whose pastry was crisp and light and whose filling was chewy with toasted nuts. I serve this one in thin slices.

## Toasted hazelnut tart

*Serves 8*

*For the pastry:*

plain flour 180g

butter 90g

egg yolk 1

icing sugar 1 heaped tablespoon

iced water a little

   (about 2 tablespoons)

*For the filling:*

skinned hazelnuts 150g

   plus 50g for the top

butter 175g

caster sugar 175g

eggs 2

plain flour 150g

vanilla extract half a teaspoon

raspberries 200g

You will need a loose-bottomed tart tin 22cm in diameter (20cm across the base).

   To make the pastry: put the flour and butter into a food processor and blitz to fine crumbs. If you prefer you can make it by hand by rubbing the butter, cut into small dice, into the flour with your fingertips. Either way, it should resemble fine, fresh breadcrumbs. Add the egg yolk, icing sugar and iced water – a tablespoon or two should be enough but add a little more if necessary. You want a firm dough that will roll without crumbling.

Toasted hazelnut tart

Tip the dough onto a lightly floured board, bring together in a ball, then wrap in baking parchment and refrigerate for 30 minutes.

Place the pastry on a lightly floured board and roll it out into a disc a little larger than the tart tin. Lift it, with the help of the rolling pin, into the tart tin, then push it tenderly into the edges and up the sides. Trim the overhanging pastry. Leave no holes or tears. Chill the pastry for 30 minutes.

Set the oven at 190°C. Place an empty baking sheet in the oven – you will bake the tart on this. Place a piece of baking parchment or foil in the pastry case, lightly flattening it to cover the pastry, then fill it with baking beans – bake for 20 minutes.

Make the filling: spread the hazelnuts out on a baking sheet and toast them in the oven for about 10 minutes, watching them carefully. They should turn a little darker and smell warmly nutty. Tip them into the bowl of a food processor and process briefly. The idea is not to reduce the nuts to fine crumbs but to a mixture of sizes, both fine crumbs and larger pieces. A mixture of grit and gravel if you like.

Remove the tart case from the oven and lift out the parchment and beans. Return to the oven for 5–7 minutes until the surface of the pastry feels dry to the touch. Lower the heat to 180°C.

Cream the butter and sugar together to a soft, light consistency, then introduce the eggs, lightly beaten, a little at a time. Mix in the flour, ground nuts and the vanilla extract. Spread half of the mixture over the pastry case, add the raspberries, then the rest of the mixture. Bake for about 30–35 minutes until the top is golden brown, the filling lightly firm. Leave to settle for a good 20 minutes before slicing.

I loved school dinners and in particular the puddings. The dented aluminium trays with their doughy cargo of yellow sponge and red jam; deep apple crumble with its curiously moreish sandy topping; and, for me at least, the quiet joy of watching rhubarb juice and custard curdle together in their dish. Best pudding of all was treacle tart. Large, shallow trays with thick pastry and a treacly middle gooey enough to pull your fillings out. Even now, the smell of treacle tart will take me back to my days as dinner monitor – a feeder even then.

No longer a receptacle for stale breadcrumbs, a treacle tart can now be found on the coolest of restaurant menus. Thick and wobbly, made with sourdough crumbs and served with an egg of crème fraîche, or dark and skinny, with a hint of black treacle, this is a recipe that refuses to die, despite it being mostly sugar. Recipes for it are a minefield. Even some of the most trusted names slip up with this recipe, producing a tart that is overly sweet, dry or mean. The pastry should be short and without sugar; the filling as deep as it is sweet. Treacle tart is what it is. A soft and chewy party of golden syrup and butter. I, for one, am helpless to resist.

A spritz of lemon juice is a pleasing addition to the classic recipe. It slices through the sweetness. And with citrus in mind, I have recently taken to stirring in a hefty dollop of marmalade, the bitter notes of the orange jam more than welcome amongst the sugar hit of golden syrup.

## Marmalade treacle tart

You will need a pie plate with sloping sides. All pie plates vary slightly in size. For the sake of accuracy, my pie plate measures 20cm across the bottom and 27cm across the top from rim to rim.

*Serves 8*

*For the pastry:*

plain flour  200g

butter  100g, cold from the fridge

egg yolk  1

iced water

*For the filling:*

golden syrup  350g

marmalade  450g

double cream  3 tablespoons

egg yolk  1

fresh white breadcrumbs  300g

Make the pastry: put the flour and butter into a food processor and blitz to fine crumbs. You could do this by hand if you like, rubbing the butter, cut into small dice, into the flour with your fingertips. It should resemble fine, fresh breadcrumbs. Add the egg yolk, lightly beaten, and the iced water – a tablespoon or two should be enough. You want a firm but easy to roll dough.

Bring the dough together into a ball, then wrap in baking parchment and refrigerate for 30 minutes.

Marmalade treacle tart

Place the pastry on a lightly floured board and roll it out into a disc a little larger than the pie plate. Lift it, with the help of the rolling pin, into the pie plate, then push it tenderly into the edges and up the sides and over the rim. Trim any overhanging pastry. Leave no holes or tears. Chill the pastry for 30 minutes.

Set the oven at 190°C and place a baking sheet in the oven to get hot. Line the pastry case with foil or baking parchment, fill with baking beans and bake for 20 minutes. Remove the beans and parchment and return the tart to the oven for 5 minutes or until dry to the touch, then remove from the oven. Lower the heat to 180°C.

Warm the golden syrup in a saucepan, add the marmalade and as soon as it becomes liquid remove from the heat. Add the cream, egg yolk and then the breadcrumbs. Tip into the baked tart case and bake for 30 minutes.

# Pudding and other matters

'Pudding' is the most jubilant of words. 'Dessert', on the other hand, hints at something altogether calmer and more serene.

Many desserts describe themselves rather well. The calm, undulating creaminess of 'syllabub'. The shattering crispness of a 'meringue'. The cuteness of a tiny dish of lemon 'posset'. Sometimes, it is fanciful. I have always felt the word 'crumble' sounds like someone walking up a long gravel drive, just as 'trifle' is probably the sound you make as you fall into a bowl of sponge and whipped cream. I am as much a sucker for their names as I am for their tastes and textures – the gentleness of flummery, charlotte, fool and blancmange.

That said, all desserts are silly things that should never be taken seriously. Hence the word 'trifle'. They have no purpose other than to amuse and delight. I love them. A mouthful of hot treacle sponge or a spoon of sweet, creamy rice. A sharp citrus water ice or a layer of cream, sponge cake and fruit. I may not eat much of them, but I would hate to be without them. To be denied a spoonful of sweet, pastel-coloured nothingness at the end of dinner would be a terrible thing.

It is oversimplifying matters to suggest that desserts are cold and puddings are hot, even though that is often the case. Or that a dessert is something to eat in summer whilst pudding only appears during the winter solstice. The names are pretty much interchangeable. 'Dessert' does somehow imply the involvement of fruit. 'Pudding' is synonymous with something warming – a serving of delicious stodge.

# Fools, syllabub and panna cotta

To this seven-year-old, there was only ever one acceptable cold dessert. A milk pudding called Instant Whip, a commercial milk pudding that came in a sachet – strawberry or vanilla flavour – to which you added milk and let it set. The utter joy of making dessert reduced to a two-minute job with a hand whisk. Instant Whip disappeared from the shelves in 2004 to be replaced by the more softly textured Angel Delight. The latter having in its favour a rather delicious butterscotch version.

Such desserts were only a step away from a classic sixteenth-century syllabub, but without the hassle of whipping cream and grating and squeezing citrus fruits. I may have moved on a little from instant packet desserts, but a love of softly whipped creamy puddings – custard-cup 'nursery' desserts – hasn't changed. What is more, I doubt it ever will.

While I reserve proper puddings – steamed sponges, baked rice, roast fruits – for warming up a chilly winter night, the desserts of summer are mere passing fancies, the stuff of dreams. Scarlet fruit crushed and stirred into whipped cream – (the fool); the juice of ripe berries soaked into soft white bread – (summer pudding); fruit juice churned into glittering granita and sorbet. The desserts of summer mark the passing of the season from pale pink early rhubarb and strawberries through the scarlet-orange apricots, peaches and then on to plums and dark, velvety raspberries. The few short weeks of the damson will be celebrated too, as will the brief finding of a supply of mulberries.

It has always been the gooseberry season I look forward to most. Fruits I picked for holiday money as a thirteen-year-old, scratched and prickled to kingdom come, but outside in the summer sunshine, happy as a lark. I still have a soft spot for their innate sourness. They make the perfect fool. A snap of sharpness to contrast with the general creaminess. The only change I have ever made to this classic summer recipe is to stir in a few drops of elderflower cordial, to introduce a further kick of acidity to the clouds of cream.

# Gooseberry and elderflower fool

*Serves 4*

gooseberries  450g  
caster sugar

elderflower cordial  a splash  
double cream  300ml

Top and tail the gooseberries, by which I mean remove the dead flower from one end and the stalk from the other. Put them in a stainless-steel pan and sprinkle over a little sugar. How much you use will depend on the sourness of your fruit. I use about 3 tablespoons for this amount of fruit if they are hard and unripe. You can always add a little more once they have softened.

Put the fruit over a gentle heat and leave to soften. Take care that the berries do not catch on the bottom – you can add a tablespoon of water if you wish, but I don't find this necessary if you keep the heat low. When the fruit is pale and swollen, stir in a splash of elderflower cordial and squash the fruit gently with a fork, leaving a rough mash rather than a smooth purée, and set it aside to cool.

Whip the cream softly, so that it rests in folds rather than in stiff peaks. Fold the crushed fruit into the cream, leaving trails of unblended fruit throughout. Spoon into glasses and let the fools rest for a while before serving.

Traditionally, custard was added to the cream and sugar of many fool recipes. I'm not sure this suits all fruits, the vanilla often masking the delicate notes of the fruit. That said, a proper custard is a worthwhile addition to an apple fool.

# Toffee apple fool

Once the sugar has been added, keep a close eye on the fruit. Let the apples colour and caramelise a little here and there – they will smell like baked apples and take on a pale toffee colour.

Toffee apple fool

*Serves 6*

*For the apples:*
cooking apples  1kg                    ground cinnamon
butter  40g                                     half a teaspoon
cloves  4                                      caster sugar  100g

*For the custard:*
double cream  225ml                 caster sugar  35g
egg yolks  4

*To finish:*
double cream  250ml               a little candied orange peel

Peel and core the cooking apples, then roughly chop or slice them. Melt the butter in a large, shallow pan – I use a 28cm deep-sided frying pan – add the apples, cloves and the cinnamon and cook over a moderately high heat for 10 minutes, covered with a lid, until the fruit is soft enough to crush to a purée. Stir from time to time, letting the apples colour a little. (If the apples get a little dry, add 2 tablespoons of water to the pan.) When the apples are soft, stir in the sugar and watch carefully as it starts to caramelise. Remove from the heat.

Discard the cloves – they have done their work – and crush the apples to a soft, fluffy purée with a fork, vegetable masher or in a food mixer. Transfer to a bowl, cover and chill in the fridge. (If you want to cool them quickly, put them in a bowl over a larger bowl of ice cubes. When they are cool, cover and refrigerate.)

To make the custard: pour the cream into a saucepan, then place over a low heat until hot (keep a close eye on it) but do not allow it to boil.

Beat the yolks and sugar until thick and pale, then pour in the warm cream. Wash the saucepan and return to the heat, then pour in the custard. Warm gently, stirring almost continuously, until the mixture has thickened a little. Transfer to a bowl using a rubber spatula, then set aside to cool before refrigerating for an hour.

When the custard and the apples are completely cool, whip the cream to soft folds, then gently mix together with the apple and custard. Finish with a slice or two of candied citrus peel.

As a gangly twenty-year-old I went to work in a restaurant in the West Country, whose menu offered a dessert known as syllabub. I had never met the word before but making it was one of my first tasks. An exercise, it turned out, in the delicate business of whipping cream. Stop too soon and you have a milkshake, one beat too many and you have butter. Even now I approach the task with mild trepidation, never taking my eyes from the cream till it is exactly at the consistency I need it. A wise cook is the one who stops before the cream is thick enough, then proceeds a few strokes at a time.

It turned out that the charmingly named syllabub was nothing more than a fool with alcohol. We made a lemon one and a fabulous raspberry version with eau de vie de framboise and crushed fruit. Many historical recipes suggest using white wine, but better now I think is to use a medium-dry sherry, with all its gorgeous notes of nuts and caramel.

## Oloroso syllabub with blood orange

I like to finish the syllabub with strips of candied peel dipped in dark chocolate. You can buy them ready-made. They are sometimes sold as 'orangettes', but they are easy enough to make yourself. I use whole pieces of orange peel (Italian grocers often have them), because they are softer and juicer than the pre-chopped sort. Take great care when whipping the cream, sherry and juice together.

*Serves 4*

blood orange  1, small
lemon  1, small
oloroso sherry  75ml

caster sugar  75g
double cream  300ml

*For the chocolate-dipped peel:*
dark chocolate  50g
candied orange peel  75g

blood oranges  2, to finish

Finely grate the zest of the blood orange and the lemon into a mixing bowl. If you are using a food mixer, use the mixer bowl. Squeeze the fruits' juices into the bowl, pour in the sherry and stir in the sugar. Mix until the sugar has dissolved, then set aside for a good two hours or even overnight.

Make the chocolate-dipped peel. Melt the chocolate in a small bowl over a pan of simmering water, removing it from the heat as soon as the chocolate is liquid. Cut the candied peel into short pieces, about 1cm thick and the length of a matchstick. Dip each piece of peel into the chocolate, place on a piece of baking parchment and leave in a cool place until the chocolate has set.

Pour the double cream into the juice, then whip until the syllabub starts to thicken. It is best to whip slowly, watching the consistency of the syllabub constantly. As it starts to thicken, the cream will feel heavy on the whisk and you should stop as soon as the syllabub is thick enough to sit in soft, gentle waves. If you whisk until it stands in peaks you have gone too far. Keep chilled in the refrigerator.

Remove the peel from the blood oranges with a very sharp knife, taking off every shred of white pith. Slice the fruit thinly. To serve, spoon the chilled syllabub into bowls, then add the slices of blood orange and the chocolate-dipped candied peel. And, by the way, you can freeze this for a wonderful ice cream.


I have always rather liked blancmange, if only for its name, which sounds like a jelly being shaken from its mould. The milky dessert fell a little in my esteem when I discovered bavarois, the French equivalent, set with less gelatine and often flavoured delicately with vanilla or framboise. And then I met panna cotta, its superior Italian sister...

Light, barely set, so fragile you feel the need to whisper in its presence, this is a dessert I longed to get right. Early attempts used too much gelatine (you could have played soccer with them), later versions too little (one particularly memorable attempt being akin to a smoothie). My problem was not trusting the quantity of gelatine required. A couple of small sheets of leaf gelatine is all you need to achieve the perfect set. Over the last few years, I have made this lightly set cream pudding with chocolate, rosewater and yoghurt. The latter usually being a bit grainy. My favourites of all are those made with buttermilk or chocolate.

Buttermilk panna cotta, apricot purée

# Buttermilk panna cotta, apricot purée

*Makes 4 small panna cotta*

leaf gelatine  2 leaves
double cream  350ml

caster sugar  100g
buttermilk  150ml

*For the purée:*
apricots  1 × 400g tin

half a lemon

You will also need four small ramekins or coffee cups.

Put the gelatine leaves in a small bowl of cold water to soften.

Pour the cream into a small, non-stick saucepan, add the sugar, then bring almost to the boil. Remove from the heat, gently squeeze the water from the softened gelatine, add to the cream and let the gelatine dissolve. Pour the buttermilk into the cream and gelatine, stir gently, then pour through a fine sieve over a jug. (Don't skip this; it is essential for a smooth result.)

Pour the panna cotta mixture into the four small ramekins or cups, place in the fridge and leave to set for 4 hours.

To make the apricot purée, put the apricots, lightly drained, into a blender and process to a thick purée. Add lemon juice to taste, squeeze by squeeze, tasting as you go.

To serve, unmould the panna cotta. An easy way to do this is to dip the dishes into hot water, run a palette knife around the edge to loosen them, then turn upside down on to a little dish. A firm shake should dislodge the panna cotta from its home. Spoon some of the apricot purée over each.

# Custards, trifle and summer puddings

To my mind, crème caramel has always been something for old people. A bag of Werther's Originals in pudding form. Happily, I now qualify for such treats and curse the ageism that stopped me eating this lightest, silkiest, glossiest little pudding.

A perfectly made crème caramel is a rare and beautiful thing. All too often they are eggy, too pale or come with tell-tale bubbles from being cooked in too hot an oven. The calmest of desserts, they are not the easiest to get right. I can honestly say that I often find the supermarket versions more reliable than homemade.

A well-made custard is unblemished, with dark, bitter-sweet caramel and a silky texture. The trick to keeping them bubble-free is to bake them in an oven no hotter than 150°C and to take them out as soon as they are set. Overcooking is the very death to something so gentle.

As much as I distrust the incessant tinkering of creative cooks – myself included – I do think the cardamom I have introduced into this is a sound idea. It is my favourite spice by far, which means I am apt to overuse it, but here it works, as indeed it does with almost any dairy-based recipe. (Try a few finely ground seeds in a vanilla ice cream or a rice pudding.)

I am often asked what I would like to eat at my final feast. Well, that meal could well end with a perfectly executed crème caramel. If they can find the cardamom, I would die even happier.

Cardamom custard

# Cardamom custards

Chill the custards thoroughly, preferably overnight, before turning out.

*Makes 4*

full-fat milk 500ml
green cardamom pods 15
eggs 2, and an extra 4 yolks

caster sugar 75g
vanilla extract a couple of drops

*For the caramel:*
caster sugar 125g

Pour the milk into a saucepan. Break open the cardamom pods and extract the seeds within. Using a pestle and mortar, grind them to a coarse powder, drop them into the milk and bring to the boil. Just before the milk starts to rise up the sides of the pan, remove from the heat, cover and set aside to infuse.

Make the caramel: put the sugar and just enough water to cover it into a saucepan and boil, over a high heat, until the caramel turns a dark butterscotch colour. If it isn't dark enough, your puddings will be pale; if too dark, they will be bitter. Pour the caramel into 4 × 200ml moulds, ensure they are evenly covered, then set aside.

Set the oven at 150°C. Put the caramel-lined moulds into a roasting tin. Lightly beat together the egg yolks, eggs and caster sugar. Place a fine sieve over the eggs and sugar, then pour the cardamom-infused milk into it. Discard the cardamom, add the vanilla extract, mix well, then ladle into the moulds.

Boil the kettle. Pour the just-boiled water into the roasting tin to come a fraction over halfway up the sides of the moulds. Place the tin in the oven and leave for 35–40 minutes until the custards are lightly set. They should quiver when jiggled – the middle set rather than liquid.

Leave to cool in their water bath, then remove and chill in the fridge for 4 or 5 hours. Unmould by sliding a palette knife around the edge of each, turning them upside down onto a dish and letting the caramel flow around them.

Note: should there be any caramel stuck in the bottom of the moulds, simply crack it into splinters with a knife and scatter over the custards.

I rarely went grocery shopping with my father. Unpacking each cardboard box and brown paper bag, every tissue-wrapped bottle or jar, was a surprise. What, I wondered, had he brought back from his Saturday morning trip to Bromyard this time? Amongst the packages were regular purchases, instantly recognisable through their white paper – a cottage loaf from the baker's, bunches of daffs or anemones from the greengrocer and a pork pie from the butcher's. Most easily spotted of all, the one I would keep till last, was the blue and white bag in which I knew I would find the trifles. These decadent treats came in rectangular waxed paper cartons, blue and white and proudly labelled with 'real dairy cream'. There would be one for each of us.

Whoever made these trifles understood the true meaning of the word. They were small and frivolous. A layer of very light sponge, a little jam, soft, almost runny custard and piped cream. Nothing fancy, rather plain even, but they were a treat beyond measure. They were the start of a lifelong love affair with trifle, a custard-cup dessert that I could eat for breakfast (and have).

I don't think I have ever published a book without a recipe for at least one trifle. From the 10-minute recipe in *Real Fast Food* to the longest trifle recipe in the world – the sweet mincemeat and orange version I did for a television Christmas special. (Proceed with caution, it will take up an entire day of your life.) They seem to be an immutable part of what I do. Whether it's lemon (*The Kitchen Diaries*), gooseberry *(Tender, Volume II)* or rhubarb *(The Christmas Chronicles)*, there is always a layered custard, sponge and cream dessert at my side.

The most popular have been those with blackcurrants and or lemon, which brings me to my point. The best trifles are those that offer something tart – a zestful contrast to the layers of whipped cream, sweet sponge and custard. It is why you will never find peaches or strawberries in any trifle recipe of mine. If a trifle is to work, it needs a hit of sharpness. I offer two here, a favourite – from 2005 – and a dazzling lemon one from the same year.

# Nigel's delightful trifle

*Serves 6*

*For the blackcurrant layer:*
blackcurrants  475g          caster sugar  2 tablespoons
water  4 tablespoons

*For the sponge and cream layer:*
plain, good-quality sponge cake          mascarpone  250g
   350g          a couple of drops of vanilla extract
a large egg, separated          whipping or double cream  250ml
caster sugar  2 tablespoons

*To decorate:*
blackcurrants  a few sprigs          crystallised violets

Pull the blackcurrants from their stalks and put them in a stainless-steel pan with the water and caster sugar. Put them over a low to moderate heat and leave them to simmer for 7–10 minutes until they are starting to burst. Once there is plenty of purple juice remove from the heat.

Break the sponge into small pieces and push it into the bottom of a large serving bowl. Spoon the hot blackcurrants and their juice over the sponge and leave to cool. During this time the sponge will soak up much of the black-currant juice.

Put the egg yolk and sugar in a bowl and mix it well, then stir in the mascarpone and vanilla.

Whip the cream, then, when it is thick enough to lie in soft folds (rather than stand in stiff peaks), fold it lightly into the mascarpone mixture. In a separate bowl beat the egg white until it is almost stiff, then fold it into the mixture.

Spoon the mascarpone cream over the cool blackcurrants and sponge. You can smooth it flat or not. Refrigerate for a good hour or so before serving, so that the whole thing has time to come together. Decorate with fresh raw blackcurrants and, if you like, crystallised violets.

Exceptionally creamy lemon trifle

# Exceptionally creamy lemon trifle

*Serves 8*

*For the syllabub layer:*

Fino sherry  65ml

lemon  1

oranges  2

caster sugar  30g

double cream  150ml

*For the custard:*

full-cream milk  500ml

vanilla pod

egg yolks  5

caster sugar  5 tablespoons

*For the sponge layer:*

plain sponge cake  175g

best-quality lemon curd  300g

Fino sherry  150ml

*To decorate:*

oranges, small  4

Pour the sherry into the bowl of a food mixer (or a mixing bowl if you are going to make it by hand), then grate into it the zest of the lemon and the oranges. Squeeze the lemon juice and add to the mixture. You won't need the orange juice, so just drink it. Set aside the sherry and juice mixture for as long as you have. Overnight is best, but an hour is better than nothing.

To make the custard, pour the milk into a saucepan, split the vanilla pod lengthways and drop it into the milk, then bring slowly towards the boil. When the milk is on the point of boiling – it will be shuddering, bubbles will be visible and maybe a little steam – remove it from the heat and leave it for about 20 minutes. This allows the vanilla to do its stuff. Lift out the vanilla pod and scrape the seeds out into the milk with the point of a small knife.

Whisk the egg yolks with the sugar until they are thick and pale, then pour in the milk and stir. Rinse the milk pan, then pour in the custard and put it over a low heat. Stir almost constantly with a wooden spoon till it thickens somewhat, getting right down into the corners of the pan. The consistency should be that of double cream. It is essential not to let the mixture get too hot, otherwise it will curdle. (If it does, then pour straight away into a clean container, plunge it into a bowl of ice and beat furiously until it comes together.) Leave to cool a little.

Cut the sponge cake into thin slices and spread each one generously with the lemon curd. Place in the bottom of a large china or glass bowl, then pour over the 150ml of sherry. Make sure the cake is thoroughly soaked. Pour the cooled custard on top of the cake and leave in the fridge to set.

Continue with the syllabub: pour the sugar into the reserved sherry and zest mixture and start beating gently. Now pour in the cream and continue beating on a lowish speed until the syllabub starts to thicken. It is crucial to keep an eagle eye on things at this point. You should stop when the syllabub will sit in thick, soft folds, only just keeping its shape.

Spoon the syllabub on top of the custard, cover with cling film and leave in the fridge for a good few hours for the flavours to marry.

Peel the oranges with a sharp knife then cut into segments, discarding the pith as you go. Pile the fruit on top of the trifle and serve.


I make a fine summer pudding. I always have. It is not ancient like so many desserts. In fact, its history is rather misty. During the eighteenth century something resembling the recipe appears to have been offered to patients 'taking the waters' at spa hotels. It used to be known as 'hydropathic pudding', which I feel is rather underselling it.

The method is straightforward: raspberries and redcurrants are warmed with a little sugar till the redcurrants burst. The resulting compote is poured into a bread-lined pudding basin and left under a heavy weight. Our gorgeous pink pudding is then turned out of its bowl – ta-da – and served with a moat of cream.

Purists demand thin white bread and only raspberries and redcurrants. I insist that a few blackcurrants bring depth and resonance to the affair, not to mention the most magnificent shade of magenta. Others may add blueberries, strawberries and cherries which I think bring little to the party. I'm sorry, but I remain unconvinced that any good is to be had from warming up a strawberry.

I first ate this most seasonal of puddings in London, at Carrier's, the much-missed Camden Passage restaurant (well, I miss it) owned by the late Robert Carrier. A fine version it was too, and it was served as an individual pudding which made it feel exceedingly special – a little box of rubies and garnets all to oneself.

While I agree the world hardly needs another recipe for summer pudding, I offer this one for what I believe to be its almost perfect balance between fruits, bread and juice. And heaven knows, I've made enough of them.

# Summer pudding

*Serves 6*

| | |
|---|---|
| redcurrants, blackcurrants and raspberries 850g | firm, good-quality white bread 7–8 slices about 1cm thick |
| caster sugar 4 tablespoons | cream to serve |

Remove the stems from the currants, put the fruit in a stainless-steel saucepan and add the raspberries.

Add the sugar to the pan and 6 tablespoons of water and bring to the boil. The currants will start to burst and give out their juice. They will take about 3–4 minutes at a cautious simmer.

Remove the crusts from the bread. Set one piece aside, then cut the rest into 'soldiers' – that is, each bread slice into three long fingers. Push the reserved piece into the bottom of a 1.2-litre pudding basin, then line the sides with the strips of bread, pushing them together snugly so that no fruit can escape, keeping a few for the top. Fill the bread-lined basin with the fruit and its juice; it should come almost to the rim. Lay the remaining bread on top of the fruit, tearing and patching where necessary so that no fruit is showing.

Put the basin in a shallow dish or bowl to catch any juice, then place a flat plate, or small tray, on top with a heavy weight to squash the fruit down. Some juice may escape, but most will sink into the bread. Leave overnight in the fridge.

The next day, remove the weight and the plate, slide a palette knife carefully between bread and basin, then turn the pudding out onto a plate. Pass a jug of cream round – it is an essential part of the pudding.

My favourite 'modern' ice cream is my own lemon, orange and basil ice cream from *The Christmas Chronicles*. The one I describe as 'pure as a winter stream, clean as ice, almost spicy'. I would be happy to eat it every day. But there are so many others I could mention. Last year, in Kanazawa, I ate an ice cream, a Mr Whippy-style cornet, that came with a showering of pure gold leaf. It was one of the first days of spring, the almond blossom was out, I had spent the morning at the Museum of Contemporary Art and early afternoon at the fabled Kenroku-en Garden. I have always adored soft-serve ice cream, but rarely more than this. An ice that stood out, amongst the thousands I have devoured during my lifetime, for the fact that something as simple as frozen custard piped into a cornet could be decorated so extravagantly. And no, it didn't taste of much, but that is not the point. The flakes of golden leaf felt like a nod, a sign of respect, to what I consider to be one of the glories of the kitchen: the art and science of ice cream.

There has probably never been a week in which I haven't eaten some form of frozen dessert. The vanilla ice-cream wafers, Orange Mivvis and choc-ices of my childhood to the expensive scoops of gelato and homemade granita and sorbet I eat now. Ices, what Elizabeth David referred to as 'the harvest of the cold months', are an almost daily part of my life. As essential to my wellbeing as coffee or green tea.


Sorbet is an ice cream without the cream. Sorbet has a powdery, sherbet quality – an acidic snap – that renders it the most refreshing of the ices. Citrus is at the top of my list, especially lemon or the rare and inaccessible bergamot, and I have made pink grapefruit too, which was as pretty as you could imagine. It is as if crushed ripe fruits have been stirred into fresh, white snow.

Its sister, granita, its coarse grains sparkling frost-like in the light, is the most beautiful of ices to make. As the mixture of sugar syrup and fruit purée freeze, you run your fork across its surface, making furrows of glistening ice. You end up with a freezer-box of ice crystals that dissolve on your tongue like snow. And not only fruit, a coffee granita is good too, especially when it comes with an unexpected spoonful of cream.

Such frozen delights don't require the ownership of an ice-cream machine, but are radically improved if you have one. Without a machine, they tend to set in a block, like a giant lolly. The slow churning of a machine can be replaced by a regular whisking as the mixture freezes – try every hour, beating the frozen edges into the liquid middle. It will help the structure.

## Strawberry granita

Refreshing as this scarlet ice is, the water ice will be improved immeasurably with a little softly whipped cream or a spoonful of crème fraîche. But then, when haven't strawberries been improved by the addition of a little dairy produce?

*Serves 4*

strawberries 500g
elderflower cordial 120ml

whipped cream or crème fraîche
    to serve (optional)

Remove and discard the leaves from the strawberries. Place the fruit in a blender or food processor and reduce to a purée. If you have neither, put the strawberries in a bowl and crush them as finely as you can with a fork.

Stir the elderflower cordial into the strawberry purée, then pour into a freezer box. Cover tightly with a lid and freeze for about an hour and a half. Check the granita's progress regularly, occasionally stirring the freezing edges into the middle. Continue freezing and bringing the frozen edges to the middle every hour or so until you have a freezer-box of crimson ice crystals.

The granita will keep like this in the freezer for a day or two. Serve, if you like, with whipped cream or crème fraîche.

## Lemon thyme water ice

Possibly my favourite water ice of all.

*Serves 4*

caster sugar 100g
water 200ml
lemon 1

lemon thyme 30g
lemon juice 200ml

Put the sugar in a small, heavy-based saucepan, pour in the water and place over a moderate heat. Using a vegetable peeler, remove the peel from the lemon in thin strips, push into the sugar and water and bring to the boil, stirring occasionally, until the sugar has dissolved.

Rinse the bunch of lemon thyme under cold running water, bash it lightly with a rolling pin, then push it down into the syrup with a spoon, cover with a lid and leave to cool. Refrigerate until thoroughly cold. You could speed up the infusion by putting the pan into a large bowl of ice.

Remove the pan from the fridge and lift out the bunch of lemon thyme, shaking it as you go. Don't worry if some of the leaves fall off into the syrup. Pour the lemon juice into the syrup, then pour into the bowl of an ice-cream machine and churn until almost frozen. Transfer to a plastic freezer-box and freeze till needed.

To make the ice without a machine, pour the syrup and lemon juice into a plastic freezer-box and mix thoroughly. Freeze for 2 hours, then stir and return to the freezer. Continue freezing and occasionally stirring until frozen.

# Roast apricot water ice

*Serves 6*

| | |
|---|---|
| apricots 600g | water 200ml |
| caster sugar 200g | lemon juice of 1 |

Set the oven at 200°C. Halve and stone the apricots and put them, cut side up, in a non-stick roasting tin or baking dish. Scatter half the sugar over them and roast for about 20 minutes, checking the sugar has melted and is browning but not burning. Remove from the oven when the apricots are fully soft and the syrup is golden. While the apricots are roasting, put the remaining sugar into a small saucepan with the water and lemon juice and bring to the boil. Remove from the heat as soon as the sugar has dissolved and leave to cool.

Tip the apricots and their roasting juices into a food processor and blend to a smooth purée, then pour in the cooled syrup and combine. Transfer the apricot mixture to an ice-cream machine and churn until almost frozen, before scooping into a freezer-box, covering tightly and freezing until needed.

To make the sorbet without a machine, pour the apricot mixture into a plastic freezer-box and mix thoroughly. Freeze for 2 hours, then stir and return to the freezer. Stir occasionally until frozen.

# Watermelon granita

Refreshing, quick and simple. An ice for high summer.

*Serves 6*

caster sugar  4 tablespoons       watermelon  1.5kg
water  4 tablespoons

Make a sugar syrup by bringing the caster sugar and water to the boil in a small pan. Lower the heat and simmer until the sugar is completely dissolved, then remove from the heat and leave to cool. You can speed the process up by lowering the saucepan into a bowl of cold water and ice cubes.

Remove the rind and seeds from the watermelon and discard. You will end up with about 1kg of flesh. Roughly chop the watermelon, then process to a thick slush in a blender or food processor.

Stir the sugar syrup into the crushed watermelon, then pour into a stainless steel or rigid plastic freezer-box and freeze for an hour. Using a fork, gently bring the crystals of frozen mixture that lie around the edges into the middle, then return it to the freezer.

Do not let the granita freeze into one vast ice cube. Instead, encourage the crystallisation by regular, gentle mixing. Continue gently stirring the frozen crystals into the scarlet liquid every hour, until the granita is entirely, but lightly, frozen into millions of tiny crystals. It should take about 4 or 5 hours.

Hand on heart, I cannot remember a day without ice cream. There is always, always, a tub in my freezer. Sometimes homemade, other times not, the best often delivered with my organic box.

Ice creams are made in this kitchen on a regular basis, their flavours following the ebb and flow of the seasons. Sometimes, they involve a homemade custard, which sounds scary but is easy enough with a little care. It is essential not to overheat your custard. This is something that needs to be made without distractions. Once the milk or cream has been mixed with the sugar and eggs and goes back into the pan to thicken over a low heat, your concentration is crucial. This is the moment to take care, watching the mixture like a hawk might watch a mouse, stirring almost constantly, then, as the custard starts to thicken, it must be cooled as quickly as possible. I like to have a bowl of ice cubes to hand. Should the mixture appear slightly grainy, I immediately pour it into a cold bowl, plunge it onto the ice cubes, then whisk furiously to dispel the heat. It usually works. Should you prefer to use ready-made custard, no judgement, but I do recommend you choose a good one, from the chiller cabinet, made with fresh cream and vanilla.

## Blackberry and apple ice cream

*Serves 4*

sharp cooking apples  1kg
golden caster sugar  200g
single or whipping cream
    400ml

egg yolks  4
blackberries  a handful

To make the ice cream, peel, core and slice the apples. Put them in a saucepan with half the sugar and stew over a low heat (they need no water, but keep an eye on them so they don't burn). Once a little juice has formed, cover and simmer gently for 15–20 minutes, stirring from time to time. Mash with a fork and cool.

Bring the cream to the boil and remove from the heat. Beat the egg yolks and remaining sugar, then stir in the hot cream. Rinse the saucepan – really important – and return the custard to it, stirring over a low heat until it thickens slightly. Cool quickly by plunging the pan into ice-cold water, stirring constantly.

Mix the custard with the mashed apples and churn in an ice-cream machine until almost frozen. Drop in the blackberries and churn briefly until the berries start to break up. Scrape into a freezer-box and freeze.

Blackberry and apple ice cream

Damson ice cream

If you don't have an ice-cream machine, pour into a plastic freezer-box, cover and freeze for an hour. Remove and beat, then return to the freezer. Repeat three or four times.

The most precious ices are those whose ingredients are in season only briefly. Bergamot, blood orange, mulberries and damsons are four that spring to mind. The latter are something I pounce on as soon as I spot them in early autumn and freeze for later. (They are almost impossible to locate out of season.)

## Damson ice cream

There are probably too many ice creams in this book, but the idea of something as fleeting and seasonal as a purple-blue damson made into an iced dessert appeals to me. So intense is the damson's flavour, it seems pointless to make your own custard. The subtleties of your handiwork will be lost against the dark, powerful fruit notes of the deepest-flavoured of all plums.

*Serves 6*

damsons  450g
caster sugar  4 tablespoons

ready-made custard  250ml

Wash the damsons, tip them into a stainless-steel pan, then pour over the sugar and 3 tablespoons of water. Bring to the boil and turn the heat down to a simmer. Continue cooking until the fruit starts to soften, its skin splits and deep purple juice has formed in the pan – about 10 minutes.

Suspend a sieve over the top of a mixing bowl, then push the fruit and juice through the sieve until only the stones are left. Scrape any purée from the bottom of the sieve (it tends to collect in large amounts) and stir into the juice. Leave to cool.

Slowly stir the custard into the damson purée. Pour into an ice-cream machine and churn till frozen.

Lemon ice cream

# Lemon ice cream

Another quick ice, this time one that doesn't need churning. Being both acidic and creamy, it carries something of both sorbet and ice cream.

*Serves 4*

double cream  500ml          good-quality lemon curd  300g
natural yoghurt  200g        juice of 2 lemons

Whip the cream until it is thick, stopping before it is stiff enough to sit up in peaks. It should lie in slovenly folds. Stir in the yoghurt, lemon curd and juice. Tip everything into a freezer-box and freeze for a minimum of 6 hours. Beat every hour with a whisk to ensure a creamier consistency.

# Marmalade and chocolate-chip ice cream

What started as an experiment ended up as a beautiful custard-coloured soft-scoop ice cream of which I am almost absurdly proud. It turns out that adding marmalade also stops the ice cream from setting like a brick. The flavours are stunning. If only cooking was always like this.

*Serves 6*

single or whipping cream  500ml     marmalade  400g
egg yolks  4                        dark chocolate  100g,
golden caster sugar  2 tablespoons      roughly chopped

Bring the cream to the boil in a saucepan. Beat the egg yolks and sugar in a heatproof bowl till thick, then pour in the hot cream and stir.

Rinse the saucepan and return the custard to it, stirring the mixture over a low heat till it starts to thicken slightly. It won't become really thick.

Cool the custard quickly – I do this by plunging the pan into a shallow sink of cold water – stirring constantly, then chill thoroughly.

Marmalade and chocolate-chip ice cream

Stir the marmalade into the chilled custard. Now you can either make the ice cream by hand or use an ice-cream machine. If making it in a machine, pour in the custard and churn according to the manufacturer's instructions. When the ice cream is almost thick enough to transfer to the freezer, fold in the chopped chocolate, churning briefly to mix. Scoop into a lidded plastic box and freeze till you are ready to eat it.

If you are making it by hand, pour the custard and the chopped chocolate into a freezer-box and place it in the freezer, removing it and giving it a quick beat with a whisk every hour until it has set.

I ate my first frozen yoghurt in Stockholm and have made it regularly ever since. The thick dairy produce freezes more lightly than custard, so the result is more refreshing. The sourness is dazzling. I like mine plain, without the rainbow of additions they are wont to scatter over the ice's pristine whiteness. There is something pure and unsullied about a tub of frozen soft-serve yoghurt, just as there is about a field of newly fallen snow.

## Mint frozen yoghurt with dark chocolate

You don't need an ice-cream machine for this. Just a freezer and a freezer-box. It helps the texture of the finished water ice if you can remember to beat the mixture with a fork every hour or so as it freezes, but this is not essential. There is something of the After Eight mint about this.

*Serves 8*

granulated white sugar  250g
mint sprigs  10g
mint leaves  10g

water  250ml
yoghurt  500ml
dark chocolate  100g

Put the sugar and half the mint sprigs, leaves and stalks, into a food processor. Pulse until you end up with moist, green sugar. Put the green sugar and water into a saucepan and bring to the boil. As soon as all the sugar has dissolved, remove it from the heat and quickly cool the mixture – either by putting the

Baked pears with Marsala

pan in a sink of cold water, or, as I do, by pouring the syrup into a bowl set in a larger one of ice cubes.

Blitz the remaining mint briefly with the yoghurt, then stir into the cooled syrup and mix gently. Pour the mixture through a fine sieve into a chilled plastic freezer-box. Freeze for a couple of hours or until ice crystals start to form on the edges, then stir or whisk them into the liquid centre and return to the freezer. Repeat once, an hour or so later, then leave until almost frozen.

When you are ready to serve the frozen yoghurt, chop the chocolate finely then melt it in a bowl placed over a pan of simmering water. Serve the mint ice in small bowls, the melted chocolate trickled over.

# A plea for hot pudding

If there is one dessert whose demise is on the cards it must be the hot pudding. Not so much crumble – without which no civilised society could exist – but those such as steamed treacle sponge and its friends. Puddings that have been around since Isabella Beeton was on the throne. A few of these are kept going by restaurants that understand we will eat such things even if we would never make them. But here's the daft thing: if ever such a pudding comes to the table, it will be gone in minutes. Spoons will appear from nowhere to scoop up the sponge, syrup and cream.

While fruit-flecked cabinet puddings and Sussex Pond will go the way of roly-poly and junket, a few will last for ever – in my book that will include treacle sponge, rice pudding and that housewives' receptacle for leftover bread – bread and butter pudding, even if it is made with vanilla-scented panettone.

## Baked pears with Marsala

*Serves 4*

*For the pears:*

| | |
|---|---|
| large pears  4 | caster sugar  3 tablespoons |
| a squeeze of lemon | butter  50g |
| sweet Marsala  3 tablespoons | |

*For the syrup:*
caster sugar  100g                    juice of a lemon
water  1 litre

Set the oven at 200°C. Peel the pears and cut them in half, dropping them into cold water with a squeeze of lemon juice in it as you go to stop them browning.

Make a syrup with the caster sugar and water and lemon, add the halved pears and simmer for 20–25 minutes, depending on the ripeness of the pears.

Put the Marsala, caster sugar and butter into a roasting tin, then add the drained pears. Bake for about 45–50 minutes, till the fruit is butter-soft. It is essential to baste them once or twice, turning them in their juices.

Remove the pears to a serving dish, then place the roasting tin with its syrup over a moderate heat. Let the syrup bubble for 1–2 minutes, giving it the occasional stir. As the sweet, buttery sauce thickens, spoon it over the pears and serve.

# Crumble

If heaven has a smell it is probably that of warm ironing and apple crumble. I can't begin to tell you how many crumbles I have made over the years (or, come to think of it, the amount of ironing I have done). There are not rules so much as preferences. I like the texture of the crumble to be made of crumbs of different sizes. Rubble rather than sand. I achieve this by splashing a little water into the crumbs and shaking the bowl gently back and forth.

The fruit should be juicy enough to bubble through the crust here and there, but not so much you end up with islands of crumble in a sea of fruit. Each to their own, but my favourites are gooseberry, damson, plum and rhubarb. Strangely, I prefer apple crumble cold, with cream.

Crumble doesn't take well to the meddlings of imaginative cooks. Finish off the jar of Christmas mincemeat by stirring the last few spoonfuls into an apple crumble; add a knife point of bun-spices to one of plum and strew a few flaked almonds over the surface of an apricot version, but that really is as far as it goes. I hate to squash innovation and experiment, but in the case of a crumble...

# A deeply appley apple crumble

*Serves 6*

| | |
|---|---|
| cooking apples 850g | golden caster sugar 75g |
| half a lemon | butter 30g |

*For the crumble:*

| | |
|---|---|
| butter 95g | golden caster sugar 45g |
| plain flour 150g | |

Peel and core the apples, cut them into plump chunks (roughly 2cm on each side) and toss them with the juice of the half-lemon and the caster sugar.

Melt the butter in a shallow pan over a frisky heat. When it starts to sizzle, tip in the apples and sugar and let the fruit colour lightly. It is essential not to move the apples around too much. Let the sugar caramelise here and there so the fruit is sticky and golden in patches. There should be a faint smell of toffee.

Lift the apples and put them in a baking dish – about 1.5 litres in capacity – together with the pan juices. Set the oven at 180°C.

Make the crumble by rubbing the butter into the flour with your fingertips (you could happily use a food processor here). When the mixture looks like fine breadcrumbs, stir in the sugar. Add 2 tablespoons of water. Shake the crumble mixture till some of it sticks together in gravel-sized lumps and tip it over the apples to cover them. Bake for 45–50 minutes till golden.

# Spiced plum crumble

One can get into a terrible row about the best accompaniment for any sort of fruit crumble. You have team custard, then those who insist on cream and others still who vote for firmer, sharper crème fraîche or yoghurt. The delightful sourness of the plums seems to me to beg for sweet, yellow double cream, but we won't get into an argument if you bring out a jug of custard. This spiced crumble is just as good cold as it is hot, even after a night in the fridge. Oh, and I do think it is worth grinding the cardamom fresh – while ground

Spiced plum crumble

cinnamon and mace keep their magic, it tends to disappear from cardamom rather more quickly.

*Serves 6*

green cardamom pods  12
ground cinnamon  1 teaspoon
ground ginger  1 teaspoon
mixed spice  1 teaspoon
plums  750g

caster sugar  50g
plain flour  150g
butter  85g
light muscovado sugar  75g
ground almonds  75g

You will also need a round baking dish measuring approximately 22cm in diameter, lightly buttered.

Set the oven at 180°C. Crack open the cardamom pods, then extract the brown seeds from within. Grind the seeds to a powder in a spice mill or using a pestle and mortar. Mix the ground cardamom with the cinnamon, ginger and mixed spice.

Halve the plums and discard their stones. Toss the fruit and caster sugar together and pile into the buttered baking dish. Put the flour in a large mixing bowl. Cut the butter into small cubes and rub into the flour with your fingertips until it resembles fine breadcrumbs. Alternatively, blend in a food processor. Stir in the muscovado sugar, ground spices and almonds, then sprinkle lightly with a tablespoon of water. Shake the bowl back and forth until you have crumbs of different sizes, then scatter over the fruit.

Bake for about 50 minutes until deep golden brown and the fruit is bubbling through the crust.

Nothing made me happier than to arrive home from school to see steam on the leaded light kitchen windows. Little rivulets of water on the fugged-up glass meant steamed pudding, possibly my favourite pudding of all. Not that it would be homemade, of course, a handmade sponge bubbling in its pot, with the comforting smell of spices and damp muslin. In our house, steamed pudding would be from a tin, its label adrift in the water, the swoosh of steam that emanated as it was opened the best sound of all. Whether sultana or chocolate, or to a lesser extent jam (well, 'they' called it jam), these weekly hot sponges were a treat beyond measure. The biggest and best being the one with a sticky hat of golden syrup.

Half a century later and you will occasionally find such old-fashioned treasure steaming up my windows. Not from a tin now though. I prefer them homemade, with butter and sugar, flour and spices and the double syrup whammy of both treacle and maple. By treacle I mean the golden variety, thick and impossibly sticky; I use it for the sweetness it brings. Maple syrup, even a small amount, introduces a mellow toffee note that is worth every penny.

We always ate it with cream from a tin. There is cream still, but it is now thick and yellow, cold from the fridge, to slide down the hot dome of steaming dough. For years I have done battle with china basins, greaseproof paper, sheets of muslin and string, which is probably why a steamed pudding is such a rare occurrence. A reusable plastic bowl, complete with a clip-on lid, is now resident in my kitchen. It carries none of the romance of the muslin-tied, crackle-glazed basin but is a hell of a lot less trouble.

## Steamed spiced treacle pudding

It is essential that no water penetrates the pudding as it steams. Cover the pudding tightly with baking parchment and foil to stop the water getting in as it cooks. Better still, buy a plastic basin with a clip-on lid. Leave the pudding to settle for 10 minutes in the hot water before turning out. It will help it keep its shape when you do so. Be generous with the golden syrup; it is important that it thoroughly saturates the top of the pudding.

*Serves 4*

butter  150g
caster sugar  150g
eggs  2, large
self-raising flour  150g
ground cinnamon  half a teaspoon

ground ginger  half a teaspoon
finely grated zest of a lemon
milk  2 tablespoons
golden syrup  2 tablespoons
maple syrup  2 tablespoons

You will also need a 1.2-litre heatproof pudding basin with a lid.

Beat the butter and caster sugar until pale and thick. Break the eggs into a bowl and mix with a fork, then gradually introduce into the butter and

Steamed spiced treacle pudding

sugar, beating all the time. Add the self-raising flour, the spices, grated zest and the milk. Pour the golden and maple syrups into the bowl, then spoon in the mixture and cover with a lid or baking parchment and foil or muslin, tied tightly with string or a rubber band.

Steam for an hour and half, leave for 10 minutes, then remove the lid or covering and loosen the sides with a palette knife. Turn out and serve with extra warmed maple syrup and double cream.

## Hot rice pudding with apple and maple syrup

'As comfortable as an old teddy bear' is how I once described this pudding, and I still think that. Especially on a frosty January evening.

*Serves 4*

pudding rice  150g
water  500ml
full-cream milk  500ml
ground cinnamon  a good pinch

apple  a large one
caster sugar  3 tablespoons
maple syrup

Put the rice in a small pan and cover it with the water. Bring to the boil, then lower the heat a little and simmer until the water has almost evaporated. Keep an eye on it.

Pour in the milk, bring back to the boil, then turn down to a simmer and partially cover with a lid. Leave for about 15 minutes, stirring regularly and keeping watch on the liquid level. It should still be very creamy. Stir in the cinnamon.

Grate the apple, peeling it if you must, then stir it into the rice, together with the sugar. Leave for 5 minutes, during which time some of the remaining liquid will be absorbed, then serve, pouring over maple syrup as you go. At least 2 tablespoons per person.

And just like that, I found myself in places that season a rice pudding with something more interesting than a bay leaf. The flower waters of the Middle East – orange blossom or rosewater – bring a soft, floral note that, when used

Creamy rice pudding with rosewater and pistachios

in small enough amounts, is deeply pleasing. Add too much though, and you are eating soap. There was rice cooked with lemon zest and toasted almonds, pistachios and honey, and once, a red-brown trickle of pomegranate molasses. In Chiang Mai I met rice with coconut milk, palm sugar and cinnamon; in Kerala, a recipe with jaggery and toasted coconut.

## Creamy rice pudding with rosewater and pistachios

*Serves 4*

pudding rice 150g
water 500ml
full-cream milk 500ml
ground cinnamon a good pinch
vanilla extract half a teaspoon

caster sugar 3 tablespoons
golden sultanas 75g
rosewater half a teaspoon
pistachios, shelled 35g

Put the rice into a medium-sized, heavy-based pan, then add the water, milk, cinnamon, vanilla and sugar. Bring to the boil over a moderate heat, then reduce the heat until the milk is bubbling gently. Leave to simmer for 25 minutes, or until tender, giving it the occasional stir.

When the rice is soft, stir in the rosewater. Chop the pistachios and stir into the rice.

And a traybake. A pastry dessert baked in a large tray can be rather useful. You can cut it into squares and serve it with custard for pudding; into fingers to tuck inside a lunchbox; or offer it at teatime with softly whipped cream. My favourite is one that has a layer of crisp biscuit-like pastry on the base, and an almond filling studded with dark berries.

## Blackberry, apple and almond slice

It is not absolutely necessary to cook the apples before adding them to the tart, but I prefer to. Letting them colour lightly in a little hot butter first will produce a particularly tender and caramelised result: a five-minute job that makes all the difference.

*Serves 8 or more*

*For the pastry:*

| | |
|---|---|
| butter 75g | self-raising flour 200g |
| caster sugar 75g | water 2 tablespoons |
| egg yolk 1 | |

*For the filling:*

| | |
|---|---|
| apples 300g | ground almonds 100g |
| butter 180g | blackberries 200g |
| caster sugar 150g | flaked almonds 3 tablespoons |
| eggs 3 | Demerara sugar 1 tablespoon |
| self-raising flour 100g | |

You will need a rectangular tart case approximately 30cm × 20cm × 3.5cm deep.

Make the pastry: using a food mixer fitted with a flat paddle beater, cream the butter and caster sugar together until light and fluffy. Mix in the egg yolk, then fold the flour into the batter together with the water to give a firm dough.

Tip the dough onto a lightly floured work surface, knead gently for less than a minute (longer will toughen it), then roll into a ball, wrap in cling film and refrigerate for about 30 minutes. You can leave it in the fridge overnight if that is convenient.

Roll the pastry out on a lightly floured board and use to line the base of the tart tin. It does not need to go up the sides. Trim any overhanging pastry. Leave no holes or tears.

Chill the pastry for a further 30 minutes. Set the oven at 190°C. Place a baking sheet or pizza stone in the oven. When the oven is hot and the pastry chilled, bake for 20 minutes on the stone or baking sheet till dry to the touch. Remove from the oven and lower the temperature to 180°C.

Peel, core and slice the apples, then cook in 30g of the butter till golden and starting to soften. Make the filling. Beat together the remaining butter and the caster sugar till pale and fluffy. Break the eggs, beat them lightly, then add them, a little at a time, to the butter and sugar. If the mixture curdles, add a little of the flour, regularly scraping down the sides of the bowl with a rubber spatula.

Blackberry, apple and almond slice

Add the flour and ground almonds to the mixture, a little at a time, beating slowly till the flour is mixed in. Spread the mixture into the pastry case, gently smoothing the surface. Add the cooked apples, drained of any butter, and the blackberries, then scatter with the flaked almonds and a little Demerara sugar.

Bake for 35–40 minutes till risen and lightly firm to the touch. Leave to settle for about 20 minutes before slicing into eight pieces or more.

# Chocolate desserts

I need to come clean here. I don't really like chocolate desserts. Chocolate cheesecakes, trifles, tarts and the like are lost on me. And yet I love, absolutely love, chocolate.

A chocolate mousse – classic, thick enough to stand your teaspoon up in – served in a tiny white pot, has a certain charm. The tricky thing is finding the occasion for it. Perhaps mid-afternoon as a little pick-me-up? Likewise, a very slim chocolate tart, if the pastry is nutty and the filling is crunchy with praline or toasted nuts. Delightful as a mid-morning treat. (The chocolate and hazelnut tart in *The Kitchen Diaries II* is a take-no-prisoners version, with fragile hazelnut pastry and a filling akin to chocolate mousse.)

A hot chocolate soufflé can be fun, even more so if you sink an egg of vanilla ice cream into its heart as it comes to the table. I always think chocolate desserts are at their most pleasing when another element, a companion, comes into play. A shot of sour fruit such as raspberry or passion fruit. A spoonful of milky vanilla ice cream. Perhaps a dusting of a sweet spice such as cardamom or cinnamon. Such additions make chocolate desserts playful. More crucially, they take away from the relentless 'chocolatiness' of it all.

That said, I have a few chocolate desserts up my sleeve. The recipes I bring out when I know I have a chocolate pudding aficionado at my table. Of which there are many.

# Hot chocolate puddings

*Serves 4*

dark, fine-quality chocolate  200g  butter  60g
caster sugar  100g  chocolate hazelnut spread
eggs  3  2 lightly heaped tablespoons

Set the oven at 200°C. Lightly butter four small ramekins or ovenproof cups. Break the chocolate into rough pieces and put it in a basin suspended over a pan of gently simmering water. Let it melt without stirring, occasionally poking any unmelted chocolate down into the liquid chocolate.

Put the caster sugar in the bowl of a food mixer, separate the eggs and add the yolks to the sugar. Beat till thick and creamy. In a separate bowl, beat the egg whites till almost stiff.

Stir the butter into the chocolate and leave to melt, then gently stir in the chocolate hazelnut spread. Fold the chocolate mixture into the egg yolks and sugar then carefully fold in the beaten egg whites with a large metal spoon. Take care not to overmix. Just firmly, calmly mix the egg whites into the chocolate, making certain there are no floating drifts of egg white.

Scoop into the four buttered dishes and place on a baking sheet. Bake for 12–15 minutes, till risen. The tops should be crackled and the centres slightly wobbly. Should you open one too early, it can go back into the oven without it coming to as much harm as you might think.

# James's chocolate and dulce de leche puddings

James came up with this recipe – a soft-crusted pudding with a fondant heart – for *Greenfeast: autumn, winter*. It remains one of the most popular puddings ever. It will stay like that for an hour or two, should you wish to make them a little ahead of time. Heatproof china ramekins are ideal for these, but you can bake them in ovenproof cups too, or even metal thali dishes. I have baked these and eaten them the following day, when they are like thick, fudgy chocolate mousses.

*Serves 2*

dark chocolate  100g
dulce de leche  2 tablespoons
eggs  2

caster sugar  100g
cantuccini to serve

Set the oven at 160°C. Break the chocolate into small pieces and leave to melt, without stirring, in a heatproof bowl suspended over a pan of simmering water. As the chocolate melts, gently stir in the dulce de leche and turn off the heat.

Break the eggs into a large bowl, add the sugar and beat until thick and fluffy. A food mixer with a whisk attachment will give the best results. Stir the chocolate and dulce de leche into the mixture. You need only two or three stirs to incorporate it. Any more and you might overmix it.

Transfer to two ramekins, using a rubber spatula. Put the ramekins into a roasting tin or baking dish. Pour enough boiling water to come halfway up the sides of the ramekins, then bake for 20 minutes until the surface is lightly crisp and the inside thick and creamy. Serve with a teaspoon and, if you wish, cantuccini biscuits.

# Five cakes for everyday
# (and four for a special occasion)

Sponge cake holds an old-fashioned magic. The quiet joy of yellow crumbs flecked with aniseed, caraway or candied peel. A loaf cake spiced with cinnamon and studded with apples. The dark, liquorice-scented mystery of ginger cake. Reassurance rather than razzmatazz.

My childhood is dotted with sponges of every hue: Victoria sandwiches filled with plum jam; cake-shop sponges stuffed with whipped cream and thickly dusted with icing sugar; coffee and walnut cakes at the village fête; and sugar-encrusted Swiss rolls. There are not many sponge cakes I haven't liked.

There is a softly fragrant recipe of which I am particularly fond. Half the flour is replaced with ground almonds. There are freckles of orange zest and nuggets of dried apricots. A fine layer of caster sugar across its surface. It is a recipe I worked on initially for *Appetite*, but have found it to be the most useful of all. A simple, shallow cake, something to bring out in wide triangles and offer with a bowl of crème fraîche.

It is my belief that no cake should be taken too seriously. Which is probably why I yawn at the baking-perfection police. Those who silently give you marks out of ten as you pass them a slice of your afternoon's work. We should take delight that someone has baked at all, not wince because their cherries have sunk.

A simple cake of butter, sugar, eggs and flour is surely treat enough, but we can do better. The recipe can come to life when its surface is pierced with a spritz of lemon juice and a gritty scattering of sugar. Once dark berries are stirred into the mixture, the cake bursts with the essence of summer. Put a layer of spiced crumble on top and you have a myriad contrasts of scents and textures.

Interrupting the quietness of the sponge with bubbles of sharp fruit – blueberries, bilberries or raspberries – has long been a baking habit of mine. The purple fruits burst, their juice stains the crumb of the cake like ink on blotting paper. In deepest summer I do this with blackcurrants, scatter flaked almonds over the top and sometimes a sprig or two of thyme.

My preferred mould in which to make such a cake is not the traditional metal tin, but a balsa wood or ovenproof baking basket. (I buy them online, as they can be tricky to track down; google Panibois to find the ones I use.) The pale wood feels sympathetic to the cake, is easy to transport on a picnic and avoids the trauma of turning the cake from its tin. Each little box is perfect for a cake for two or three. I am aware this doesn't suit everyone, so I have also tested the recipe in the usual 20cm tin.

## A blackcurrant cake for midsummer

Blackcurrants are rippled through the soft, almond-rich crumb of this pretty cake – the very essence of summer. I sometimes add a few rose petals and an extra handful of raspberries at the last moment, or perhaps a light scattering of caster sugar and a sprig of rosemary.

*Serves 8–10*

| | |
|---|---|
| butter 175g | ground almonds 100g |
| golden caster sugar 175g | grated orange zest 1 teaspoon |
| eggs 2, large | vanilla extract a few drops |
| self-raising flour 175g | blackcurrants 250g |

You will need a 20cm loose-bottomed cake tin or four 13cm × 10cm wooden cake baskets.

Line the base of the cake tin, or the baking baskets, with baking parchment. Set the oven at 170°C.

Cream the butter and sugar together in a food mixer until pale and fluffy. Beat the eggs lightly then add, a little at a time, to the creamed butter and sugar, pushing the mixture down the sides of the bowl from time to time with a rubber spatula. If there is any sign of curdling, stir in a tablespoon of the flour.

Mix the flour and almonds together and, with the mixer at a slow speed, fold in in two or three separate lots. Add the orange zest and vanilla, and once they are incorporated add the blackcurrants.

A blackcurrant cake for midsummer

Scrape the mixture into the cake tin and bake for a good hour. (If you are using small baking baskets start testing after 45 minutes.) Test with a skewer – if it comes out relatively clean, then the cake is done. Leave the cake to cool for 10 minutes or so in the tin, run a palette knife around the edge, then slide out on to a plate, or serve the little cakes in their baskets.

A sponge cake is particularly appropriate on a summer's day, brought out on a pretty plate, its surface glistening with sugar or crowned with petals. Perhaps a loaf or layer cake whose light crumb has been soaked through with elderflower cordial, cherry juice or lemon. I feel 'drizzle cake' is a rather negative name for something so refreshing and full of spritz. (Sleet aside, drizzle is surely the least appealing type of rain.) The ethereal quality of the sponge appeals on a sultry afternoon, as does the citrus scent and gritty crunch of the lemon-drenched sugar that sits aloft, like sugar on a fruit pastille.

I don't tinker for tinkering's sake. I debate long and hard before adding another element to a much-loved, traditional recipe. One afternoon in the summer of 2011 I had a whim to include a handful of mint leaves in a lemon cake, but the herb's clean, cool notes failed to come through. I had another go with leaves of thyme from a pot on the kitchen windowsill. As the cake came from the oven, the scent of herbs and citrus was clear and bright. I liked it. Apparently, I wasn't the only one. There are now versions of this delicate, summery cake everywhere. Tart though the recipe is, a spoonful of yoghurt, soured cream or thick kefir on the side is gorgeous.

# Thyme and lemon cake

*Serves 6–8*

| | |
|---|---|
| butter 180g | eggs 3, large |
| caster sugar 180g | a lemon |
| self-raising flour 90g | thyme leaves 1 teaspoon |
| ground almonds 90g | |

*For the top:*

| | |
|---|---|
| lemons 3, large | water 2 tablespoons |
| caster sugar 4 tablespoons | thyme leaves half a tablespoon |

You will need a 20cm loaf tin, lined with baking parchment.

Set the oven at 180°C. Cream the butter with the sugar in a food mixer till pale and fluffy. Sift together the flour and baking powder and mix with the ground almonds. Lightly beat the eggs, then add them to the butter and sugar in two or three batches, beating them thoroughly each time. If the batter appears about to curdle, stir in a little of the flour mixture.

Grate the zest from the lemon and mix it with the thyme leaves. Reserve the lemon for later. Pound the two together with a pestle or in a food processor or spice mill. Fold into the cake mixture with the flour, baking powder and almonds.

Spoon into the lined tin and bake for 50 minutes. Squeeze the lemons, including the reserved one. While the cake bakes, dissolve the sugar in the juice of the lemons and water over a moderate heat and stir in the thyme leaves. As the cake comes from the oven, spike the surface with a skewer and spoon over the syrup. Leave to cool, then serve in thick slices, with yoghurt or kefir.


We had driven for hours through the winding lanes of Devon, got lost once or twice and stopped for afternoon tea. The whole affair, the plump brown pot and pretty cups, the warm scones (no sultanas!) and pot of jam, the bread and butter cut in triangles and my glass of orange barley water, was an enormous luxury. The on-a-whim extravagance from my dad, an unspoken apology for losing his temper with Mum's eccentric map-reading.

So moist and ginger-laced was the accompanying cake that my father politely asked for the recipe. His request being equally politely turned down, I made a note to make one just as good. I never did, until a few years ago, Dad long gone, when I had several goes at something that packed a similarly sticky crumb. I stirred in chopped crystallised ginger. Little jewels, twinkling like carnelians at the bottom of the cake.

I don't often ice my cakes, but there is something enormously nostalgic about this thin, glossy surface, the one that sticks to your fingers as you eat. The way it leaves you with no alternative but to lick them.

# Deep double ginger cake, orange icing

Don't be alarmed at the runny texture of the uncooked cake mixture. It is how cakes of this genre are made. The finished cake, iced or not, will keep for several days wrapped in paper and foil.

*Serves 8*

self-raising flour 250g
ground ginger
   2 level teaspoons
ground cinnamon
   half a teaspoon
bicarbonate of soda
   a level teaspoon
salt a pinch
golden syrup 200g

syrup from the ginger jar
   2 tablespoons
butter 125g
stem ginger in syrup 3 lumps
   (about 60g)
sultanas 2 heaped tablespoons
dark muscovado sugar 125g
eggs 2, large
milk 240ml

*For the icing:*
icing sugar 250g
orange juice 2–3 tablespoons

poppy seeds 2 teaspoons

You will need a square cake tin measuring approximately 20cm × 22cm, lined on the bottom with baking parchment.

Set the oven at 180°C. Sift the flour with the ginger, cinnamon, bicarbonate of soda and the salt. Put the golden and ginger syrups and the butter into a small saucepan and warm over a low heat. Dice the ginger finely, then add it to the pan with the sultanas and sugar. Let the mixture bubble gently for a minute, giving it the occasional stir to stop the fruit sticking to the bottom.

Break the eggs into a bowl, pour in the milk and beat gently to break up the egg and mix it into the milk. Remove the butter and sugar mixture from the heat and pour into the flour, stirring smoothly and firmly with a large metal spoon. Mix in the milk and eggs. The mixture should be sloppy, with no trace of flour.

Deep double ginger cake, orange icing

Scoop the mixture into the lined cake tin and bake for 35–40 minutes, or until a skewer, inserted into the centre of the cake, comes out relatively clean. (There should be no raw mixture on it.) Unless you are serving it warm, leave the cake in its tin to cool, then tip out on to a sheet of baking parchment.

Make the icing: put the icing sugar into a bowl, then beat in the orange juice, either with a fork or using a small hand whisk. It should be thick enough that it takes several seconds to fall from the spoon. Spoon over the cake, sprinkle with the poppy seeds and leave to set.

Wrap it in paper and foil and leave to mature for a day or two before eating.

In the late 1970s I worked in a hotel in the Lake District. Each morning, we baked banana cake to serve, sliced and buttered, on ivy-patterned plates for afternoon tea. Each secretly snaffled piece left me underwhelmed by its sweet and waxy texture. I have played with various banana cake recipes over the years. Some were a little heavy, like bread pudding. In other attempts, the fruit was too shy. The most successful, and the one I now make time and again, is the one in which I included dark chocolate chips among the bananas. Chocolate and banana are exceedingly good friends. The addition of cardamom sugar on top is a recent one and one I am particularly pleased with.

## Chocolate muscovado banana cake

*Serves 6–8*

plain flour 250g
baking powder 2 teaspoons
butter, softened 125g
light muscovado sugar 235g
ripe bananas 400g
  (peeled weight)

vanilla extract a teaspoon
eggs 2
cardamom pods 10
caster sugar 2 tablespoons
dark chocolate 100g

You will need a loaf tin approximately 24cm × 12cm × 7cm deep, lined with baking parchment.

Chocolate muscovado banana cake

Set the oven at 180°C. Sift the flour and baking powder together. Using a food mixer, cream the butter and sugar together till light, fluffy and pale coffee-coloured.

Put the bananas in a bowl and mash them with a fork. The texture of the cake will be more interesting if the mixture is lumpy rather than crushed to a purée. Stir in the vanilla extract. Beat the eggs lightly with a fork, then combine them with the butter and sugar mixture. Introduce a spoonful of flour at any sign of curdling.

Crack open the cardamom pods with a heavy weight – I use a pestle – extract the seeds and grind them to powder. Mix together the caster sugar and cardamom. Chop the chocolate into small pieces approximately the size of coarse gravel, then stir it and the bananas into the butter and sugar. Gently fold in the flour and baking powder. Scrape the mixture into the lined baking tin, sprinkle the cardamom sugar over the top then bake for about 50 minutes. Check the cake is ready – it should feel lightly firm to the touch. Insert a metal skewer into the middle of the cake; if the skewer comes out with any wet cake mixture on it, it needs a little longer in the oven.

Gooseberry crumble is my favourite pudding. There, I have said it. (Frankly, it's a weight off my mind.) A few summers ago, while writing a story for the *Observer*, I worked out that piling a layer of crumble on top of a fruited sponge cake is a thoroughly good thing. The layers of sponge, fruit and crumble work in harmony, each bringing something of worth to the party. The best variations on the recipe are those with fruit that has a decent snap of acidity, such as rhubarb, gooseberries, blackcurrants or plums.

I now make a gooseberry crumble cake each summer, sometimes tinkering with the recipe so that it is more cake than crumble, or vice versa. I think I have the ratio about right now, and the two layers carry enough natural sweetness to balance the wincing sourness of the gooseberries. Once you involve double cream or vanilla ice cream, the cake I developed as a teatime cake becomes a first-class dessert.

# Gooseberry (or blackcurrant) crumble cake

*Serves 8*

butter 125g
caster sugar 125g
plain flour 75g
baking powder 1 level teaspoon

ground almonds 75g
eggs 3, medium
gooseberries (or blackcurrants),
    topped and tailed 325g

*For the crumble:*
butter 80g
plain flour 110g

Demerara sugar 3 tablespoons

You will also need a 20cm deep-sided springform cake tin, lined with baking parchment.

Cream the butter and caster sugar together until light and fluffy. This is best done using a food mixer. Stir together the flour, baking powder and ground almonds. Break the eggs into a bowl and beat with a fork or small whisk.

Make the crumble. Rub the 80g of butter, in small pieces, into the flour, then stir in the Demerara sugar and set aside. Set the oven at 180°C.

Add the beaten egg, a little at a time, to the creamed butter and caster sugar. If the mixture starts to curdle, add a few tablespoons of the flour mixture to bring it together. Mix in the flour, baking powder and almonds.

Transfer the batter to the prepared cake tin and smooth the surface. Scatter the gooseberries or blackcurrants evenly over the mixture. Trickle a teaspoon or two of cold water over the crumble and shake the dish so the crumbs form a mixture of fine and coarse lumps. Tip the crumble over the gooseberries or blackcurrants, then bake for 50 minutes to one hour, until lightly firm.

Remove the cake from the oven and set aside to rest until cool. Run a palette knife carefully around the edge of the cake after 15 minutes or so, to loosen it. Remove the cake from the tin and serve.

# Special cakes

All cakes are special. You could make me a cake from a packet mix and I'd still thank you. That said, some cakes are more special than others. The method may be more time-consuming, the ingredients out of the ordinary, or you may need a specific cake tin. These are the recipes you keep up your sleeve for when the time is right.

I knew cake was more than a mere treat from the moment I first stuck a bottle-brush fir tree in the snowy icing of Mum's Christmas cake. Early birthday cakes endorsed a suspicion that some cakes are more than just butter and sugar, eggs and flour. They carry congratulations and blessings, well-wishing and love. They are frosted not just with icing sugar but with nostalgia and sentiment, concern and respect. Cakes are frivolous and silly, fun and trivial.

Some people can turn a plain cake into an object of wonderment by their dexterity with a piping bag. If you need convincing of their art just check out a few cake decorators on Instagram. There are cakes I keep for birthdays, celebrations and other occasions where the surprise appearance of a fancy cake feels appropriate. In my book this will amount to anything for which I have to buy a new cake tin, make a filling or frosting or pick a posy from the garden.

The cakes that follow are simple enough. I am not going to have you spinning sugar or making chocolate caraque. Let us leave that for the hobby cooks. This is a handful of recipes I feel go above and beyond the usual quiet charm of sponges and loaf cakes. Useful, a little time-consuming, but worth the extra trouble we take. And they taste wonderful.

My favourite cake fell into this 'special' category. The recipe is in *The Christmas Chronicles*. You must first poach some small, sweet apples till translucent. A cake batter is made with butter, dark sugar and ground, toasted hazelnuts. Once baked, the surface of the cake is flooded with icing you have spiced with cardamom and decorated with toasted seeds and a snow of dried pink rose petals. It is everything I want a cake to be and takes an entire afternoon.

I now make it with plums. The preparation time is almost halved. Ripe, they require no initial cooking. Unripe, you are still saved the peeling and coring time. Should you be working with unripe fruit, the poaching time is brief. Even the most recalcitrant imported plum will soften to a jammy morsel after a while in the apple syrup below.

## Wholemeal plum cake, spiced icing

*Serves 8*

ripe plums  500g

*For the cake:*

| | |
|---|---|
| butter  200g | self-raising wholemeal flour  150g |
| light muscovado sugar  75g | baking powder  1 teaspoon |
| golden caster sugar  75g | ground cinnamon   half a teaspoon |
| skinned hazelnuts, 100g | salt  a pinch |
| eggs  4 | |

*For the icing:*

| | |
|---|---|
| icing sugar  150g | sesame seeds  1 teaspoon |
| lemon juice  3 teaspoons | poppy seeds  2 teaspoons |
| cardamom pods  6 | dried rose petals  2 teaspoons |
| ground cinnamon  a pinch | |

Set the oven at 160°C. Line the base of a 23cm springform baking tin with baking parchment.

Halve and stone the plums and set aside.

Make the cake: dice the butter, then put it in the bowl of a food mixer with the sugars and beat for a good 5 minutes till light and fluffy; the colour of latte. Regularly push the mixture down the sides of the bowl with a rubber spatula to ensure even creaming.

While the butter and sugar cream, toast the hazelnuts in a dry pan, watching carefully and moving them round the pan so they colour evenly. Grind to a fine powder in a food processor.

Beat the eggs lightly with a fork, then add, slowly, with the paddle turning, to the butter and sugar. Combine the ground hazelnuts, flour, baking powder, cinnamon and salt, then add to the batter, mixing it together thoroughly.

Wholemeal plum cake, spiced icing

Scrape the batter into the lined tin and gently smooth the surface. Place the plums on the surface of the cake. They will sink into the cake as it bakes. Bake for 55 minutes to an hour, until the cake is spongy to the touch. (Test for doneness with a metal skewer. It should come out a little damp, but without any raw cake mixture sticking to it.)

Remove the cake from the oven and leave to settle for 20 minutes. Run a palette knife around the inside of the tin to loosen the cake, then carefully undo the spring clip and transfer the cake to a plate.

Make the icing: sift the icing sugar into a bowl, stir in the lemon juice and add a little water – just a drop or two – if necessary to bring it to a thick pouring consistency. Crack the cardamom pods, remove the black seeds and grind them to a fine powder, then stir into the icing. Stir in the ground cinnamon and pour over the cake. Lightly toast the sesame seeds in a dry pan until golden, then mix them with the poppy seeds and dried rose petals and scatter them over the icing.

If your plums aren't perfectly ripe, cook them briefly first.

unripe plums  500g
butter  30g
unfiltered apple juice  250ml

Halve and stone the plums. Melt the butter in a shallow pan and add the fruit, cut sides down. Pour in the apple juice and bring to the boil. Lower the heat and cook for 10 to 15 minutes, until the plums are translucent and tender to the point of a knife. The apple juice will have virtually disappeared. Watch the fruit carefully towards the end of cooking, making sure it doesn't collapse. Remove from the heat and continue as above.

Much-loved and time-honoured, the coffee and walnut cake is a perfect thing. A recipe to which there is nothing to add and nothing to take away. Recipes for it are two a penny and remarkably similar. Good luck with finding the original. It's a village-fête cake, the sort of cake you secretly hope to find when you prise the lid off the cake tin.

The coffee and walnut is included in this collection for many reasons (easy to master, a good keeper, much appreciated, I could go on), but mostly because it is my favourite cake and I want you to have a recipe for it. A decade ago, mine would have been crowned with a ring of walnut halves. A contemporary version loses the nuts but keeps a single swirl of cappuccino-coloured frosting.

## Coffee and walnut cake

*Serves 8–10*

butter 175g
golden caster sugar 175g
eggs 3, large
self-raising flour 175g

baking powder 1 teaspoon
instant coffee granules 2 teaspoons
walnut pieces 65g

*For the buttercream:*
butter 200g
icing sugar 400g

instant coffee granules 2 teaspoons

You will need two 20cm loose-bottomed sponge tins, their bases lined with baking parchment.

Set the oven at 180°C. Beat the butter and caster sugar till pale and fluffy. This is most easily done with a food mixer. Break the eggs into a bowl, beat them briefly with a fork, then add them a little at a time to the butter and sugar, beating well after each addition.

Mix the flour and baking powder together and gently mix into the butter and sugar, either with the mixer on slow speed or by hand, with a large metal spoon. Dissolve the coffee granules in a tablespoon of boiling water, then stir into the mixture. Chop the walnuts and stir them in gently.

Divide the cake mixture between the lined tins, lightly smooth the tops, then bake for 20–25 minutes. Remove from the oven and leave to cool.

To make the buttercream, beat the butter with a food mixer till soft and pale, then add the icing sugar and beat till smooth and creamy. Stir a tablespoon of boiling water into the coffee granules, then mix into the buttercream.

As soon as the cake is cool, turn one half upside-down onto a plate, spread with two-thirds of the buttercream, then place the second half on top. Spread the remaining buttercream around the edges and around the sides.

My theory about carrot cake's enduring popularity is that people somehow kid themselves they are eating vegetables rather than cake. (I have news for them.) Whatever, the carrot cake has much to commend it. The root vegetables help to keep it moist; the crumbs are large and the texture open. Once the only option in health food cafés, word spread and carrot cake is enjoying something of a renaissance. I admit I initially set out to make a version without the cream-cheese filling and failed. It turns out the frosting is essential to the balance of the cake. Without it, each mouthful feels worthy and somehow missing the whole point of why we eat cake.

The fluffy, spice-freckled crumbs can stay, but I felt for a long time that the cream could be less sweet, a touch softer, perhaps flecked with sweet spices. All this without destroying its reason for being.

Introducing mascarpone to the cream cheese makes the frosting less 'clarty' in the mouth. Cutting the sugar works too. Though an attempt to swap sugar for honey gave an unwelcome medicinal note. But the addition of a spoonful of finely grated orange zest and a flick of ground cardamom was the touch I had been waiting for.

## Carrot and mascarpone cake

*Serves 8–10*

eggs  3
self-raising flour   250g
bicarbonate of soda
   half a teaspoon
baking powder  1 teaspoon
ground cinnamon  1 teaspoon
salt  a pinch

sunflower oil  200ml
light muscovado sugar  250g
carrots  100g
beetroot  100g
juice of half a lemon
walnuts  75g
sunflower seeds  75g

Carrot and mascarpone cake

*For the frosting:*
mascarpone cheese  250g
Philadelphia cream cheese  200g
unrefined icing sugar  150g
orange  grated zest of 1, medium

cardamom pods  10
crystallised roses or violets
2 tablespoons

You will need 2 × 22cm round cake tins.

Set the oven at 180°C. Lightly butter the cake tins, then line each with a disc of baking parchment.

Separate the eggs. Sift together the flour, bicarbonate of soda, baking powder, cinnamon and salt. Beat the oil and sugar in a food mixer until well creamed, then introduce the egg yolks one by one. Grate the carrots and beetroot into the mixture, then add the lemon juice. Roughly chop the walnuts and add them together with the sunflower seeds too.

Fold the flour into the mixture with the machine on slow. Beat the egg whites till light and stiff, then fold tenderly into the mixture using a large metal spoon (a wooden one will knock the air out).

Divide the mixture between the two cake tins, smooth the top gently and bake for 35–40 minutes. Test with a skewer for doneness. The skewer should come out with a few crumbs attached but not sticky with raw mixture.

Remove from the oven and leave to settle for a good 10 minutes before turning the cakes out of their tins on to a cooling rack.

To make the frosting, put the mascarpone, Philadelphia cheese and icing sugar into a food mixer and beat till smooth and creamy. It should have no lumps. Mix in the orange zest. Crack the cardamom pods, remove the brown-black seeds and grind them finely in a spice mill or with a pestle and mortar and stir into the icing. Crush the sugared roses or violets, add them to the sugar and stir in.

When the cake is cool, sandwich the halves together with about a third of the frosting. Use the rest to cover the top of the cake. I don't think you need be too painstaking; a rough finish will look more appropriate here.

I have recently taken to decorating homemade cakes with a few edible flowers. Nothing too big, you are not trimming a hat for Ascot. Just a few primroses in spring, rose petals, or the flowers of scented geraniums, which we should really call pelargoniums. A sprinkling of marigold petals is pretty on the dark mahogany of an autumn ginger cake. (Nasturtiums belong in a salad.) Some of the smallest pelargoniums are charming, with the scented leaves and diminutive, purple-pink blossoms. I keep a few purely for decorating 'special occasion' cakes. A few on the cake that follows would charm.

# Apricot and lemon curd cake

The first time I took this still-warm cake from the oven (on a chilly spring day in 2020), the scent of citrus and butter wafted up, reminding me of why I bake rather than buy. There are three elements here: the apricot sponge itself; the lemon curd; and the crumble that crowns the cake. This is not a recipe to hurry. Instead, it's a piece of baking to take your time over, an hour or two of quiet hands-on time in the kitchen, perhaps with the radio on and no distractions. The finished cake will keep for several days in a cake tin. We ate it as both teatime treat (with a pot of fresh mint tea) and as dessert, with a spoonful of thick yoghurt nudging the crumble crust. The recipe makes a little more curd than you need, but it will keep for a week in a stoppered jar in the fridge. A truly splendid thing to find when you've just toasted an English muffin. I feel I should add that this is not a cake to eat warm, as it will crumble when sliced. Better, I think, to give it time to settle, a good hour or more, before cutting it into thick, generous slices.

*Serves 8*

*For the lemon curd:*

| | |
|---|---|
| unwaxed lemons  4 | eggs  3 |
| caster sugar  200g | egg yolk  1 |
| butter  100g | |

*For the cake:*

| | |
|---|---|
| butter  125g | eggs  3, medium |
| caster sugar  125g | soft dried apricots  75g |
| self-raising flour  75g | icing sugar for dusting |
| ground almonds  75g | |

Apricot and lemon curd cake

*For the crumble:*

| | |
|---|---|
| butter  80g | Demerara sugar |
| plain flour  110g | 3 tablespoons |

You will need a 20cm × 10cm × 7cm rectangular loaf tin lined with baking parchment.

Make the lemon curd: finely grate the lemons' zest, then squeeze their juice. Put the lemon zest and juice, the sugar and the butter, cut into cubes, into a heatproof bowl set over a pan of simmering water, making sure that the bottom of the bowl doesn't touch the water. Stir with a whisk from time to time until the butter has melted.

Mix the eggs and egg yolk lightly with a fork, then stir into the lemon mixture. Let the curd cook, stirring regularly, for about 10 minutes, until it is thick and custard-like. It should feel heavy on the spoon. Remove from the heat and stir occasionally as it cools.

Make the cake: set the oven at 180°C. Cream the butter and caster sugar together until light and fluffy. This is best done using a food mixer. Stir together the flour and ground almonds. Break the eggs into a bowl and beat with a fork or small whisk. Chop the apricots finely using a food processor.

While the butter and sugar are creaming together, make the crumble. Rub the 80g of butter, in small pieces, into the flour, then stir in the Demerara sugar and set aside.

Add the beaten egg, a little at a time, to the creamed butter and caster sugar. If the mixture starts to curdle, add a few tablespoons of the flour to bring it together. Mix in the flour and chopped apricots.

Transfer the batter to the prepared loaf tin and smooth the surface. Spoon in 250g of the lemon curd and smooth the surface. Trickle a teaspoon or two of cold water over the crumble mix and shake the dish so the crumbs form a mixture of both fine and coarse lumps. It makes for a more interestingly textured crumble. Tip the crumble over the lemon curd, then bake for 50 minutes to 1 hour, until lightly firm.

Remove the cake from the oven and set aside to rest until almost cool. Remove the cake from the tin, peel away the parchment, dust the cake with icing sugar and serve.

# The stillness of cheesecake

A slice of cheesecake arrives on a small white plate. Cool, calm, silent. A sour whiff of buttermilk, the caramel sweetness of vanilla. Your fork slides through with barely a sigh.

The sweet, fudgy filling can cloy after a mouthful. This pale and graceful pastry needs a jolt of jam or fruit to waken it, and us, from its vanilla-scented slumber. A tart fruit compote will work – gooseberry, plum or apricot – or a little mound of baked rhubarb at its side.

Better still, I think, is to spread a layer of soured cream over the surface. Nothing to interfere with the purity and peace that lies ahead.

You can make cheesecake with mascarpone, ricotta or quark, curd cheese, cream cheese or fromage blanc. At a push, you could get the recipe to work with sieved cottage cheese. Ricotta will give you a lighter, more open texture, but it may lack structure and weep in the oven. Mascarpone alone will be too rich, too bland, too expensive and a bit sticky. If you crave the creamiest cheesecake, and I feel sure you do, then you must use not just 'cream cheese', but 'full-fat cream cheese'. Be aware that anything 'light or 'low-fat' will be full of air and water and your cake will collapse.

I have eaten cheesecake in New York, Vienna and Berlin and the Jewish pastry shops of Le Marais in Paris. I have devoured, and indeed published recipes for, baked cheesecake with a pastry case, others on a crushed crumb crust and others still that were set by gelatine rather than by eggs and the heat of the oven. There may have also been an 'instant' version. Cheesecake for the impatient.

As a teenager, I set about making my first with cottage cheese, sugar-crusted Nice biscuits and a tin of mandarin oranges. I recall the recipe had gelatine in it. I remember this rather slim cake for being a success, albeit disappointingly shallow and overly sweet.

All the cheesecakes I grew up with were held together with gelatine. A mousse on a bed of crumbs. I won't deny the appeal of its airy texture, citrus zing and the way the crumbs stuck to the moussey filling. For *Tender, Volume II*

I mastered the uncooked cheesecake without using gelatine, specifically to go with a glowing damson compote whose juices bled like the arteries on a roadmap into the cheesecake. It is something of a stretch to call this a cheesecake, so light and frothy was its texture, but that is what it was. I still make it, occasionally, to bring to the table on a late summer's afternoon, with a compote of crimson plums.

An uncooked version is a good place to start. They are unthreatening to make and seem to please everyone other than the harridans who insist a cheesecake is only worthy of the name if it cooked. Despite the complication of gelatine, it is where I started.

I should add a few words about biscuit-crumb bases. I must have tried every plain biscuit in the book. A quest, I suppose, to find something more interesting than the classic wheaten digestive. After crumb crusts of chocolate digestives, oatcakes and Hobnobs, choc-chip cookies and gingernuts, Rich Tea and imported graham crackers, I have come to the conclusion that there is nothing better than the old fashioned Nice. Crisp, light and sweet, the gritty sugar crystals of this biscuit flatter the vanilla curds without adding confusing flavours (gingernuts), excess heaviness (digestives) or too much sugar (Hobnobs).

Over the years, I have reduced the amount of butter I use in the crumb base. Too much and you have nothing to contrast with the fatty body of the cake. And there's something else. There is temptation, and occasionally emphatic instructions, to press the crumbs firmly into the cake tin. I think we should resist. Tamp down too firmly and your crumbs will compact into a hard, buttery disc. A more pleasing result will come from patting them down gently with the back of a spoon, giving a crust that crumbles, like coarse, sweet sand, onto the plate.

## Light and mousse-like lemon cheesecake

With the inclusion of gelatine and the care we must take with beating and folding in the egg whites, this is something of the scenic route to cheesecake. It is, however, gorgeous. Poised somewhere between a lemon mousse and a traditional cheesecake, it will quiver on your plate, and delight rather than clog your taste buds. I'm sure there are those who would argue it is not really a cheesecake at all and I wouldn't argue with that, but I include it here for its light and sharp character. (The body of the mousse will get firmer with each passing hour in the fridge – overnight is just about perfect.)

Toasted, flaked almonds add a welcome note of crispness to the base of a cheesecake and lighten the crust. My feeling is that the base should be delicate and barely there, so I avoid pressing the crumbs into the cake tin too firmly, as it tends to compact the mixture. Unlike the rest of the genre, this needs no accompaniment of soured cream or tart fruit. To get your slice of cake to the plate in one piece, serve with a cake slice rather than a palette knife.

*Serves 8 (at least)*

*For the crust:*

flaked almonds  70g

plain biscuits  150g,
    such as Nice or Marie

butter  65g

*For the mousse:*

eggs  4, medium

caster sugar  150g

lemons  2, large

gelatine  5 sheets (9g)

full-fat cream cheese  250g

double cream  250ml

rose petals  a handful (completely
    optional, but rather lovely)

You will also need a round 20–22cm cake tin with a removable base, lined on the base with a disc of baking parchment.

In a dry, shallow pan, toast the flaked almonds until golden, then remove from the heat. Crush the biscuits to fine crumbs, either in a plastic freezer bag with a rolling pin or using a food processor.

Melt the butter, then add the crumbs and flaked almonds, and mix thoroughly. Transfer the mixture to the lined cake tin, pressing it in a thin layer over the base. Chill for an hour.

Separate the eggs. Put the whites in a large mixing bowl. Beat the yolks and sugar together using an electric mixer with a whisk attachment until thick and pale. Grate the lemon zest finely, then add the zest to the yolk mix.

Juice the lemons – you will need 125ml. Soak the gelatine in a bowl of cool water. Warm the lemon juice in a small saucepan and remove from the heat. Lift the softened gelatine from the water (it should be a soft, quivery mass, only just solid enough to pick up) and drop it into the warm juice. Stir until it is dissolved.

Add the cream cheese to the yolk-and-sugar mixture, beating until completely smooth, then add the lemon juice and gelatine. Whip the cream until it's thick enough to sit in soft waves (not quite thick enough to stand in stiff peaks), then fold gently into the mixture. Beat the egg whites until stiff, then fold them in carefully and thoroughly.

Pour the mixture into the chilled cake tin (it should come almost to the top), then cover tightly with cling film and chill overnight. (Make sure you don't have anything garlicky or oniony in the fridge – such airy, mousse-type dishes are likely to pick up the scent.)

The next day, run a warm palette knife around the edge of the cake to release it from the edges, then remove it carefully from the tin. Decorate with the rose petals if you wish.

Note that the cake is wobbly and fragile, so keep it chilled until you intend to serve it, and use a cake slice, rather than a knife, when you do so. To remove it from its tin, stand the tin on a low, stable jar or container slightly smaller than the base, tenderly slide the sides of the tin down, slowly releasing the cake, then lift the cake by its base and place on a plate. (I would leave the cake on its base for slicing.)

# The thick and fudgy cheesecake

If I could have just one cheesecake (an unthinkable scenario), it would be of the deep, fudgy variety, heady with vanilla freckles, so thick and 'clarty' it sticks to the roof of your mouth. I developed such a cheesecake for the first volume of *The Kitchen Diaries* and most of my subsequent ones (sour cherry, 2011, Christmas mincemeat, 2012, and gooseberry cheesecake slice, 2018) have been riffs on that. The exception was the over-the-top white chocolate and peanut butter recipe that was, by my own admission, somewhat hardcore. Sweet, gooey and intensely sticky, it could clog an artery at twenty paces. (It's fabulous, by the way.)

This recipe that follows has stood the test of time. I would never be so arrogant as to say this is the perfect cheesecake. However, it really is rather

A fudgy lemon cheesecake

good and probably closest to what we think of when we want the quiet thud of cheesecake on the table.

# A fudgy lemon cheesecake

*Serves 8*

butter 70g
Nice or digestive biscuits 200g
mascarpone 500g
full-fat cream cheese 200g
golden caster sugar 150g

eggs 3, large, plus an extra yolk
lemon 1
double cream 150ml
vanilla extract half a teaspoon

Melt the butter in a saucepan. Crush the biscuits to a fairly fine powder. You can do it in the traditional way, with a plastic bag and a rolling pin, or in a food processor. Tip the biscuits into the melted butter and stir briefly till the crumbs are coated. Set the oven at 140°C. Press two-thirds of the buttered crumbs into the base of a deep 20–22cm loose-bottomed springform cake tin. Set aside in a cold place to become firm. The freezer is ideal.

Put the kettle on. Put the mascarpone, cream cheese, caster sugar, eggs and extra egg yolk in the bowl of a food mixer (you will need the flat beater attachment). Finely grate the lemon zest into the cheese and sugar, then beat until thoroughly mixed. Squeeze the lemon. Fold the cream, juice of the lemon and vanilla extract into the cheesecake mix.

Wrap the base of the tin with foil, covering the base and sides with a single piece with no joins, then pour the cheesecake mixture into the tin. Lower the cake tin into a roasting tin. Pour enough of the boiled water from the kettle into the tin to come halfway up the sides of the cake tin. Slide carefully into the oven. Bake for 50 minutes then switch off the oven and leave the cake in place to cool.

When the cake has cooled, chill for a good couple of hours in the fridge. (Overnight won't hurt.) Undo the spring clip, release the cake from its tin and slide onto a plate. Press the reserved crumbs onto the sides of the cake and serve.

A Basque-style cheesecake

# The light, creamy, black-capped 'Basque' cheesecake

In San Sebastián with James, late winter 2016. After a standing lunch of grilled prawns and chilled Fino, we followed the curve of La Concha Promenade, then wandered through the cobbled streets of Donostia. There was no plan, no tourist map in our hands. Just the assurance that should we get lost, it would be brief and perhaps it wouldn't be such a bad thing anyway. Late in the afternoon – at my insistence – we stopped at a pastelería for coffee and something sweet. A morsel to keep us going until our inevitably late dinner.

I chose a slice of cheesecake, its centre as soft as syllabub, its crust scorched. A cheesecake with no pastry or crumb crust to support its curds, no berries rippled through the deep, vanilla-scented custard. A cake that wobbled mousse-like on the fork. I was surprised not to miss the crunch of pounded crumbs. Not only was it not missed, the biscuit crumbs suddenly felt like an interference. Grit in the oyster. The smoky bitterness of the blackened crust was all the contrast I needed.

Back at home, I set about making a similar Basque-style cheesecake. I am used to keeping an eagle eye on progress, to ensure not a freckle of brown appears on my cheesecake's surface. It took six attempts to perfect the wobble and char, but I think we are here now.

## A Basque-style cheesecake

*Serves 8*

full-fat cream cheese  650g
caster sugar  220g
lemon  1
vanilla extract  half teaspoon
eggs  4, plus an extra yolk

double cream  250ml
soured cream  150ml
cornflour  30g
sea salt  a generous pinch

Set the oven at 220°C. Line the inside of a high-sided 20cm springform cake tin entirely with baking parchment, making sure you bring it up the sides. It will pucker around the edges, but no matter. Place a pizza stone or baking sheet in the oven to heat up.

Put the cream cheese and caster sugar into the bowl of a food mixer and beat for a few seconds until mixed. Grate the lemon zest into the cheese, then add the vanilla extract.

Break the eggs into a small bowl, add the extra yolk and beat lightly with a fork to combine the yolks and whites. Introduce the eggs to the cream cheese, beating at slow speed, then pour in the double and soured creams. Push the mixture down the sides of the bowl with a rubber spatula and briefly continue mixing. At this point it may look too liquid but worry not.

Stir in the cornflour and salt, making sure it is thoroughly combined, then pour the mixture into the lined cake tin. Slide carefully into the oven, place on top of the hot stone or baking sheet and bake for 45 minutes, until the cake has risen a little and its surface is dark brown. The centre may quiver when shaken. A thoroughly good thing. Now turn off the heat and leave the cake to settle for a further 10 minutes. Remove the cake from the oven and leave to cool, then place, still in its tin, in the fridge.

When completely cold, remove the cheesecake from its tin and serve in thick slices, perhaps with a small dish of extra soured cream.


I see cheesecakes with green tea, chocolate or caramel stirred through them, and I think they are fun, but something tart that slices through the fatty filling seems more appropriate than adding yet another level of sweetness.

You can add fruit to the cheesecake mix too, blueberries being the most popular choice. You do need to be careful when introducing fruit to the mix before cooking however. Raspberries or blackberries can produce too much moisture and disturb the texture of the cake. Strawberries are too sweet and bring nothing of interest to the party. A layer of gooseberry or plum purée spread over the crumb crust before the filling goes in is a better idea, though you should expect a faint line of curdling where the cheese mixture meets the fruit. Best of all I think is a spoonful of tart, poached fruit on the side.

# A fruit compote for cheesecake

damsons or blackcurrants 500g       water 4 tablespoons
caster sugar 150g

Remove the stalks from the fruit and the stones from the damsons, then tip into a saucepan with the sugar and water. Bring to the boil, lower the heat and leave the fruit to simmer for 5–8 minutes (maybe a few minutes longer with the damsons) or till the syrup is deep purple and the skins are starting to burst. Cool, chill and serve with cheesecake.

# Four chocolate cakes

There is probably a chocolate cake for everyone. The multilayered, buttercream-filled sandwich cake; the fudgy bûche de Noël; bouffant cream and cherry confections from the Black Forest; and dense pound cakes the colour of peat. There are sunken cakes that ooze like an overripe Brie, others whose texture is akin to a chocolate truffle, and plain sponges redeemed by a pencil-thin layer of apricot jam and ice-crisp chocolate icing. All that is without even touching on roulades and chocolate cupcakes.

My very first slice of chocolate cake came home from a party in a paper napkin. I held the precious slice of pale cake, decorated with buttercream and Smarties, in my hand in the back of the car. It wasn't much of a chocolate cake, now I come to think of it. The filling was buff rather than a rich, glossy chestnut. It tasted of chocolate buttons, treats that have the extraordinary knack of tasting stale even when they aren't. It was the most wonderful thing I had ever tasted.

I like chocolate cake that is shallow, fudgy and crumbly. It is something I eat mid-morning or afternoon, never after a meal. Just a thin slice, please, preferably around 11am with an espresso and a diminutive glass of iced water.

If I'm honest, I rarely eat any sort of chocolate cake, but the making of it remains full of small and wonderful pleasures: the sight of chocolate melting in the bowl suspended over simmering water; pushing the thin squares down into the deep glossy-brown puddle; folding the fluff of beaten egg white into the batter of butter and sugar and flour and darkest 70 per cent; and finally, wiping the sticky crumbs from the knife and watching everyone's eyes light up as you pass them the smallest slice on a pretty plate. I sometimes think that is as close to chocolate cake as I need to get.

I offer four possibilities here: one with a soft centre; another speckled with hazelnuts and sherry-soaked sultanas; a deep hazelnut sponge with flecks of bitter chocolate and a wave of buttercream; and finally a shallow, flourless version with nibs of toasted nuts and a whiff of Marsala.

# Chocolate espresso cake

In the mid-1990s, there was a fashion for 'squidgy' chocolate cakes. The sort of recipe which, whilst having a classic crumb-like texture around the edge, was soft and mousse-like within. It wasn't my sort of cake at all, but as I've said, a cake is something you make for others, so I pursued my own version of the popular soft-centred chocolate cake by introducing a splash of espresso to calm a genre that I felt was just altogether too 'chocolatey'. Within weeks of publishing, readers were sending me pictures of the cakes they had made from my recipe and stopping me in the street to mention it. I think it was the first time I had such a reaction over a piece of baking. The generosity of comments was deeply encouraging, and I was grateful for them. In its own way the cake was a turning point. I believe we have collectively moved on now, but I include it in this collection, in its original form, for those who like their cakes with a moussey middle. Serve it with a jug of cream and a little glass of iced water.

*Serves 8*

| | |
|---|---|
| fine, dark chocolate, chopped 180g | golden caster sugar 200g |
| coffee 3 tablespoons | baking powder 1 teaspoon |
| butter 140g | cocoa powder 2 tablespoons |
| eggs 5 | plain flour 90g |

Line the base of a 20–23cm shallow springform cake tin with baking parchment. Melt the chocolate in a heatproof bowl set over a pan of simmering water. As soon as it starts to soften, add the coffee and leave it for 2–3 minutes. Stir very gently, then, when the chocolate has melted, add the butter. Stir until it has melted. Set the oven at 180°C.

Meanwhile, separate the eggs, beat the whites with an electric mixer until stiff, then fold in the sugar. Mix the baking powder with the cocoa and flour. Remove the chocolate from the heat, quickly stir in the egg yolks, then slowly, firmly and gently fold the melted chocolate into the egg whites. Lastly, stir in the flour and cocoa mixture.

Hazelnut chocolate cake with sultanas and rosemary

Stir the mixture tenderly with a wooden spoon, taking care not to knock out any air. It should feel light and wobbly. Don't overmix, just enough to fold in the flour. Scoop into the lined tin and bake for 35 minutes. Leave to cool in its tin, then turn out.

One afternoon, late in 2017, I made what was to become my favourite chocolate cake of all. Shallow, fudge-like and spiked with sherry-soaked golden sultanas and shards of chocolate, its surface gritty with caster sugar scented with rosemary. A cake for an autumn afternoon, perhaps with coffee or smoky roasted tea.

There was the first faint nip of cold in the air. A pinprick to remind me winter was on its way. A fire, several gardens away, had sent a long, lazy curl of smoke into the darkening sky. My fancy turned to the thought of dabbing sweet crumbs, roasted nuts and dark chocolate from a plate with my finger and thumb.

## Hazelnut chocolate cake with sultanas and rosemary

This is a chocolate cake I can get behind. Intense, but not overly sweet, it is damp without being gooey, rich without being heavy. A thin slice is enough, served with soured cream or crème fraîche or perhaps a spoonful of fig jam. The cake keeps soundly, for a good day or two, wrapped in foil or cling film. You will need a spoonful, no more, of crème fraîche on the side. And (I mention this only because I am asked so regularly), yes, the diminutive weight of flour is correct.

*Serves 10*

| | |
|---|---|
| golden sultanas  90g | caster sugar  150g |
| medium-dry sherry  60ml | butter  150g |
| skinned hazelnuts  175g | dark chocolate  300g |
| plain flour  20g | eggs  6, separated |
| cocoa powder  10g | |

*For the herb sugar:*

| | |
|---|---|
| rosemary leaves  2g (about 20 leaves) | caster sugar  2 tablespoons |
| | golden sultanas  2 tablespoons |

Put the 90g of sultanas in a small bowl, pour in the sherry and set aside for 2 hours, stirring occasionally. Line the base of a 24cm springform cake tin with a disc of baking parchment. Set the oven at 160°C.

Toast the hazelnuts in a dry, shallow pan till golden brown and fragrant. Tip all but 20g of them into a food processor and process to fine crumbs. Mix the flour and cocoa together.

Using a food mixer, beat the caster sugar and butter together till light and fluffy. Put a small pan of water on to boil, place a small dish on top of it, break the chocolate into the dish and let it melt over the simmering water, without stirring.

For the herb sugar, process the rosemary and caster sugar to a coarse powder and add the golden sultanas.

Slowly introduce the egg yolks to the creamed butter and sugar, beating constantly. Whisk the egg whites until almost stiff. Mix the melted chocolate into the butter and sugar, then carefully fold in the ground hazelnuts, drained sultanas and the flour and cocoa. Lastly, fold in the beaten egg whites, making certain there are no lumps of unincorporated whites. (This can be quite hard going, but you should fold the two mixtures together lightly until thoroughly mixed.) Scrape the mixture into the lined cake tin.

Finally, scatter the reserved hazelnuts, golden sultanas and rosemary sugar over the surface. Bake for 40–45 minutes until lightly firm, the top slightly cracked. Remove from the oven and leave to cool before carefully removing from the tin.


Daft as it sounds, I often find chocolate cakes too dense and relentlessly 'chocolatey'. (I would rather be teased by chocolate's charms than smothered by them.) It is probably why I don't like chocolate truffles very much. Proof, if ever we needed it, that you really can have too much of a good thing. As popular as the soft-centred chocolate cake is, my interest lies elsewhere. A cake that has tiny nibs of chocolate through its crumb is more my style. It is the crunch of the freckles of dark chocolate that appeals.

I spent a while, and a lot of 70 per cent cocoa butter, on playing with cakes in which chocolate was used more as a 'seasoning' than as the main ingredient. (A pound cake marbled with chocolate. Mocha icing on an almond sponge. A chocolate Battenburg – a failure, and an entire day of my life I will never get back.) None quite hits the spot. The answer lay in adding intense chocolate nibs to a hazelnut sponge. The crumb was soft and giving, the crunchy nibs of chocolate melted on your tongue like those in a choc-chip cookie. Rather than a buttercream-filled sandwich, the cake was topped with a wave of smooth cinnamon-spiced ganache. My sort of cake.

## Chocolate-chip hazelnut cake with chocolate icing

*Serves 10*

| | |
|---|---|
| butter 250g | eggs 4, large |
| golden caster sugar 250g | self-raising flour 125g |
| skinned hazelnuts 75g | ground cinnamon half a teaspoon |
| dark chocolate 120g | strong espresso 4 teaspoons |

*For the chocolate buttercream:*

| | |
|---|---|
| dark chocolate (70 per cent cocoa solids) 250g | butter 125g |
| | ground cinnamon a knifepoint |

Set the oven at 180°C. Line the base of a deep, loose-bottomed 20cm cake tin with baking parchment.

Put the butter, cut into small pieces, and the sugar into the bowl of a food mixer, then beat till white and fluffy. Toast the hazelnuts in a dry pan, then grind to a coarse powder, less fine than ground almonds but finer than if you chopped them by hand. Chop the chocolate into what looks like fine gravel.

Break the eggs into a small bowl and beat them gently. Slowly add them to the butter and sugar mixture, beating all the time. (The mixture may curdle at this point but no matter, simply add a tablespoon or two of the flour.)

Stop the machine. Tip in half the ground nuts and half the flour, beat briefly at slow speed, stop the machine again, then add the rest of the nuts and flour, the chopped chocolate and the cinnamon and mix briefly.

Gently fold in the espresso, taking care not to knock the air from the mixture, then scoop into the lined cake tin using a rubber spatula. Smooth the top and bake for 35–45 minutes, covering the cake with foil for the last 10 minutes if it appears to be browning too quickly.

Test the cake with a skewer after 35 minutes. It should come out moist but without any raw mixture sticking to it. If it has raw cake mixture on it, pop the cake back in the oven for 10 minutes. Remove from the oven and leave to cool in its tin. Run a palette knife around the sides of the cake and release it from its tin. Peel the paper from the bottom of the cake.

To make the chocolate buttercream, snap the chocolate into small pieces and put it in a small bowl placed over a pan of simmering water. Leave it to melt, with little or no stirring, then add the butter, cut into small pieces, and the cinnamon and stir gently to mix. Remove from the heat and leave to cool until thick enough to spread. (I sometimes put mine in the fridge for about 15 minutes.)

Spread the chocolate cream over the top of the cake and leave for an hour before cutting.

What I often miss in a slice of chocolate cake is contrast, which is probably why I would prefer a simple chocolate cornflake cake to a slice of gooey gateau. We need a little respite from all the richness. It is why the thin line of apricot jam in a Sachertorte is so essential. (And why it has to be a sharp, acidic fruit jam rather than raspberry or black cherry.)

All I ask is the crunch of a toasted almond, a crisp chocolate chip or a nugget of sweet-sour fruit such as chopped dried apricot or a dark and brandy-laden raisin amongst the soft, cocoa-rich interior. Deep in the dark days of last winter (the first week in January 2021 to be exact), I set out to remedy this by introducing tiny nibs of toasted almonds to a densely textured chocolate cake. But here's the thing, the nuts must, absolutely must, be toasted. The difference is subtle but, I think, worth every second of our time.

## Marsala almond chocolate slice

Roasted nuts, dark chocolate. A marriage made in heaven. The cake will appear, as you take it from the oven, to be not quite ready. The middle will be slightly sunken and feel less springy than the sides. That is as it should be. As it cools, the texture settles and the result is deeply fudgy and really rather pleasing. It is, incidentally, flourless and will keep, covered with kitchen foil, for several days.

Marsala almond chocolate slice

*Serves 8*

| | |
|---|---|
| skinned almonds  120g | caster sugar  120g |
| dark chocolate  125g | vanilla extract  a few drops |
| butter  175g | Marsala  50ml |
| eggs  4 | cocoa powder  30g |

You will also need a rectangular loaf tin measuring approximately 20cm × 10cm × 7cm (measured, as always, across the base).

Set the oven at 160°C. Line the base and sides of the loaf tin with baking parchment.

In a dry, shallow pan, toast the almonds over a moderate heat till golden. Shake them regularly to encourage as uniform a colour as possible. Tip them into a food processor and reduce to coarse crumbs. Ideally, some of them almost as fine as ground almonds, others a little larger, like fine gravel.

Break the chocolate into small pieces, roughly dice the butter and put them in a mixing bowl. Place the bowl over a small pan of simmering water (the base of the bowl should be just shy of the water level) then leave to melt. Give it no more than the occasional stir.

Separate the eggs and put the yolks into the bowl of a food mixer, add the sugar and whisk till thick and creamy. (You can use a hand-held whisk if you don't have a food mixer.) Stir in the melted chocolate, the vanilla extract, the Marsala, cocoa powder and then the toasted, ground nuts.

Beat the egg whites till almost stiff. I do this by hand. (Stop whisking when they are thick enough to sit in soft mounds rather than whisking to stiff peaks.) Using a large metal spoon, fold the whites into the chocolate mixture, stopping as soon as the whites are no longer visible. (It is essential not to overmix.) Transfer to the cake tin using a rubber spatula and bake for 35–40 minutes until the edges are lightly firm to the touch, the middle still a little soft. Listen to it. The cake should be making a very faint crackling sound. (If it's silent, you've overcooked it.) Remove from the oven and leave to settle and cool.

To serve at its best, cut it after about an hour, and serve in thick wedges, with crème fraîche or thick double cream.

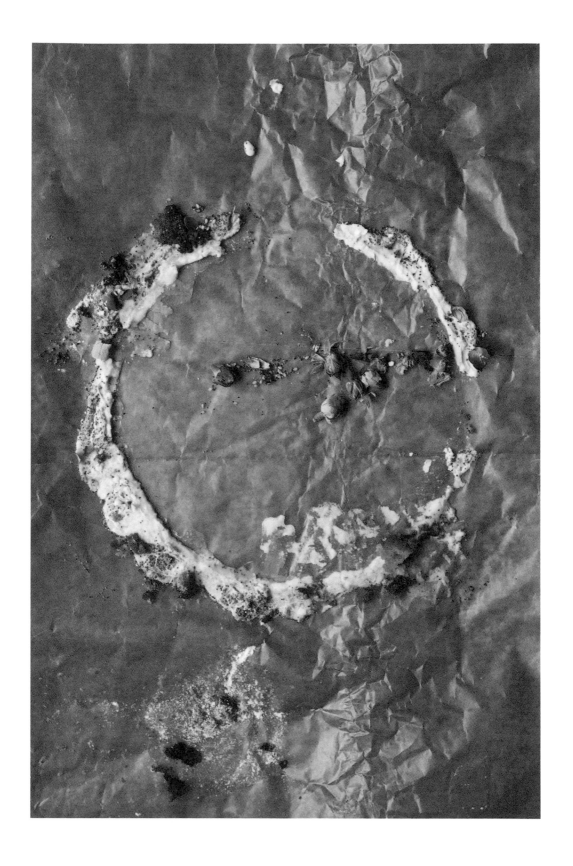

# The ritual of tea

I am not sure when the drinking of tea and coffee became such an honoured ritual in my house – the elevation of the mundane to that of a deep and cherished pleasure – I only know that it has.

Coffee and tea are treated as essential markers in my working day – the everyday turned to a miniature celebration – during which I stop work, put the worn and much-used paraphernalia of tea and coffee – a pot, a cup, a tiny oval plate of cake or a biscuit – on an old flea-market wooden tray and move to another room. A room far away from the work in hand. It is only then, out of sight and reach of desk, hob and kitchen sink, that I can really feel the benefit of the steaming brew in my cup. (The most effective break is often the one I don't really have time to take.) In all honesty, I probably make more fuss over a pot of coffee than I do over making dinner.

It probably sounds more than a little pretentious to turn the taking of a hot drink into an 'event'. In my defence I will point out that I am far from the only person to cherish such moments. There is something deeply pleasing about the Swedish tradition of 'fika' – the art of going out, or at least stopping work, for coffee and cake. It is a habit into which I have happily slipped. Japan takes such matters with something of a considered reverence too. I consider these few minutes stolen from the working day as deep breaths of fresh air with which to refocus, take stock, get my head together. The point, and I suspect the reason why this has become such a crucial part of my day, is that I return as energised and focused as others coming home from a run. Whoever happens to be around at the time gets to share these rituals too, with a biscuit or slice of cake in hand. The timing is dependent not on the striking of the church bell audible from my desk, but on an inner clock that I have listened to intently for most of my life.

I long to be the sort of tea drinker who enjoys a mug of sweet, milky tea, but I am not. I take both tea and coffee without either dairy or sugar. Coffee is espresso or filtered, the latter emerging drip by slow drip from a paper-lined cone into a small copper pot. Espresso is a morning thing – my daybreak heart-starter. Pour-through is an altogether more languorous mid-morning affair. And yes, I grind my own beans. Tea is invariably green, roasted hojicha with breakfast or something lighter, brighter and more verdant in the afternoon.

There is something of a small collection of mugs in my kitchen and each is given its 15 minutes in the sun. Several have a specific role – there is a Sunday morning mug, for instance, and another cup specially for yuzu tea. (Please don't tell me you haven't a favourite mug.) I am sure there is a reason why a cup of coffee or tea tastes better in one receptacle than it does in another, but I am unsure of the science behind it. My only answer is that sometimes things just feel right. That is my only response to the question of why I prefer green tea in one cup and roasted hojicha in another. Sometimes the choice may have to do with the shape, on other occasions it is the weight of a cup that suggests its contents – to my mind delicate green teas need an equally delicate teacup. Others may gravitate towards a favoured mug given to them by a friend or loved one. And I warm to the idea of a pair of mugs, two friends that take tea together. I am not sure how I would feel if one were broken though. A mug in mourning for its mate.

I can only imagine the life of those who have time to take afternoon tea, *Downton Abbey* style (does anyone, really?), but for me the time for these rituals is instead snatched from the working day. Twenty, maybe 30 minutes to refresh, rejuvenate and get back on track. Each cup is accompanied by cake or cookie. A slice of fruit cake in winter, a scruffily torn wedge of panettone in spring, something from the golden biscuit tin – a highly decorated drum originally filled with German lebkuchen, now demoted to the home of dark chocolate digestives. If guests are here, they might get a friand – the oval sponges I so love making (the most instantly gratifying baking out there), speckled with dark chocolate or crystallised orange peel.


I suspect we buy biscuits for the nostalgia they bring rather than for their quality. I remain devoted to a dark chocolate digestive (and yes, I do believe the chocolate used to be crisper and shinier than today) and the Tunnock's caramel wafer. A custard cream is fine too, though fig rolls seem to have rather lost their edge. I know I go on about it, but I still hanker after the long-lost Abbey Crunch, which few people under fifty have ever heard of let alone tasted.

Put nostalgia and convenience to one side and there is little reason to ever buy a commercial biscuit. Occasionally, on a rainy autumn afternoon, I get the urge to bake a batch of handmade biscuits and then spend the evening wondering why anyone would ever buy them. The sheer butteriness of a home-baked version is worth every second of our time (clue, add twice as much salt as the recipe asks for, it really does bring out the flavour of the butter). Handmade biscuits possess a crumbly, fragile texture unattainable in a factory-produced affair. I make few, but eaten warm from the baking sheet, soft or crisp, chocolatey or nutty, melting or satisfyingly chewy, they are a true treat for the soul.

# A light, crisp biscuit

Dunking a biscuit into a glass of honey-sweet wine is something I reserve for weekends. An activity that on another day feels strangely illicit. Muscat wines such as Tokaji and Beaumes de Venise will keep for ages, tightly corked, in the fridge. You don't actually need to finish the bottle. Really, you don't. And yes, there are Italian cantuccini, the pistachio or chocolate-flecked biscuits as hard as bones – biscuits made specially for dipping into sticky wine. I eat them, and every time I do, I long for something lighter, crisp rather than hard, prettier and more delicate.

Almonds feel somehow essential here. Either ground to a powder or in the form of marzipan – moist nuggets of nut paste threaded through the dough. I took the latter idea to make featherlight biscuits, studded with pine nuts, and made them lightly fragrant with a grating of lemon zest. Of course, they work with coffee too, though I think better with a jewel-coloured tea in a fine cup – rosehip, mint, chamomile or verbena.

# Pine kernel and lemon cookies

Eaten an hour or so after baking, these are soft, chewy and cookie-like; a few hours later and they become crisp and biscuity – the sort of thing to serve with coffee or a glass of sweet golden wine. Lemon zest and toasted pine kernels lend an Italian note. The sugar sparkles, brandysnap-like. They will keep for a fortnight in a biscuit tin, should you find yourself with that sort of willpower.

*Makes 15–20 biscuits*

| | |
|---|---|
| pine kernels 100g | zest of a lemon |
| marzipan 250g | plain flour 35g |
| caster sugar 200g | egg whites 70ml |

Lightly toast the pine kernels in a shallow pan until pale gold in colour, then set aside. Break the marzipan into hazelnut-sized pieces and put them in the bowl of a food processor, then process briefly to large crumbs.

Add the sugar to the marzipan, then finely grate the lemon zest and add to the bowl with 35g of the pine kernels. Process for a few seconds to combine and to roughly chop the pine kernels.

Stir in the flour. In a separate, medium-sized bowl beat the egg whites until almost stiff, then fold in the crumb mixture, mixing until thoroughly combined.

Set the oven at 175°C. Line a baking sheet with baking parchment. Take one heaped tablespoon of the mixture, roll it into a ball and then drop it into the reserved toasted pine kernels. Roll the cookie dough in the pine kernels, then place it on the lined baking sheet.

Bake for 10–12 minutes until the cookies have spread. They should look slightly underdone.

Remove from the oven and leave for 10 minutes to settle before transferring them carefully to a cooling rack with a palette knife.

I have amassed quite a collection of hazelnut cookie recipes. The chunky, crumbly biscuits in *Tender, Volume II*, soft, sandy and best eaten warm, and the more fragile, maple syrup-scented version in *The Kitchen Diaries III*. In late autumn 2020 I moved the recipe on a little. A more complex affair, which fitted in with the extra time some of us had on our hands during the second pandemic lockdown.

The heart and soul of these tender, golden cookies is praline, made by toasting the hazelnuts and grinding half to fine crumbs and the remainder 1–2 minutes longer, to an intensely nutty paste. The latter stirred into a buttercream to sandwich the little cookies together. This is not a recipe to rush, but one to take your time over, on a freezing winter's afternoon, radio on, the wind outside blowing the leaves into drifts.

# Hazelnut buttercream cookies

Sweetly crisp when first out of the oven, they soften delightfully when filled with the praline buttercream. The dough will keep in the fridge or the freezer, so you can slice off as much as you need and batch bake. The praline cream will keep for a few days in the fridge.

*Makes about 30 cookies*

*For the praline:*

| | |
|---|---|
| skinned hazelnuts 250g | vegetable oil a little |
| caster sugar 125g | |

*For the cookies:*

| | |
|---|---|
| butter 225g | salt half a teaspoon |
| soft brown sugar 100g | skinned hazelnuts 15, halved |
| plain flour 200g | |
| cornflour 50g | |

*For the butter icing:*

| | |
|---|---|
| butter 125g | the reserved praline paste above |
| icing sugar 250g | |

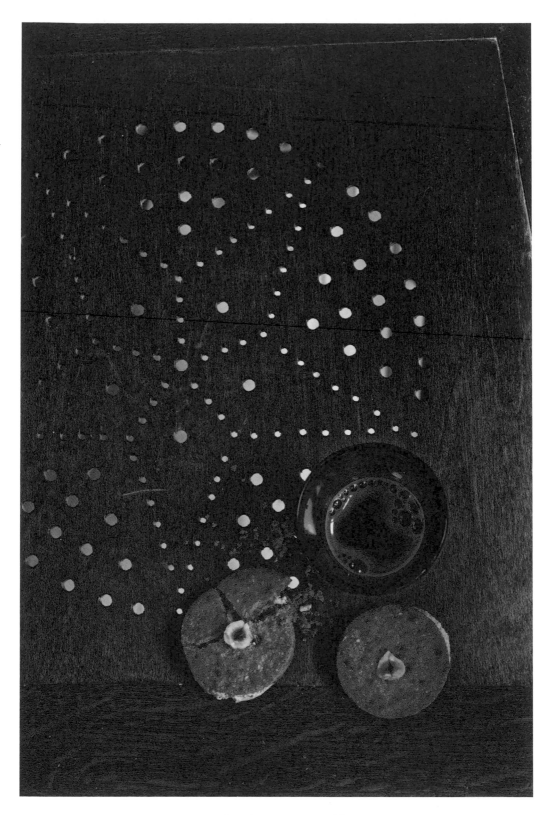

Hazelnut buttercream cookies

Tip the 250g of hazelnuts into a wide, shallow pan (I use one 28cm in diameter) and toast them over a moderate heat till golden. You will need to shake the pan regularly – you want them to brown evenly. Sprinkle in the sugar and leave it to melt. I know it is tempting to stir, but don't. Lightly oil a baking sheet with a little vegetable oil. As the sugar becomes syrupy, gently move the nuts around, making sure they are all lightly coated. As the caramel darkens to a deep and glossy brown, remove the pan immediately from the heat and tip the hazelnuts onto the oiled sheet.

Leave the nuts for 15 minutes to cool and set. Break them into small knobbly pieces, put them in the bowl of a food processor and process for a minute or so to fine crumbs. Stop the machine, remove 120g and set aside. Continue processing until the remaining crumbs have turned to a thick, coarse paste. You need to watch carefully, as this change in texture happens quite suddenly. Using a rubber spatula, scrape the paste into a small bowl and set aside.

To make the cookies: set the oven at 160°C. Put the butter and sugar into the bowl of a food mixer with a flat paddle attachment and beat at moderate speed till soft and creamy. It will mix more evenly if you push the mixture down the sides of the bowl once or twice with a rubber spatula. Meanwhile, mix the flour, cornflour and salt together then stir in the reserved 120g of praline.

With the paddle slowly turning, add the flour mixture a few spoonfuls at a time. When everything is well mixed, scoop the dough out onto a piece of aluminium foil, baking parchment or cling film, whichever is handy. Roll the dough into a fat sausage about 28cm in length and 6cm in diameter, wrap loosely and place in the fridge for an hour. (Please don't be tempted to skip this, otherwise your cookies will spread alarmingly.)

Take a slice of the dough, approximately as thick as a pound coin (just over 3mm) and place it on a parchment-lined baking sheet. Now repeat with as many cookies as you can get on your sheet. Place half a hazelnut on half of the cookies. Bake in the oven for 12–15 minutes then remove. If you want neat edges, use a 6cm cookie cutter to trim each whilst they are still warm, then transfer with a palette knife to a cooling rack. Continue with the next batch.

To finish, cream the butter till soft, stir in the icing sugar, then, when smooth, stir in the reserved praline paste. Sandwich the biscuits together with the buttercream.

If there is one biscuit that seems to have pleased more than others, it is the batch of rose, marzipan and dark chocolate cookies that appeared in my column in the *Observer* in winter 2019. My original intention was to come up with a biscuit suitable for putting in a pretty box to give as a Christmas gift, but it turned out that the best moment to eat these soft, rose-scented cookies is when they are still warm, when the butterscotch notes of the brown sugar are still in evidence and the chocolate chips have yet to set. It is essential not to overbake them, so they are crisp outside, but retain a certain softness within. Practice, as ever, makes perfect. Helpfully, the raw dough will keep in the fridge, wrapped in baking parchment, for several days, so in theory you could slice and bake a batch at will.

## Chocolate chip, rose and marzipan cookies

*Makes about 18–20 cookies*

| | |
|---|---|
| butter  125g | bicarbonate of soda |
| caster sugar  85g |    half a teaspoon |
| light muscovado sugar  85g | crystallised rose petals  20g |
| egg  1, large | marzipan  200g |
| milk  1 tablespoon | dark chocolate  150g |
| plain flour  250g | vanilla extract |

You will also need a baking sheet, lined with baking parchment.

Set the oven at 200°C. Cream the butter and sugars together until they are light and the colour of milky coffee. You can do this by hand, but the lightest results are to be had from using a food mixer fitted with a paddle beater. Break the egg into a small bowl, mix the white and yolk together with a fork, then combine, beater still turning, with the butter and sugar. Add the milk to the mixture.

Mix the flour and bicarbonate of soda together and fold into the creamed butter and sugar mixture. Finely chop the rose petals, break or cut the marzipan into small pieces and add both to the mixture. Chop the chocolate into small nuggets, then fold into the cookie dough with a couple of drops of vanilla extract.

Roll the mixture into spheres approximately the size of a golf ball, setting them out on the baking sheet, leaving room for them to spread. (I cook eight at

Chocolate chip, rose and marzipan cookies

a time on a 30cm × 30cm baking sheet.) Bake for 12 minutes, until each cookie is pale and lightly risen. Remove the tray from the oven and leave to settle for 5 minutes before transferring to a cooling rack. Continue with the next batch. The cookies will keep in a biscuit tin for several days.

Flapjacks – homely, cheap, unfancy – carry the scent of butter, golden syrup and oats, the sort of smell that says 'everything is going to be fine'. My mother would occasionally bake a batch in time for my return from school, where a tray would sit, warm and treacly, on the back of the Aga. Twenty years later, working in the kitchens of a much-loved London café, I baked them every day as they became our bestselling item.

As dear as the plain version is to me, with all its buttery scent and memories, I now embellish them a tad with seeds and a little dried fruit. You can use whatever appropriate seeds you have to hand, but in the interests of texture I try to use a mixture of sizes. An equal weight of large pumpkin and sunflower seeds, with just 10g each of diminutive linseed and sesame, probably works best, but they are helpfully interchangeable. I often use golden sultanas, dried cherries, mulberries or candied orange peel, but you could also use apricots, raisins or dried cranberries. Basically, whatever is in the cupboard.

## Oat, nut and seed flapjacks

*Makes 12 flapjacks*

butter 150g
golden syrup 4 tablespoons
soft brown sugar 70g
porridge oats 150g

jumbo oats 100g
mixed seeds 65g (see above)
pistachios 25g (shelled weight)
dried fruits 90g (see above)

You will also need a shallow baking tin – a roasting tin will do – about 22cm × 24cm, lined with baking parchment. Melt the butter in a deep saucepan. Set the oven at 170°C. Add the golden syrup to the melted butter, then stir in the sugar and let it melt.

Stir both sizes of oats into the melted butter and sugar together with a generous pinch of salt. Remove the pan from the heat, then stir in the dried seeds, nuts and fruits.

Tip the mixture into the baking tin and gently smooth the surface level, but do not compress or compact the mixture. Bake in the oven for 25 minutes. The flapjack is done when it starts to turn a darker gold around the edges. The centre should be firm and springy to the touch.

Remove the tin from the oven and, if you wish, score, without cutting right through, into twelve rectangular pieces. I prefer to break mine into rough pieces of assorted sizes as they cool.

I tend to forget about the years I worked in a bakery. This may be because of the zombie state I worked in after rising each morning at 4am or perhaps simply because it was the 1970s. We made Danish pastries whose laminations of flaking dough and butter were sandwiched with apricots, and old-fashioned pound cakes dotted with caraway seeds and dustings of cinnamon. A favourite part of my job was making crumbly Parmesan biscuits the diameter of a two-pound coin. My tongue would tingle from the deep hit of umami and I would find myself going back time and again till it was sore.

## Parmesan biscuits

The recipe was so easy to remember it has stayed with me to this day (equal butter-cheese-flour, an egg and bake at 180°C for 10 minutes). They take barely 10 minutes to make and not much more than that to bake.

*Makes about 20 bisuits*

plain flour  125g
cold butter  125g
finely grated Parmesan  125g

egg yolk  1
a little ground chilli powder

Set the oven at 180°C. Put the flour into a mixing bowl, cut the butter into small chunks and rub the ingredients together with your fingertips until they look

Parmesan biscuits

like fine, fresh breadcrumbs. It is essential that you don't go too far with this, and that you stop rubbing in as soon as the flour and butter look crumb-like.

Add the grated Parmesan, the egg yolk, a pinch of chilli powder and a little salt. Even with all the Parmesan, the flavour will be improved by a good fat pinch. Now gently bring the dough together with your hands, squeezing and softly kneading it till it looks like coarse pastry.

Twist the dough in two and roll each into a fat cylinder about the diameter of a two-pound coin. Slice each roll into thick discs, about 0.5cm thick – less than the thickness of your little finger.

Place each slice on a baking sheet and bake for 10 minutes. They are ready when pale gold and crumbly. Lift them carefully from the baking sheet – they will be very tender – and allow them to cool on a rack.

You can keep them for a day or two in an airtight container.


Friands are fairy cakes for grown-ups. They carry something of the lightness of our childhood favourite but with the tenderness and moist crumb that comes from using ground almonds. I have been making friands since the summer of 2011, when my first recipe for them was published in the *Observer*. Inside each tiny cake was a blackberry or two, a little fruit bomb lying in wait to surprise and delight. Since then, I have used slices of purple fig with almonds; raspberries with ground hazelnuts; and baked them in both classical round tins and in shell-shaped madeleine moulds (and charming they were too). For Christmas I stir in crystallised orange peel and nibs of dark chocolate.

The most useful of cake recipes – they can be out of the oven in half an hour – friands also keep in good condition for a day or two. (One of the upsides of adding ground almonds to a cake recipe is the extra shelf-life they will add.) As tradition insists, mine usually appear as small, round cakes, baked in muffin or small bun tins, but last year I rethought the recipe to produce one larger shallow cake. The result was a fruit-laden almond sponge with a crisp, nut-brown top, a soft centre and cake-like outer edge. A spoonful of crème fraîche is pleasing with this, as is a trickle of double cream.

# Browned butter, blackberry and hazelnut friand

My blackberry friand recipe is baked in one large dish rather than as individual cakes. I like it this way, undecided whether it wants be pudding or cake, served warm from the oven, in generous, fruit-studded spoonfuls. Keep a careful eye on the browning butter. It should be a rich nut-brown, but no darker. If there are any brown speckles – the burning milk solids – pour the butter through a fine sieve before using it.

*Serves 4*

butter 180g
skinned hazelnuts 100g
plain flour 50g
icing sugar 180g

grated lemon zest 1 teaspoon
egg whites 5
blackberries, raspberries 250g

Set the oven at 180°C. Line a 24cm baking dish with baking parchment. Melt the butter in a small pan over a moderate heat. Watch carefully as the butter first froths and then calms down and starts to turn a deep gold. Once the butter becomes walnut-coloured and smells nutty and toasted, remove immediately from the heat and set aside.

Toast the hazelnuts in a shallow pan until they are golden. Move them regularly around the pan to help them to brown evenly. Tip the nuts into a food processor and reduce to fine crumbs.

Sift the flour and icing sugar into a large mixing basin, then stir in all but one tablespoon of the ground hazelnuts. Stir in the lemon zest. In a separate bowl, beat the egg whites until they reach a soft, sloppy foam.

Make a deep well in the flour and sugar, then add the beaten egg whites and the melted butter. Combine everything lightly but thoroughly, then pour into the prepared dish. Scatter the blackberries and raspberries over the surface, then the reserved ground hazelnuts.

Bake for 35 minutes until risen and golden brown. The surface should be lightly crunchy. The inside soft and spongy. Remove from the oven and leave to settle for 10 minutes before serving.

Browned butter, blackberry and hazelnut friand

Bringing a cake to the table is itself a symbol of hospitality. (You don't bake a Battenburg for yourself.) 'Would you like a slice of cake?' is a sentence that lies at the very heart of generosity and welcome. Ditto 'I'll just put the kettle on'. A little cake, be it cupcake, fairy cake, muffin or madeleine, is, on the other hand, like offering a token, a sort of culinary billet-doux. To make traditional friands, use the recipe above, spoon the mixture into a twelve-hole bun tray or fairy-cake cases and reduce the baking time to 10–15 minutes.

## Chocolate and candied peel friands

I use a whole piece of crystallised orange peel for this, then chop it finely. They are not always easy to track down, these large slices of fruit preserved in a gossamer-thin coat of crisp, white sugar, but they are more juicy than the usual chopped candied peel – Italian grocers are a good hunting ground and, should you be in London, Fortnum & Mason have a year-round supply. If they prove elusive, you could use ordinary candied peel, but the effect won't be quite as perfumed.

*Makes 12 friands*

crystallised orange peel  60g
dark chocolate  60g
butter  180g
plain flour  50g

icing sugar  180g
ground almonds  100g
grated orange zest  1 teaspoon
egg whites  5

Set the oven at 200°C. Lightly butter twelve shallow bun tins or madeleine tins.

Finely chop the crystallised orange peel and the chocolate and set aside. Put the butter in a small pan and melt over a moderate heat, then watch it carefully until it becomes a dark, nutty gold. Take care not to let it burn. Leave to cool.

Sift the flour and sugar into a large mixing bowl, then add the ground almonds. Add the orange zest, then add the chocolate and crystallised orange peel. Beat the egg whites to a soft, moist and sloppy foam – they shouldn't be able to stand up. Make a well in the centre of the dry ingredients then pour in the egg whites, together with the melted butter. Mix lightly but thoroughly, then pour into the buttered tins.

Bake for 10–15 minutes, remove from the oven, then leave to settle before carefully removing from the tins with a palette knife.

# The brownie

Of course, there was much discussion over where to put the brownie recipe. In the end I decided not to include it in the chocolate cake chapter as we really shouldn't think of something so dense and fudgy as a cake. It is, after all, only a short step away from a chocolate truffle.

I can honestly say that my 'very, very good chocolate brownies' are without question my most popular recipe. By which I mean my most commented on and most Googled. The recipe came about because I was asked for a story to go with a special Glastonbury Festival issue of the *Observer* magazine. Brownies were the first thing I thought of. Unimaginative, but you do want something that will get better in a small tin over a few days (no one is going to be taking a Victoria sponge, believe me). If, when I'm long gone, people are still making my brownies, for whatever reason, I shall not have lived in vain.

## My very good chocolate brownie recipe

No nuts, no flavourings, just a 24-carat brownie as dense and fudgy as Glastonbury mud. Whatever else you add is up to you.

*Serves 12 (or two with the munchies)*

caster sugar  300g
butter  250g
chocolate (70 per cent
   cocoa solids)  250g

eggs  3, large, plus 1 extra egg yolk
plain flour  60g
finest-quality cocoa powder  60g
baking powder  half a teaspoon

You will need a baking tin, about 23cm × 23cm, preferably non-stick, or a small roasting tin.

Set the oven at 180°C. Line the bottom of the baking tin with baking parchment. Put the sugar and butter into the bowl of a food mixer and beat for several minutes till white and fluffy. You can do it by hand if you wish, but you need to keep going until the mixture is really soft and creamy.

My very good chocolate brownie recipe

Meanwhile, break the chocolate into pieces, set 50g of it aside and melt the rest in a bowl suspended over, but not touching, a pan of simmering water. As soon as the chocolate has melted, remove it from the heat. Chop the remaining 50g into gravel-sized pieces.

Break the eggs into a small bowl and beat them lightly with a fork. Sift together the flour, cocoa and baking powder and mix in a pinch of salt. With the food mixer running slowly, introduce the beaten egg a little at a time, speeding up in between additions. Remove the bowl from the mixer to the work surface, then mix in the melted and the chopped chocolate with a large metal spoon. Lastly, fold in the flour and cocoa mixture, gently and firmly, without knocking any of the air out. Scrape the mixture into the prepared tin, smooth the top and bake for 30 minutes.

The top will have risen slightly and the cake will appear slightly softer in the middle than around the edges. Pierce the centre of the cake with a fork – it should come out sticky, but not with raw mixture attached to it. If it does, then return the brownie to the oven for 3 more minutes. It is worth remembering that it will solidify a little on cooling, so if it appears a bit wet, don't worry.

# Just one more bite before I go

I am lucky to enjoy such rich, deep, sweet sleep. Five and a half hours in which I am dead to the world. I wish it was six but my body refuses the offer of more. Insomniac friends are amazed how quickly I fall asleep – about five minutes – and that I almost never wake during the night. I can sleep on trains, planes (though rarely do) and in the car. Neither do I seem to be affected by noise or light, which is just as well with my bedroom being on a bus route. But there is one caveat to this, and it is an utterly delicious one.

My night's sleep is only at its fullest when it is preceded by a tiny midnight snack.

By snack, I mean a morsel, nothing more. (We are not talking full bacon sandwich here.) A rough-textured oatcake spread with a nubby wave of peanut butter; a craggy lump of Parmesan; an anchovy fillet or two nicked straight from the tin. Once in a blue moon, it will be something sweet though without too much of a sugar hit – a teaspoon or two of ice cream perhaps or, heaven, a spoonful of leftover pudding. The quantity is diminutive but not austere. The ritual, unlike that of drinking tea or making coffee, is (alas) over in seconds. But a tiny bite of something before I retire is an essential part of going to bed. Any insomniacs may like to try it, just in case it works.

Opening the fridge door is a dangerous thing to do at midnight – all manner of treasures lie hidden, sleeping under saucers in china bowls. Yet opening the fridge as I lock up for the night is something I do without thinking. You know... just to check all is well. A fingerful of hummus, a spoonful of cold plum crumble or joy of joys... a cold sausage next to the mustard jar. It goes without saying that this nugget of joy must never ever be of a virtuous nature. That would be to lose the point.

Of course, if I had a few minutes longer, then I might just put the kettle on for a cup of miso soup – the instant stuff from a sachet – or most likely, make myself a slice of toast, crumbling tiny flakes of salt in the deep, shining pools of butter. A nightlight glowing in the dark.

# Index

rice, salmon, Japanese pickles 263
smoked haddock and mussel pie
    320–1
smoked mackerel pie *310*, 311

FISH SAUCE:
chicken and cucumber salad with
    lime and fish sauce 204
and a cure for a cold, a hangover,
    everything really 254
minced lamb with lime and
    coriander 232, *233*
mussels, coconut and noodles 242–3
noodles with prawns 261–2

FISHCAKES:
crab and harissa croquettes 271–2,
    *273*
dill and haddock fishcakes, parsley
    sauce 270–1

FLAGEOLET BEANS:
a little stew of flageolet, broad
    beans and peas 161, *162*

FLAPJACKS:
oat, nut and seed flapjacks 471–2

FONTINA:
cheesy chips 147–8
cheesy greens and potatoes 141–2
potato cake with Fontina and herbs
    134–6, *135*

FOOLS:
gooseberry and elderflower fool 368
toffee apple fool 368–70, *369*

FRANGIPANE:
plum frangipane tart 351–2

FRIANDS:
browned butter, blackberry and
    hazelnut friand 475, *476*
chocolate and candied peel friands
    477

FRITTERS:
green Thai bubble and squeak
    fritters 139–41, *140*

FROSTING, CAKE:
carrot and mascarpone cake 430–2,
    *431*

FRUIT COMPOTE:
a fruit compote for cheesecake 447

FRUITS, DRIED:
oat, nut and seed flapjacks 471–2
sticky, seeded malt loaf *70*, 71–2


G

GARAM MASALA:
chicken with tomatoes, yoghurt
    and garam masala 241–2

GARLIC:
couscous and tomatoes 164–5
prawns, black garlic and dill butter
    226–8, 267
roast garlic, lemon and Parmesan
    mash 164
salad dressing 22
the stickiest wings 195–6
wild garlic and basil cream 160

GINGER:
baked tomatoes with ginger and
    coconut 121–2
deep double ginger cake, orange
    icing 419–21, *420*
pickled red cabbage and ginger
    285–6
roast butternut soup with
    mushrooms and ginger 34–5
the stickiest wings 195–6

GOCHUJANG:
baked aubergines with gochujang
    and tomatoes 112–13, *114*
the chicken wing feast 277–9, *278*
greens with gochujang 142–3

GOOSEBERRIES:
gooseberry and elderflower fool 368
gooseberry (or blackcurrant)
    crumble cake 424

GRANITA:
strawberry granita 385
watermelon granita 387

GRAVY:
roast chicken with roast potatoes
    and roasting juices 191–4, *192*

GREENS:
cheesy greens and potatoes 141–2
greens with gochujang 142–3
noodles and greens 157–8


H

HAM:
ham with juniper and cider 283, *284*

HARICOT BEANS:
baked aubergines with gochujang
    and tomatoes 112–13, *114*
noodles with lentils and soured
    cream 159
a quick pancetta and bean soup
    with spaghetti 40, *41*

HARISSA PASTE:
crab and harissa croquettes 271–2,
    *273*
pappardelle with mushrooms and
    harissa 156

HAZELNUTS:
browned butter, blackberry and
    hazelnut friand 475, *476*
chocolate-chip hazelnut cake with
    chocolate icing 455–6
hazelnut buttercream cookies
    466–8, *467*
hazelnut chocolate cake with
    sultanas and rosemary 452, *453–4*
toasted hazelnut tart 358–60, *359*
wholemeal plum cake, spiced icing
    426–8, *427*

HERBS:
grilled sausages, herbed chickpea
    mash 228–30, *229*
hazelnut chocolate cake with
    sultanas and rosemary 452, *453–4*
herb cream 24–5
herb dressing 25
herb flatbread 68–9
herb pancakes with spinach and
    mushrooms 166–8, *167*
potato cake with Fontina and herbs
    134–6, *135*

# A note on the type

The text is typeset in Lyon, designed by Kai Bernau in 2009. Like many great serif typefaces, Lyon draws from the work of the French type designer Robert Granjon (1513–1590), one of the finest letter makers of the Renaissance. Though less well known than his contemporary Claude Garamond, his work includes a much broader range of styles and he is known for the typeface Civilité as well as for his italic type form. Lyon's elegant looks are matched with a curious, anonymous nature that allows the text unobtrusively to shine through.